	DATE DUE	
FEB 25 1998 S'		
WITHDRAWN		

Charles Tomlinson

Plage Paysage (1974)

Charles Tomlinson
Man and Artist

Edited by Kathleen O'Gorman

University of Missouri Press

Columbia, 1988

Charles Tomlinson: man and artist.
    Bibliography: p.
    Includes index.
    1. Tomlinson, Charles, 1927–   —Criticism and
interpretation.   I. O'Gorman, Kathleen.
PR6039.0349Z63   1988   821'.914   87-19076
ISBN 0-8262-0656-5

This paper meets the minimum requirements of
the American National Standard for Permanence of Paper
for Printed Library Materials, Z39.48, 1984.

For permissions, see p. 252

Contents

III. The Painter

IV. Postscript

List of Abbreviations

A   With Octavio Paz. *Airborn / Hijos del Aire*. London: Anvil Press Poetry, 1981.

AS   *American Scenes and Other Poems*. London: Oxford University Press, 1966.

BW   *In Black and White: The Graphics of Charles Tomlinson*. Cheadle: Carcanet Press, 1976.

CP   *Collected Poems*. Oxford and New York: Oxford University Press, 1985.

F   *The Flood*. Oxford and New York: Oxford University Press, 1981.

Images *Words and Images*. London: Covent Garden Press, 1972.

N   *The Necklace*. 1955. Reprint. London: Oxford University Press, 1966.

NNY   *Notes from New York and Other Poems*. New York: Oxford University Press, 1984.

PI   *The Poem as Initiation*. Hamilton, New York: Colgate University Press, 1967.

PL   *A Peopled Landscape: Poems*. London and New York: Oxford University Press, 1963.

R   With Octavio Paz, Jacques Roubaud, and Edoardo Sanguineti. *Renga: A Chain of Poems*. 1970. Reprint. New York: George Braziller, Inc., 1972.

RC   *Relations and Contraries*. Poems in Pamphlet 9. Aldington, Kent: Hand and Flower Press, 1951.

S   *The Shaft*. Oxford and New York: Oxford University Press, 1978.

SA   *Some Americans: A Personal Record*. Berkeley and London: University of California Press, 1981.

SIB   *Seeing Is Believing*. 1958. Reprint. London: Oxford University Press, 1960.

SP   *Selected Poems: 1951–1974*. Oxford and New York: Oxford University Press, 1978.

WI   *The Way In and Other Poems*. London: Oxford University Press, 1974.

WrW   *Written on Water*. London: Oxford University Press, 1972.

WW   *The Way of a World*. London: Oxford University Press, 1969.

All quotations in the book are cited by page number.

Donald Davie

Foreword

My name occurs often enough in the pages that follow—notably in a very generous page from the hand of C. T. himself—that it may be understood how I cannot write about him at this late stage in a friendship of forty years, except personally. And yet this must be handled with some delicacy; for C. T. himself is a person of fastidious reticences. It is characteristic that his relationship with his elder daughter—a relationship unusually warm and intimate—should be registered in his poetry only through an elaborate allusion to a very elaborate and artificial poem by Andrew Marvell. Moreover, in this justly admired piece, which is examined more than once by the essayists in this book, the relationship of father to daughter has hardly been established before we are led to think of it as *any* father to *any* daughter. Other relationships as close or closer—with his other daughter, with his parents, preeminently with his wife—are in his poetry overtly treated nowhere at all. And one would not have to be an especially coarse-fibered reader to wonder if this poet's family life were not, while thoroughly decorous of course, somewhat formal and dry (the very opposite is the case).

In this all but unbroken silence about the claims and comforts of the kindred, there is an austerity that some readers find chilling. And sure enough, when Tomlinson's poetry has been complained of, one recurrent complaint has been that it lacks "human warmth." It would be easy to rebut this after a fashion by alleging that readers who thus complain have been led astray by the fashion of yesterday for poetry that was, or made profession

Donald Davie is Andrew W. Mellon Professor of Humanities at Vanderbilt University and recipient of American Academy of Arts & Sciences and Guggenheim Foundation fellowships. He has written numerous collections of poetry, literary criticism, and aesthetic theory and has edited collections of essays and of poetry.

1

of being, "confessional." But this would be wrong: the demand for "warm humanity" from poets is much older than that and is to be heard from people not especially enamored of the verse confessions of the late John Berryman or the late Sylvia Plath. It derives, we may well think, from a misconception that is ineradicable and endemic—the supposition that when life moves over into art the transition is imperceptible or ought to be. Not just in Tomlinson's art but in all first-rate art, surely, the contrary is true: the transition is perceptible and is meant to be; and the more responsible the artist, the more pains he will take to ensure that we recognize the changeover. Moreover, the change, as we experience it, may indeed seem analogous to a drop in temperature, a draft of cold air at which we shiver. For, by a familiar constellation of notions, one that Tomlinson appeals to quite often, "cold" goes along with "keen." And if art is a realm of unusually keen, as we say unusually "heightened," perceptions and apprehensions, no wonder if we know we have got there, into that realm, by suddenly feeling chilled.

However, it makes as much sense, and perhaps more, to say that Tomlinson's responses, as we find them registered in his poems, are unusually warm. How ardently this sensibility responds to landscapes and skyscapes, to a single tree or a stand of trees, to the swell of a hillside, to the behavior of running water! Yes, but—so one kind of reader will reply—ardor in these relations is misplaced; misplaced and surely *dis*placed— from the circle of interhuman relations, where ardor is proper, on to these nonhuman entities, trees and hillsides, where it is wasted. The assumption is, we see, that for such ardor to be expended on the outdoors it must have been parsimoniously husbanded, withheld; it is not conceived that the warmth for hillsides is a spilling over from warmth husbanded indeed, but generously expended too, in the domestic circle and the wider circle of friendships. It may be asked, Does this grudging reader exist? He puts in no appearance in the pages that follow, our essayists having decided (I take it) that it is a waste of time trying to meet his demands, to satisfy his needs. They are right, and I shall not waste more time on him. But he exists, right enough; and those who have followed Tomlinson's career are very much aware of him. For he has reviewed every one of Tomlinson's collections to date, and he will review the next, and the next. The point of remembering him is to emphasize that Tomlinson's has been no primrose path to recognition and fame; that he has suffered neglect and sometimes malicious misunderstanding, like any artist who goes his own way without bowing to fashion; and that he pays a price for the dignity with which he keeps his private life private.

It says something for the tact and delicacy of Alan Ross that he was able to prevail on C. T.'s privacy enough to elicit what is surely a very warmhearted account by him in his answers to Ross's questionnaire. It's in this piece, for instance, reprinted here, that we encounter for the first time the poet's father, portrayed only sketchily, it's true, but intriguingly; we have the impression of a character sufficiently odd and angular to have made an abiding impression on his son and to have furnished some poets (but not this one) with materials for poems. Unwontedly frank though Tomlinson is in this piece, still he relies on us to read between the lines. And this is easier for someone like myself who, as he acknowledges, grew up in a socioeconomic milieu hardly distinguishable from his. Without going into the sometimes comical, sometimes pitiful intricacies of English social distinctions, it may be said that we both grew up— and at much the same time—on or very near a crucial fault line in the English social system, the line where the aspiring and self-respecting proletarian, on his way modestly "up," meets the unfortunate or feckless petty bourgeois drifting "down." There is no zone in the social hierarchy—or there was not when we were young—where reticence is more at a premium, where the injunctions to "keep yourself to yourself," to "keep up appearances," to "keep your self-respect," are more often heard and attended to. To keep our own counsel, especially about the intimate relations that matter most, was I think bred into us both in our boyhoods, in such a way that Tomlinson's reticence about such things was probably never, for him, a matter of choice—it did not occur to him to act otherwise.

And yet, for both of us but especially for him when I first knew him, a powerful example presented itself of how one might respond differently. I am thinking of D. H. Lawrence. The household of Lawrence's *Sons and Lovers* is more luridly lit than the households where C. T. and I grew up. But it is not far distant on the social scale; and Mrs. Morrell's struggle to keep her head high was familiar to me, and I suppose to him, from womenfolk closely akin to us. The explosive force of Lawrence's writing comes in part, surely, from the strength of the reticences, the taboos, that he had to break down or break through—and I have in mind not the sexual taboos, which everyone knows about, but the social ones. Plainly this was one dimension of Lawrence's achievement where Tomlinson was not going to emulate him. But otherwise Charles in his twenties, and his wife Brenda also, admired Lawrence very much indeed—and not just as artist but as moralist too, insofar as that distinction can be made. Charles to my knowledge has never disowned this early allegiance, and I see no reason why he should. But some to whom I have spoken of it have been surprised, and even a little amused, seeing I suppose a wide gulf fixed between Charles's fastidiousness and what they think of as "the Lawrencian." Yet Lawrence too was fastidious, if not in the way of reticence, in the matter of honing clean his perceptions of the nonhuman world, recognizing all the while how he must let the items of that world resist him, in an otherness that the avid perceiver must respect. And so, not just for the historical record but in order to give Lawrence his due, his donation to Tomlinson should be recognized. In *The Necklace*, Tomlinson's second collection but the first where his writing is assured, everyone acknowledges the presence of Wallace Stevens. But if Tomlinson learned from any literary source to perceive the visible and tangible world with such sensitivity, he learned it from the author of *Etruscan Places* and *Sea and Sardinia* more than from the author of *Harmonium*. The English predecessor and (for a time) master needs to be honored. It was through Lawrence's eyes that Tomlinson took his first sightings of Liguria and Tuscany. Equally, it was through Lawrence's eyes that he first looked at New Mexico; and if his response to the dance-centered cultures of the Hopi and other Indian nations is more knowledgeable and more patient than Lawrence's was, still his respectful delight in them remains, so far as I can see, within the parameters that Lawrence first inscribed.

In his lecture, "The Poet as Painter" (reprinted here), Tomlinson ascribes his awareness of the visual world, which is also an arena for the play of elemental energies, not to any literary source but to the experience of following, and sometimes of fishing, the canals that webbed the district of his birth and nurture—Burslem, Hanley, the Staffordshire potteries. The account is compelling and fascinating; and of course we believe him. But in doing so, we need not shut out our knowledge that once again it was Lawrence who first made palpable to the English imagination (I do not forget Arnold Bennett) that region of the industrialized North Midlands where we, all three, grew up: Lawrence in Nottinghamshire, Tomlinson in Staffordshire, I in South Yorkshire. Lawrence's great essay "Nottinghamshire and the Mining Countryside," along with innumerable passages in his stories and novels, maps the terrain in which Tomlinson and I spent our boyhoods—industrialized without being urbanized, even at its most desolate still reached for by long fingers of the manorial and agrarian England, which it had never completely supplanted. In such a landscape—just because it is marginal, lies at and over a frontier—a young person's sensory apparatus (if it is the right young person) becomes hypersensitive. It did so in Lawrence's case, and in Tomlinson's.

When Alan Ross asks about this, C. T.'s answer seems to me, drawing on my own experience, exactly right. "When people ask me if I rejected my surroundings, I have to reply that they rejected me. Meaning that so much of them was just too thin a soil to support the weediest growth." Of course one is conditioned by the surroundings one grows up in. And if, when grown, you suppose yourself not irremediably crippled as a sentient being, then you have to be grateful to the conditioning that has, as a matter of observable fact, permitted you to survive that long. And so when Tomlinson, in *The Way In* (1974), makes his peace with his native place—in poems occasioned I think by enforced returns to Stoke while attending his parents through their last declines—this greatly enriches, and makes more poignant, the process of his poetry to that point and thereafter. But of course this is quite different from saying, "He should never have left." He had to leave, and he was right to leave; only his having once left permits him now, compassionately and mournfully, to return. Without the initial breach, no reconciliation would be called for, or would be possible.

If someone protests, "But not all have the chance to leave!" that cannot be denied. But if some are to be crippled, to achieve not even "the weediest growth," can that impose on me the duty to cripple myself, stunt my own growth, so as to keep common cause with them? Some voice loud in support of "social justice" seems to demand as much. C. T., again like Lawrence before him, refuses that blackmail. On this matter, his politics or his social philosophy, our essayists for the most part keep silent. And it is just as well; for if they broached this topic, the most they could provoke would be parrot-cries like "Elitist!" It should be said, however, that Tomlinson has thought on these matters and has a perfectly consistent position, first and last. "Social justice"—we may suppose he approves of it. Meanwhile, however, *sauve qui peut*; he is an artist and must look out for himself, in a society where no one guarantees the artist, qua artist, a livelihood.

That provincial bringing up, in a very particular part of the English provinces, had an advantage that not I certainly, and perhaps neither of us, recognized until much later. It gave us a standpoint, or a point of leverage, on the history of the last two hundred and fifty years. We did not have to consult the books in the local reference library, we had only to ask idly about local landmarks and the names they bore, to recognize that the landscapes we grew up in had been determined not in the nineteenth century but in the eighteenth. For Charles, Etruria Vale; for me, Wentworth Woodhouse. Though later we would thrill to Wordsworth's and Ruskin's condemnations of what indeed were damnable, industrially blasted landscapes, still in the end what did they know—Ruskin, raised in an affluent South London suburb, Wordsworth among the dalesmen? We knew, or could learn merely by talking with our fathers, a phase of history anterior to any that Wordsworth or Ruskin knew: the first phase of the Industrial Revolution, when individuals strove with some success to preserve and hand on societal and craftsmanlike decencies in the face of the mechanized technologies that were tried out in provincial England sooner than anywhere else in the world. It was Charles more than anyone else, I am anxious to admit, who made me recognize that industrial technology—in its earliest, perhaps its "innocent" phase—did not always, nor necessarily, drive out the crucial perceptions of design, even of elegance. As long tongues of pre-industrial England licked into my Barnsley, as into his Stoke, we were made to envisage—in some measure, we actually experienced—a marriage between the pre-industrial and the industrial. At all events, however it might be for our contemporaries raised in Hertfordshire or Hampshire, we were in no danger, if we kept our wits about us, of envisaging the English eighteenth century exclusively or chiefly in images of sedan chairs and Ralph Allen's crescents in Bath. The eighteenth century that we knew, through anonymous local tradition filtered down to us and through the less-than-ancient ruined monuments that punctuated our walks, was a time when elemental energies—of fire, earth, and water— were, as precariously harnessed by primitive technology, alive and evident to all people as seldom before or since. I remember clearly how, quite late in our friendship, something of this was brought home to me—in Charles's vivid espousing of Cowper's unfinished poem, "Yardley-oak." I applaud Mr. Wilcox for bringing out, in the first pages of his essay, some of this deeply pre-romantic allegiance of Tomlinson's imagination.

Thinking along these lines, we thrust the poet back among the historical contingencies that have conditioned his ways of feeling. We see him as a creature of his times as well as of quite specific locations, and of the nation that he was born to. It is easy to overlook this in the case of a poet like this one, who has moved so eagerly, with such ready sympathy, with such enviable ease and even authority, into cultures (and therefore languages, of course) that were to begin with, and must always in some measure remain, foreign to him. It could be argued that this is to do him a disservice, cramping him back into confines he has splendidly transcended. But this is not how Tomlinson himself feels. From the first, and increasingly as time has passed, he has been restive about considerations of his work that, however laudatory in their intention and their effect, type him too exclusively as a philosophical poet, one who is more or less haughtily removed above the accidents of time and place and nation. On the contrary I think he is happy, and even anxious, to be seen as an individual mired in history, stuck in and stuck *with* the particular span of years he has lived through. This, an increasing involvement with history and an increasing confidence in dealing with it, is one theme that has been too little regarded in this artist's development. As early as *A Peopled Landscape* (1963; and the title incidentally is a protest or a remonstrance—against the opinion that the scenes in his poetry had not, and never would have, people in them), there is the very important poem, "Up at La

Serra," which engages directly with politics at the level where politics takes on human meaning—in a small municipality where, in the context of the social options actually open to the citizens, communist aspirations for instance might seem attractive, even noble, and not necessarily in the short term self-defeating. By the time of *The Way of a World* (1969), Tomlinson has acquired the confidence, in poems about Scriabin and Trotsky, to consider head-on the momentous historical fact of the Russian Revolution; just as, in later poems about Danton and Charlotte Corday, he confronts the French Revolution—prototypical, in being the first *total* revolution, social as well as political. If we expect from a great poet, or from one who would be great, engagement with history and with the tragicomedy of mankind's attempts to second-guess the direction of history's momentum, Tomlinson has passed that test. And he acquired the confidence to meet that challenge from experiencing, first in his bones and thereafter in his memories, the history that prepared for those revolutions and made them inevitable.

Part I

The Man

Landscape with Bathers (1971)

George Oppen

1. To C. T.

One imagines himself
addressing his peers
I suppose. Surely
that might be the definition
of "seriousness"? I would like,
as you see,
to convince
myself
that my pleasure in your response
is not
plain vanity
but the pleasure of being heard,
the pleasure
of companionship, which seems
more honorable.

[Written originally in a letter to Charles Tomlinson, who, in his reply, suggested this division into lines of verse. The poem is, therefore, a collaboration.]

George Oppen received the Pulitzer Prize in literature in 1969 and the award of the Academy and Institute of Arts & Letters in 1980. His numerous books of poetry include his *Collected Poems: 1929–1975*.

Michael Hennessy

2. Chronology

1927	(8 January) Alfred Charles Tomlinson born at Stoke-on-Trent, Staffordshire, England, son of Alfred Tomlinson (an estate agent's clerk) and May Lucas Tomlinson.
1945–1948	Obtains B.A., Queens' College, University of Cambridge. Studies with Donald Davie; develops interest in American poetry.
1948	(23 October) Marries Brenda Raybould. (Two daughters: Justine Benedikte, Juliet Virginia.)
1948–1951	Teaches elementary school in London "while trying to paint in the evenings" (*SA*, 98). Exhibits paintings in London and Manchester.
1951	*Relations and Contraries* published by Hand and Flower Press: "quatrains, sonnets, a working through traditional verse forms . . . but the traditional verse forms didn't really let me say anything very new."[1]
1951–1952	Travels in Italy; works briefly as private secretary to Percy Lubbock. "During [this] trip the urge to paint began to recede before the urge to write poetry."[2]
1952–1955	Researcher, Royal Holloway College and Bedford College, London.

Michael Hennessy is Associate Professor of English at John Carroll University. His publications include essays and reviews on Tomlinson, Auden, and Shakespeare. He is also author of a composition text, *The Random House Practice Book*.

1. Hamilton, "Four Conversations," p. 83.
2. Octavio Paz, from *BW*, p. 11.

1954   Obtains M.A., London University.

1955   *The Necklace* published by Fantasy Press, introduced by Donald Davie. Contained poems written "between December 1950 and March 1953 . . . [W]ould not have appeared . . . had Donald Davie not contributed an introduction" (*SA*, 12).

1956   Receives Bess Hokin Prize for Poetry.
(August) Poems of *Seeing Is Believing* "virtually completed" (*SA*, 13).
(Autumn) "Critics have spoken of the presence of [William Carlos] Williams in both *The Necklace* and *Seeing Is Believing*, but I did not seriously begin to read Williams until the autumn of 1956" (*SA*, 13).

1956–present   Lecturer (later Reader and then Professor) in English Poetry, University of Bristol.

1957   (February) "Late in February 1957 I wrote my first poems in emulation of the three-ply cadences that Williams used in the two books of his I had read [*Desert Music* and *Journey to Love*]" (*SA*, 16).

1958   *Seeing Is Believing* published in New York by McDowell, Obolensky, "thanks . . . to Hugh Kenner" (*SA*, 17).

1959   (October) Visits William Carlos Williams at his home in Rutherford, New Jersey.
(December) Visits Yvor Winters at his home in Palo Alto, California.

1959–1960   (November-May) Traveling fellowship in the United States from the Institute of International Education. A "journey across America that lasted some five months" (*SA*, 27). Tomlinson, his wife, and their daughter travel from New York to New England and California, and return to New York via New Mexico, the Deep South, and Washington, D.C.

1960   (April) Visits Marianne Moore at her apartment in Brooklyn, New York, and William Carlos Williams in New Jersey.

Seeing Is Believing published by Oxford University Press. Thirteen new poems added since the 1958 edition; one poem deleted.

Receives Levinson Prize for Poetry.

Versions from Fyodor Tyutchev (with Henry Gifford) published by Oxford University Press. Thirty-seven translations from Russian.

1962   Receives Union League Civic and Arts Foundation Prize.

Edits the May issue of *Poetry Chicago* on contemporary poetry.

1962–1963 Visiting Professor, University of New Mexico. Travels in the Southwest and Mexico and writes "American Scenes" and "Mexican Poems," which appear in his 1966 collection. "The year 1963 proved in many ways an *annus mirabilis*. I met both 'objectivists' [Louis] Zukofsky and George Oppen [during August in Brooklyn, New York]. And those meetings were preluded by two others—with Robert Duncan and Robert Creeley" (*SA*, 46).

1963   (January) Visits Georgia O'Keeffe at her home in Abiquiu, New Mexico.

(22 June–27 July) Stays at Kiowa Ranch, where D. H. Lawrence had lived, near Taos, New Mexico. "I / sat high / over Taos / on a / veranda / Lawrence had / made in / exile here. . . ." (*SA*, 53).

(August) Visits Zukofsky and Oppen in Brooklyn, New York.

A Peopled Landscape published by Oxford University Press. Contains sixteen poems in imitation of the three-ply form of Williams.

Castilian Ilexes: Versions from Antonio Machado (with Henry Gifford) published by Oxford University Press. Twenty-five translations from Spanish, several of which adopt Williams's three-ply form.

1964   Receives Inez Boulton Prize for Poetry.

Edits the January 1964 issue of *The Review*, a special

number on the Black Mountain poets, and the December 1964 issue of *Agenda*, devoted to the work of Louis Zukofsky.

1966   (April) Reading tour of New York State for the Academy of American Poets.
The Necklace reissued by Oxford University Press.
American Scenes and Other Poems published by Oxford University Press.

1967   (Summer) Meets Ezra Pound at Festival dei Due Mondi at Spoleto, Italy. "It is strange to have met the innovators of one's time only when age had overtaken them" (*SA*, 116). Also meets Octavio Paz for the first time.
(Autumn) Olive B. O'Connor Professor of Literature, Colgate University. Delivers Phi Beta Kappa Lecture, later published by Colgate as *The Poem as Initiation*.

1968   Receives Frank O'Hara Prize.
Receives National Translation Center Grant, University of Texas, Austin, to translate the poetry of Ungaretti.

1969   (30 March–3 April) Tomlinson, Octavio Paz, Jacques Roubaud, and Edoardo Sanguineti write the first European renga, "in the basement of the Hotel St. Simon [Paris], which at once evoked a train of associations with Persephone and the underworld" (*R*, 36).
Travels to Hungary for three weeks at invitation of Hungarian Poets, Essayists, Novelists. Reads own poetry and meets Hungarian poets and intellectuals.
Edits *Marianne Moore: A Collection of Critical Essays* published by Prentice-Hall.
The Way of a World published by Oxford University Press.

1970   *Ten Versions from Trilce* (with Henry Gifford) published by San Marcos Press. Ten translations from the Spanish of César Vallejo.

1971   *Renga* (with Octavio Paz, Jacques Roubaud, and Edoardo Sanguineti) published by Gallimard, Paris. Tomlinson's English translation published by Braziller, New York, in 1972, and Penguin, London, in 1979.

1972   *Written on Water* published by Oxford University Press.
Words and Images, graphic pieces and poems, published by Covent Garden Press.
Edits *William Carlos Williams: A Critical Anthology* published by Penguin.
(September) Exhibits graphic work, Ely House, London.

1974   Fellow of Royal Society of Literature.
Castilian Ilexes: Versions from Antonio Machado reissued in Penguin Modern European poets.
Aquilia Records: Song cycle "I have seen Eden," words by Charles Tomlinson, music by Stephen Srawley, recorded by Jane Manning.
Honorary Fellow of Queens' College, Cambridge.
The Way In and Other Poems published by Oxford University Press.

1975   One-man show of graphics at Clare College, Cambridge.
BBC television film: "The Poetry and Graphics of Charles Tomlinson."
In Black and White: The Graphics of Charles Tomlinson published by Carcanet Press (Introduction by Octavio Paz).
Reading at Rotterdam International Poetry Festival.

1976   Receives Cheltenham Poetry Prize.
Edits *William Carlos Williams: Selected Poems* published by Penguin.
(1 October–1 November) Bicentennial Reading Tour: New York, Princeton, Williamstown, Wisconsin, Chicago, Minnesota, Stanford, Pittsburgh, Haverford, Washington, D.C.

(2 November–16 November) Three Witter Bynner Lectures (Albuquerque).

1976–1977   Receives Leverhulme Fellowship to work on *The Oxford Book of Verse in English Translation*.

1978   *The Shaft* and *Selected Poems: 1951–1974* published by Oxford University Press.
(November) Opening at Hayward Gallery, London, of Arts Council of Great Britain Touring Exhibition, "The Graphics and Poetry of Charles Tomlinson," which toured throughout England until 1981.

1979   Reading at International Poetry Festival in Genova, Italy.
Edits *Octavio Paz: Selected Poems* published by Penguin.
Receives Cholmondeley Award for Poetry.

1979–1980   (December–January) Travels to San Francisco for MLA lecture. Visits Georgia O'Keeffe. Delivers Franklin Dickey Memorial Lecture in Albuquerque.

1980   Readings in Utrecht and Amsterdam.
Marianne Moore reading at Bryn Mawr. Readings at Colgate, Princeton, Pennsylvania, New York.
Airborn / Hijos del Aire (with Octavio Paz) published in Mexico by Martín Pescador.
Edits *The Oxford Book of Verse in English Translation* published by Oxford University Press.

1981   Exhibits 31 graphics at Exeter University.
Honorary Doctor of Literature at Keele University.
Exhibition of graphics at Keele University.
(May) Travels to USA: Honorary Doctor of Literature at Colgate University. Chapin Memorial Lecture on translation in New York.
(Autumn) Visiting Fellow, The Council of Humanities, Princeton University.
(October) Travels to Albuquerque to deliver Witter Bynner Centenary Lecture: "Ovid in Augustan Translation"; poetry reading.

The Flood published by Oxford University Press.
Some Americans: A Personal Record published by University of California Press.
Airborn / Hijos del Aire (with Octavio Paz) published by Anvil Press.

1982   Receives Wilbur Award for Poetry.
(January–February) Delivers Clark Lectures at Cambridge on "Poetry and Metamorphosis."
(August) Travels to Mexico for International Festival of Poetry in Mexico City.
Isaac Rosenberg of Bristol published by Bristol Historical Association.

1983   *The Sense of the Past: Three Twentieth Century Poets.* The Kenneth Allott Memorial Lecture, published by Liverpool University Press.
Addresses MLA (New York): "William Carlos Williams and Measure."
Exhibits graphics at Poetry Society, London.
Poetry and Metamorphosis published by Cambridge University Press.
(August) Reading at International Poetry Festival in Rome.
(November) Reading at Mondello Prize Festival in Palermo.
Translations published by Oxford University Press.

1984   Juror for Neustadt Literary Prize at Norman, Oklahoma.
Notes from New York and Other Poems published by Oxford University Press.
Rotterdam International Festival of Literature: reading and paper on "Poetry and Inspiration."
Collaboration with Raymond Warren in a song cycle for voice and piano, a work for spoken voice with flute and percussion, and a choral work—the latter given a prize and performed in the town hall at Leuven, Belgium.

1985   Edits enlarged edition of *William Carlos Williams: Selected Poems* for New Directions.

Collected Poems published by Oxford University Press.
Eden: Graphics and Poetry published by Redcliffe Press.
Cambridge International Festival of Literature: reading and paper "On First Reading Ezra Pound."
Delivers lecture to Boston Seminar on Translation: Readings at Boston, Middlebury, Brown.
Three week tour, reading in Germany at Universities of Tübingen, Erlängen, Freiburg, Heidelberg, Mannheim.
Delivers lecture, "Poetry and Music," at Leuven European Festival, Belgium.
Exhibits at Keele University: "Charles Tomlinson: A Celebration" of books, manuscripts, photographs, and graphics.
Keele University inaugurates a unique archive of the poetry of Charles Tomlinson, to be recorded over three years by the poet. Three cassettes issued commercially.

1986   One-man show of graphics opens new gallery at Regent's College, London.
Honorary Doctor of Literature from University of New Mexico.
"Shelley in Italia," lecture given at Shelley Conference, in San Terenzo, Italy.

1986–1987   Four graphics in touring exhibition: "Surrealism in English Art."

1987   Ten graphics to Colby College Gallery, Maine.
(April) Lamont Professor at Union College, Schenectady, N.Y.
Reading and lecture at Colgate University, N.Y.
First reading in Clore Gallery, Tate, with John Ashbery.
The Return published by Oxford University Press.
(September) Visiting Professor at McMaster University, Canada. Selection of graphics at McMaster Art Gallery.

Poésies Choisies—selected poems in French published by Janjard, Paris.

(December) Edmund Blunden Lecture in Hong Kong.

Selected poems in Italian, *Nella pienezza del tempi*, published by Garzanti.

Alan Ross and Charles Tomlinson

3. Words and Water

Charles Tomlinson has been Reader in English Poetry at the University of Bristol since 1968. He lives with his wife and two daughters, both musicians, half an hour's drive from the nearest railway station in a steep, narrow valley—like a slightly open book—consumed by green. The stream from his garden (in which he himself grows the vegetables) runs in due course into the Severn estuary. From his house—two old cottages joined into one—no other buildings can be seen. He is a tallish, spare man whose austere features—at least in repose—are deceptive. His books of poems, ranging from *The Necklace* (1955) to *The Shaft* (1978), have earned him a distinctive place in contemporary English poetry. He is one of the most scholarly and traveled of English writers, a gifted translator, and a graphic artist whose works are at present being shown in London after a two-year tour. I spent a day with him in Gloucestershire during August, the thickly wooded, watered landscape at its lushest, almost too good to be true. When I got back to London I wrote out a number of questions and posted them off.

AR   Your poem "The Marl Pits," where, as in "At Stoke," you recall a childhood landscape, ends with the line "And words and water came of the same source" (*WI*, 11). Light, air and water have always been the guiding elements of your poetry and you suggest in the same poem that the struggle to reach them freed you from your background. Could you describe this background and the process of escape?

Alan Ross is the editor of *London Magazine*. His recent books include *Death Valley* and *Blindfold Games*. "Words and Water" was originally published in *London Magazine*, n.s. 20 (January 1981): 22–39.

CT It was working class, beginning in a street of back-to-back houses—in the place Larkin assigned Mr. Bleaney's sister to, though she may have been a good deal sprier than her brother's creator ever realized. I was flying from Heathrow recently and the girl who was examining passports took one look at mine and said, "I come from there, too. Don't you miss the oatcakes?" I envied the people on the other side of that street because their yards ran right to the rear wall of a potbank. It was oddly comforting to think of the people out of that very street working away in there, and the wall gave out a warmth all the year round. Our background was a bit complicated by the fact that we were a Tory family in a Labor stronghold—rather like that of my friend Donald Davie in Barnsley. Only we were lower down the social and intellectual scale—his mother was a school teacher, and mine was a mill girl from Leicester. My father wasn't only Tory but also Jacobite. At least, in certain moods he was, when he could get himself to believe a notion of his aunt's that the Tomlinsons came of a by-blow of one of the Stuarts and were thus on the way to being heirs to the throne. Not a working-class fancy, you might think, and it wasn't. My father was a mysterious example of *déclassement*—of a fall from petty bourgeois status: partly by way of his marriage, partly by the loss of his job as manager of a jam pot factory (he blamed cheap Czechoslovakian glass), partly through a strange self-injuring streak that manifested itself more and more as a desire to repress the articulate side of his nature. Even at that, he liked to run things, was active as an organizer of local fishing clubs, and for years he contributed fishing notes to the *Evening Sentinel* under the pen name of Grayling. It was politics that aroused his most belligerent and least likable feelings. His father was a great admirer of Lloyd George, and to this I attribute his dislike of Welshmen. It ran into high fantasy—like his Jacobite sympathies when he reflected on who it was should be in Buckingham Palace instead of "those damned Windsors—and that's not their real name, you know." When we were on the beach at Rhyl he once said, "You see those chaps there with their shoes on—they're Welshmen. They never take their shoes off in public." "Why not?" I asked him. "Because they've got cloven hooves." I think he almost believed that.

What I had to escape wasn't only Stoke but also my father's

stale stoicism, which was half him and half the place. I escaped through schooling. There were some fine teachers in the schools who always noticed bright children and encouraged them. The only troubles I had there were the horrific bullying, mathematics, and illness. I got heart trouble at five, then pleurisy and rheumatic fever at nine, which cost me two years' absence. But once I was back in the swim, I made it to the local high school and simply reveled in learning languages: languages meant another world out there (not that you could get out there, since there was a war going on). And the Jewish teacher of German—a refugee from Hitler, who had studied at Berlin and Heidelberg—meant another world where people talked about Rilke and Kafka and Mann as everyday facts. Need you wonder that when a decade or so later the Larkin-Amis line about no myth kitties and no more poems on foreign cities looked like prevailing, I felt that my world—the world I'd been reaching out to since I was twelve—was under attack and I smelt in the air once more all the stalenesses I'd detested.

AR   In the poem "Class," you relate that a midland accent once cost you a job: "diction defeated my best efforts . . . you had only to open your mouth . . . to show where you were born and where you belonged" (*WI*, 11). For most writers, whatever the limitations, their adolescent surroundings exercise increasing pull. Have you resisted yours rather than drawn from them? I ask, even though your Stoke poems seem to me among your best.

CT   Put it this way—I have both resisted and drawn from my adolescent surroundings. When people ask me if I rejected my surroundings, I have to reply that they rejected me. Meaning that so much of them was just too thin a soil to support the weediest growth. Even though I helped in the fish and chip shop round the corner, I've no nostalgia about all that. What it came to in terms of literary culture was the *Daily Express*, the *News of the World*, the *People*.

One thing I haven't said about Stoke is that it was a long, narrow town and, on foot or by bike, you could easily get out into surrounding country—lush to the south and harsh moorland to the north. The place was still invaded by farms and fields side by side with pitheads and the housing estates. So I knew the countryside intimately from early on. And like so many others I was a member of a fishing club—of two or three, in fact—and we fished the canals on the outskirts of the city and went to matches or fished alone, all over Staffordshire. That's what contemplation was for me—fishing. Silently watching water and willing the fish to appear—or not willing, just letting the fish drift up, luring them in a peculiar will-lessness into one's mental orbit. It's a wonderful discipline for a boy—just learning to sit still and keep your shadow off the water, to sit in silence and take in things under the surface. A good place to start as a poet—or a painter.

The experience of fishing went together with the experience of prolonged illness—those two years I spoke of—when you were alone upstairs, and in the quiet and a peculiar transparency of consciousness you could hear all the goings-on of the house proceeding—could even hear the clink of shunting wagons from the sidings beyond—and, although for long periods you didn't see people, you were very conscious of the world pulsing on as a fact quite distinct from yourself and yet in which you had a share. It was almost as if you were the invisible man and that, by imagining, you could more or less see what was happening down there and out there—almost as if you were out there, but unseen yourself. So my background—and my physique, if you like—made a contemplative of me, but it wasn't myself I was contemplating: it was what Coleridge in "Frost at Midnight" calls "all the numberless goings-on of life." That much of this took place for me in the Staffordshire countryside was also important.

AR   In an earlyish poem, "The Art of Poetry," you wrote

> At first, the mind feels bruised.
> The light makes white holes through the black foliage
> Or mist hides everything that is not itself.
>
> (N, 14)

and later, in the same poem,

> There must be nothing
> Superfluous, nothing which is not elegant
> And nothing which is if it is merely that.
>
> (N, 14)

You are arguing, I imagine, for words to earn their keep?

CT   Two things were at work in that poem. I was, as you say, arguing for words to earn their keep. I was also arguing with one of my mentors and with a certain aspect of his elegance—I mean Wallace Stevens. That second bit you quote is a playful demur, phrased after his "Snow Man," where he writes about the listener who "nothing himself, beholds / Nothing that is not there and the nothing that is." I was worried that this kind of thing could lead to rather self-conscious writing, and Stevens himself didn't always avoid that. In arguing for words to earn their keep, I was arguing for a kind of exactness in face of the object, which meant an exactness of feeling in the writer. It meant that you must enter into a relationship with things, that you must use your eyes and see what they were offering you—what, at first, you might not notice. I suppose I learned this lesson from Ruskin—chiefly from the evocations of leaves, clouds, water in *Modern Painters*, but he only extended on a conscious plane what I already intuitively knew from watching water when I went fishing as a child. The wind-prints you saw there and the state of the light told you about a lot more than just the way to catch fish.

AR   You were, I think, taken up rather earlier and more enthusiastically in America than in England, yet it seems to me that you are a particularly English poet in feeling, if less in subject matter and technique. Can you account for such American interest?

CT   The immediate reason is that one of the very few critics who wasn't looking the other way when I published *The Necklace* in 1955 was Hugh Kenner. He wrote an excellent review for *Poetry* (Chicago). The editor, Henry Rago, asked me for new work and I had a considerable quantity—the better part of a book that I couldn't place here. "I cannot see the difference between these poems and prose," C. Day Lewis wrote to me from Chatto's. Well, Henry Rago could, and the same was true of Frederick Morgan at *The Hudson Review*. When Kenner came to this country in November 1956, he returned to the States with *Seeing Is Believing* in his satchel—I'd tried it on practically every publisher in this country—and he placed it with his own publisher,

McDowell, Obolensky. So that much was Kenner's doing. He also talked about my things to Marianne Moore (who had been a considerable influence) and to Williams (who was to be subsequently). Perhaps the Americans responded to a certain tonality that owed something to Stevens and Moore—poets who saved me from the Dylan Thomas infection. And, also, like you, they could see, I think, that I was a particularly English poet—that was the impression I got when Henry Rago talked to me about my work. It was a real thrill and honor to have so much poetry in his magazine, and to win some of its prizes, during his marvelous editorship. When he died, what a falling off was there. The magazine began to feel like a chi-chi boutique. A great decade was over.

AR From Stoke you went to Cambridge, having been just too young for the war. Was this a good time for you, in terms of friends, influences, your own writing?

CT At Cambridge, as in another, more august case, imagination seems to have slept. I wrote very little there until later on when I almost wrecked my degree chances because of a passion for writing film scripts. I was film mad. I think it was all the visual experience films offered—even rather poor films. It takes a lot to drag me to the cinema these days, but I still love the moment when the curtains divide and the dream screen opens. It's all the novelettish stuff dressed up in "technique" and the sexual twaddle that usually follows that puts me off. Thin stuff for all the visual compulsion.

It's difficult to talk of Cambridge tidily. I was still in touch with old friends from Stoke, and I'd made a new friend, Donald Reid, from Blackpool. The Stoke group—there were five of us from the same high school—was passionate about music and so was Donald. And I mean music. Not that pop-pudding all the kids from every class of our society slop around in today. We were fascinated by the power and precision of Toscanini—as Ted Hughes tells me he was as a youth. It's been difficult to listen to other people's Beethoven ever since—we even got to like the terrible biscuit-tin noises those boxy recordings reduced the timpani to. Donald, who had actually played timps with the Blackpool Symphony Orchestra, knew Benjamin Britten, and whenever he came to Cambridge—people still thought him terribly modern in '45—we used to go and see him. I remember his once saying, "I've just played through the Brahms symphonies in piano score, and they're as bad as I always thought they were." It took me twenty years or more to get back to Brahms after that.

The big figure at Cambridge in those days was Leavis, of course. I realize in retrospect just how much one learned from him—but I couldn't stand the charismatic presence always demanding more of one's soul than one wanted to give. I had to stop going to his lectures and read it all in his books. I also had the feeling that the *Scrutiny* group somehow distrusted living artists: you have only to look at the "creative" work in the review—eventually trickling down to none at all—to realize how lazy they got when confronted by others than the mighty dead. But Leavis was a force—there's no denying it—and Cambridge treated him abominably.

AR   A number of your early poems are about the Lerici coast of Italy. How did you get there? Does Italy still seem more home to you than elsewhere in Europe?

CT   I'd just begun my fourth year as an elementary school teacher in London. I had a poem in *Botteghe Oscure*, the magazine that came out in Rome, directed by Princess Marguerite Caetani. She'd asked me about myself—probably all she wanted was a contributor's note, but I sent up a howl about being trapped in Camden Town and how terrible it all was. So she asked a friend of hers to have a look at me and at my drawings. To cut a long story short, it was through him I got the job as Percy Lubbock's secretary near Lerici. It lasted three weeks. He suddenly decided he didn't want a secretary—this was the accent business in "Class." I've told the story at more length in an autobiographical volume due from the University of California press, *Some Americans*. Thanks to the kindness of Lubbock's stepdaughter, we—and I really must say "we," since I had long been married: a girl from Stoke, of course—we were allowed to stay on in a villino that adjoined the gardener's house. Through the gardener and his wife, we got to know their relations—up at La Serra, the nearby village, and the link with La Serra has gone ever since. A number of friends went as migrant workers to Germany, but one of them who stayed put, Paolo Bertolani, published a rather successful book last year—*Racconto della Contea di Levante*—about his life as a boy and about the ghosts and the folk life of his bit of the coast. When I first knew him, he wasn't quite twenty—unemployed, writing poems, and spending every spare penny on books. He's ended up in the police force—an unusual, but as it turns out a fruitful, place for a writer. Yes, Italy is still more home than elsewhere in Europe—and not just Liguria. My choice of a town would always be Siena.

AR You have been teaching at Bristol now for nearly twenty-five years, with visiting lectureships in America. Has the life of an academic seemed natural to you, or, had things been different, would you have preferred another way of earning your living, or preferred even to have lived the life of a full-time writer?

CT The beauty of teaching is that you are paid to read good books and you keep in touch with the younger generation and often, by the right few words at the right moment, you can be very helpful to them. I could never have been a full-time writer. I just don't have the sort of popular appeal that would earn me a living. On the other hand, I don't simply write—I write and paint. The two combined with teaching are more than a full-time occupation. The sheer physical exhaustion of it all is devastating. At times, one's nerve ends simply ache.

AR Since the Oxford University Press first published you in 1960, you have brought out another seven volumes of poems with them, at roughly three-year intervals. During the same period you have produced translations from Tyutchev, Machado, Vallejo, and Paz, and your *Oxford Book of Verse in English Translation* has recently appeared. How useful to you has been your involvement in translation? In what way do you usually set about it?

CT To begin with, I'd better say that I don't much believe in translation theory. In the 1930s show last year there was a picture of a strong man shifting two mangles. I tend to think of the recent spate of translation theory books as resembling the man with the mangles: you lift all this machinery and carry it a certain distance and let it go with a great clunk. And still you can't write a decent translation of two lines of Catullus. I began translating because Henry Gifford, who has an enviable linguistic ability, said to me, "Just look at this poem by Tyutchev—it seems to have a lot in common with your own work." So he took me through it step-by-step, wrote me out a transparency, as he called it, and we set to work on our little volume of Tyutchev, sadly out of print now. To start with, you must have some common ground with your text, and I think in differing ways that's what happened when I tackled Machado and Vallejo with Henry and more recently Pushkin's *Bronze Horseman*. In the Pushkin, for example, there occurs an extraordinary combination of formality and passion that recommends itself immediately. In all these ventures, it's really been my friendship of twenty-five years with Henry, the sharing of and kindling to his discoveries, that has supplied the base. He can take one into a language even when one doesn't know it—like Russian—and he can stop one fumbling when one does—as in the case of Spanish, though I didn't really know much Spanish when we embarked on Machado. I've learned it since. In a way, translation for me has often been a celebration of our friendship, and it's given me, of course, insights into ways of broadening one's own scope as a poet. Without Machado's "Poem of a Day," for example, I could never have written "Up at La Serra," which seems to me my first important attempt at a political poem. What I've learned from doing *The Oxford Book of Verse in English Translation* is this: we have a great literature of poetic translation that nobody reads. It's a scandal that there isn't a cheap edition (as there was in the nineteenth century) of Pope's Homer or Garth's Ovid that contains some of Dryden's greatest poetry. I learned also—and this is something I want to explore when I give the Clark Lectures at Cambridge in '82—that it's possible for poets to do some of their finest work in translation. Dryden and Shelley prove that, in their contrasted ways. You might even say in Dryden's case that translation—particularly of Ovid and Lucretius—permitted him to surpass himself as no other literary mode could have. The poets also—and it is as true of Rossetti and Chapman as it is of Dryden, Pope, Shelley, Pound—say marvelous things about translating, in a way the men with the mangles never do. I learned something else from *The Oxford Book*: there are translators of poetry lurking under every stone, quite ferocious in their urge for self-promotion. Translation can become a soothing mechanical habit for non-poets—something like knitting.

AR You have edited essays on Marianne Moore and William Carlos Williams. How did these come about?

CT They came about because I thought people ought to know more of Williams and Moore and because there were classic essays about them out of circulation: Eliot's two fine essays on Moore, for example, and Paul Rosenfeld and Gorham Munson on Williams. I might as well have spared myself the effort, to judge from reception and sales. The trouble is, in the supermarket conditions of today's bookshops, if everyone doesn't come forward cheering, in no time at all a book disappears from the shelves and is dead. That's what happened to the Moore and the Williams.

AR Have the works of any of your friends or contemporaries had any special influence on you?

CT I can think straight off of three contemporaries who are close friends and whose examples have deeply affected me in different ways. My oldest friend is Donald Davie. As my supervisor in my last year at Cambridge, he kept me on the rails and really restored for me a love of learning that the place had done much to sap. He criticized, with generosity and trenchancy and humor, most of my early work. If he hadn't written the introduction to *The Necklace*, no one would have published it here. Yet how different the poems in that volume were from his poems of the time. I think stylistically we've always been very distinct as poets, but we have this in common—a vocabulary and a certain moral ethos that owes a lot to the eighteenth century. Years ago, we were reading Smart and Cowper and saying here were great practitioners you could learn from. For both of us, and increasingly so, Dryden has been one of the major figures—I mean we'd place him beside Chaucer. What Donald had to say about diction and syntax in his first two critical books put me on the alert just when I needed direction: *Articulate Energy* confirmed and focused vague thoughts I'd been having about syntax as I got to the end of *The Necklace*. It was a book that showed one a way forward as a poet. And, of course, Donald is just very good company. When he emigrated to America, if the world weren't science mad, his going would have been lamented in the newspapers as those of our physicists were.

I promised you three friends. George Oppen and Octavio Paz are about as different from each other as they are from Donald. I'm not sure that either of them has influenced my style of writing—I'd found a style long before I knew them. But they are men of total integrity, and the way they've lived their lives— George mostly privately, Octavio more in the public eye—is a lesson to anyone. I'm not sure the English have ever taken their measure properly. George's quite considerable body of poetry, beginning in 1934, then encountering a twenty-five year silence, really gets accomplished from 1962 on when he published *The Materials*. It was in reviewing that, I came to know him. There is no sign of him in Enright's *Oxford Book of Contemporary Verse*, where all those skillful east-coast verse musings get more than their fair innings. But then, I can't see the English have ever genuinely known what Pound and Williams were at, either. Eliot somehow slipped into the fold. We *are* an incurious race. When Octavio Paz came as Simón Bolívar professor to Cambridge, I had the impression that very few people there knew who he was. Why, somebody I was talking to had even got him muddled up with Mario Praz. What I owe most to Octavio is his instinctive sense of what I was up to in my graphic work and his ability (even in everyday talk) to make a situation (and I'm quoting Arnold from memory) of which the creative power can avail itself. You feel, after talking to Octavio, that you want to sit down and *make* something. We've just done a little sonnet sequence together by post called *Airborn*—due soon from Anvil. It was an attempt to achieve a work a bit more intimate than that experiment, *Renga*, which we did for Gallimard in '69 with two other poets, Sanguineti from Italy and Roubaud from France. That's out in Penguin now.

AR   An exhibition of your graphics is at present on tour. When did you start this kind of work? Can you describe the process?

CT   When I came down from Cambridge in '48 and got stuck in elementary school teaching in London, I spent most of my evenings drawing and painting. I showed one or two things in summer exhibitions at the Leicester Gallery and at Gimpel Fils. There was even the offer of a job in a Brook Street Gallery run by a gentleman called Rubin. The idea was that he would own my pictures in return for which I would receive a wage—I was also to help in the gallery. The contract was being typed by Mrs. Rubin, so I went for an anxious walk to contemplate the ducks in Regent's Park. I got back to Brook Street and the typewriter was still rattling and above its noise I said a belated no, much to Rubin's fury. After that, and over the years, I kept up a certain amount of drawing. It wasn't easy to fit in—for one thing I was writing *Seeing Is Believing*, for another I was preparing myself for academic work by taking an M.A. in English. Once I got the job at Bristol, there was even less time, with lectures to prepare and the demands of teaching. However, during the vacations I kept trying but got myself into an odd formal problem. I wanted to bring out the resistant presence of objects, and there always came a certain moment when I found the separating outlines becoming too coarse. I couldn't reconcile sensation and form without forcing the picture into a willed unity. The marks of those paintings were a darkened background and an uneasy black line round all the forms. Black obsessed me, drove me away from painting, you might say—that and the need to earn a living. So I thought it was all over. And for twelve years it was.

Then in 1968 I'd been gazing at some reproductions of Hércules Seghers—landscapes that looked almost like moonscapes, almost monochrome in effect, suggesting that you could use black if only you knew how. I did a few things that summer—some in black, some in sepia. They weren't much good, but they helped unclog the blockage. The summer after that—God, what a time it takes to do these things!—I managed to make a very *exact* series of drawings in Indian ink, of cattle and bird skulls, and I kept at it, off and on, till the next summer. It was then I went from drawing to collage and decalcomania. Decalcomania is the surrealist device whereby you spread out paint on one surface, cover it with another surface, press, draw off and then see what you've got. I'd read Óscar Domínguez's recipe for this in which he says, "Spread out black gouache." Actually, I was using tempera tins left over from my London days—but it *was* black. So I started to use black directly. I altered the decalcomania with brush, and I cut it up with scissors and recombined it. This started a real flood of pictures. It was tremendously exhausting, but by 1972 there were enough to put on an exhibition at Oxford University Press to coincide with a new book of poems, *Written on Water*. Not that the art press or the literary press took any notice, but Michael Dibb, who directed the John Berger TV documentaries, *Ways of Seeing*, went to the show and told me that one day, when he had some money, he wanted to do a V film about the pictures and their relation to the poetry. There was another show at the Cambridge Poetry Festival in 1974. In 1975 Michael Dibb made his film—three-quarters of an hour's worth that had to be tailored to fit a fifteen-minute slot. All the same, he managed to give it a splendid continuity. The rest was stored on the BBC shelves and somebody destroyed it.

The present Arts Council exhibition was entirely instigated by Jonathan Barker, their poetry librarian, who showed the reproductions in a volume called *In Black and White*—a selection of my graphics introduced by Paz and done by Carcanet Press—to Andrew Dempsey, the Deputy Director of Exhibitions. Andrew came down to look at my studio—namely the table in our sitting room—and I rescued all the pictures from under the bed and behind the piano. He looked at them, liked them, got an excellent designer, Philip Miles, and, together with Jonathan, we assembled a selection of poems and graphics. The frames are numbered like a book, and we hoped my publishers might make one of the show, but they soon realized it would cost too much. It's at the end of a two-year tour—at Swiss Cottage Library from 3 January to 1 February.

AR   More than most English poets, you show an interest in, and relate your poems to, painting. Which contemporary painters have most attracted you?

CT   I don't feel we are living in a great age of painting. My real affections go back to the explosion from 1910 or so up to the twenties, and then the recovery of energies by the school of New York. If I were picking out favorites, it would be the analytic cubism of Braque and Picasso, then Juan Gris; some of the surrealists—Magritte, early Ernst, early Matta, Miró. I like Arshile Gorky. Then there are "traditional" Americans like Demuth and Georgia O'Keeffe. The list would be endless. Perhaps it's enough to say Cézanne is my favorite "modern" painter—for sheer quality of painting as great as Titian—and there's all that he has inspired among the writers: Rilke's superb letters about him to Clara Rilke, Merleau-Ponty's essay, Adrian Stokes's piece of 1947, Philippe Jaccottet's meditation in *Paysages avec Figures Absentes*, Williams's scattered remarks. His problems were our problems—the negotiation between self and world when the romantic inflation of self has failed.

AR You live surrounded by green—hills, trees, fields—and with the constant sound of water. Your poems are full of shadows, half-lights, glimmerings. Is this the landscape you would have chosen for yourself?

CT It's perfect. It's a perfect fulfillment of chance—finding the place, and then almost being chosen by it, to make it articulate. But I do love other landscapes—the deserts of New Mexico and Arizona, for instance, the pueblos along the Rio Grande, the vastnesses of upstate New York, the cultivated lands of Provence and Tuscany. Of course, there are certain big cities too that fascinate—New York itself, Chicago, Paris, not to mention London.

AR Personal relationships, domestic life, friends even, are rarely evident in your poetic country, which has rather the air of an unpeopled Eden. Yet plainly they are an assumption behind all your writing. Is their absence from your poems a kind of diffidence? Are objects—animals, stone walls, skulls, churches, valleys—more real to you, or at any rate more conducive to poetry?

CT If you take a rather different sort of poetry from mine— George Herbert's say—there aren't many people present: the whole thing is between him and God, the poems are prayers and contemplations and self-discoveries—very different from the social world of Pope. Now the sort of poems you speak of, in my case, are also in their way a kind of religious poetry—a finding of what my friend, the French poet Philippe Jaccottet, calls *ouvertures*—openings through place into mystery. Place—this place—speaks to me more than the dogmas of any religion, and it speaks of very fundamental things: time, death, what we have in common with the animals, what things are like when you stop talking and look, what Eden is like, what a center is. But that is only one kind of poem I write—there are political poems like "Assassin," "Prometheus," "Over Elizabeth Bridge" and polemical poems like "Against Extremity," "The Chances of Rhyme." There are funny poems—some in every book practically. There are cityscapes like the long one in *American Scenes* about Washington Square, San Francisco. If the poems of contemplation are heard, are weighed rightly, they neighbor those other poems. Indeed, the poems of contemplation are written in a language so dense in the usages of community that I can never think of them as being merely private or passive or just concerned with "stilled" moments: they are full of the weave of time, they map the continuous negotiation we all make in being involved in a world of things whose full nature keeps eluding us. I also think that in those particular poems I am addressing somebody, that I am taking some other person with me as I write down the words they are going to mouth over. But they do call on a certain relinquishment and distrust of the ego, a certain anonymity, as one feels oneself into relation with all those "numberless goings-on of life" that are intricated in time, place, death, otherness. Yet, as I say, these poems need to be seen in relation with very diverse ones—like my French Revolution sequence in *The Shaft*, for example.

AR You list your recreations in *Who's Who* as "music and walking." You have your daughters to play for you at home and you have marvelous walking country all round. Is there anything you miss, living where you do?

CT I don't miss a thing. It's a marvelous place and a marvelous base. I teach in a major city. I see as much of London as I wish. In the course of a year or so, I've been, at odd moments, in Italy, New Mexico, New York, Holland. Of course, I spend a lot supporting OPEC. But my real problem is time, not place. This is the most unclaustrophobic valley in all Gloucestershire and the county itself is so varied. My next book, *The Flood*, due in June, explores the place as far as the Severn estuary and the people who have lived there. That's a great area too.

AR Do notions of committed poetry have any meaning to you? I assume all poetry to be "committed" in one way or another, but the term is bandied about these days as if it had a narrower significance: a commitment to political action of some kind, a vague radicalism.

CT "Notions of committed poetry" makes me think again of my friend George Oppen, who lived through the thirties as a member of the Communist Party but refused to write "political" poetry. He says that he saw men who needed feeding, and since you couldn't feed them by writing poetry, he went into poor-relief work. He also said that he didn't believe in the honesty of a man's declaring, "Well, I'm a poet and I will make my contribution to the cause by writing poems about it." His reply to that one was, "I don't believe that's any more honest than to make wooden nutmegs because you happen to be a wood-maker. If you decide to do something politically, you do something that has political efficacy. And if you decide to write poetry, then you write poetry, not something that you hope, or deceive yourself into believing, can save people who are suffering." I really let George answer that question for me, but I'll add this: what people understand by "political poetry" usually means urging liberal sentiments that your audience agrees with anyway—knowing in advance what it is your poem has to say and then joining your auditors in a bath of self-righteous indignation. I am thinking of the Vietnam poems that were so much to the fore in public readings in America in the sixties, and pretty corny little things they look now, to quote W. C. Fields. I'm always struck by the contrast between Vallejo's poems in which he identifies himself with the Peruvian *chollo*, without urging solutions or attitudes, and his utterly banal journalism, reporting Russia in the thirties. And one further point: in poems like "Assassin" (which came out in *London Magazine*) and "Prometheus," not to mention "Over Elizabeth Bridge" (another *London Magazine* piece), I've written poems about political situations. I began as early as "Up at La Serra" in *A Peopled Landscape*, where I see a young boy trapped in a situation in which unemployment is the chief threat. And in my last book, I try to imagine what it was like to be Charlotte Corday, Danton, J. L. David, at the time of the French Revolution. But the measure of these poems oughtn't to be whether they're committed to political reality (though they are), but whether I've preserved the language there in which such things can be written of—whether my duty to language has been maintained and I've thus succeeded in reconciling public and private concerns.

Auricular (no date given)

Part II

The Poet

Perspectives

Joel F. Wilcox

4. Tomlinson and the British Tradition

The British poet Charles Tomlinson has been supposed by some readers to be the particular property of Americans because of his affinity for the ways of our poetry. His appreciation of William Carlos Williams, as signified by his use of Williams's familiar triadic line, indicated to the American that his own poetry would be received in England one day.[1] At the same time Tomlinson was building his reputation, there were the trips to the United States, the tenure in New Mexico, and the visits to Williams, Marianne Moore, and Yvor Winters so engagingly recounted in his book *Some Americans*. Indeed, a few Americans doubtless look on Tomlinson's "adoption" of America as proof of their suspicion that the contemporary British poetic landscape is barren.[2] If nothing else, Tomlinson's "Americanism" is novel, so much so that we are apt to underrate his place in the British tradition and his contribution to its development.

The poet himself has asserted that the formative influences on his development derive from the British poetic tradition and that his favorites were the Augustan and romantic poets. He says though the "distinguishable American presences in my own work . . . were . . . Pound, Stevens, and Marianne Moore . . . the tradition of the work went back to Coleridge's conversation poems" ("Some Americans," 287). Furthermore, he characterizes his work as "a phenomenological poetry, with roots in

Joel Wilcox is Assistant Director of the Undergraduate Academic Advising Center at the University of Iowa. He is a specialist in Renaissance studies, principally the poetry and translations of George Chapman.

1. Charles Tomlinson, "Some Americans: A Personal Record." *Contemporary Literature* 18 (1977): 289–90. Hereafter cited in the text by abbreviated title and page number.
2. For a brief account of some misjudgments of contemporary British poets by Americans, see the concluding pages of Donald Davie's *Thomas Hardy and British Poetry*.

Wordsworth and in Ruskin."[3] Whatever promise of future recognition Williams interpreted for himself from Tomlinson's
style, Tomlinson himself had feared that Williams would dislike
his volume *Seeing Is Believing* because the influences in it were
English and European ("Some Americans," 291).

Influences can make for a risky discussion in the case of a
living poet. After all, Harold Bloom's theory (*The Anxiety of Influence*) that a strong poet consciously misreads his predecessors
tempts a critic to take a poet's pronouncements concerning influences he has felt and turn them on their head. I propose a different attitude toward literary influence here. I would like to focus
less on the direct than the indirect influence, assuming enough
of the principle of plenitude that, given the developments in poetics up to his time, a poet such as Charles Tomlinson must in-
evitably have come along. "Influence" in this sense, therefore,
suggests the matrix in which a mind may develop, from which it
may depart in directions of its own choosing. I therefore confine
my exploration of influences on Tomlinson in the British tradition to the Augustans (including Wordsworth!) and Ruskin.

To begin with, how would Charles Tomlinson have read the
Augustan poets? Tomlinson collaborated in some measure with
his former tutor, Donald Davie, on Davie's 1958 edition of *The
Late Augustans*, a carefully chosen selection with an excellent introductory essay. If Tomlinson shares the view of Davie and
F. R. Leavis (one of the critics he quotes with some regularity),
he would believe that the Augustan poets have tended to get
rather less acclaim than is their due. Much of this has to do, no
doubt, with prejudices we inherit from the romantics and the
Victorians, but some damaging prejudices may have come as a
result of misinterpretation of the lines of tradition that the Augustans followed. Leavis claimed, for instance, that rather than
place Pope in the line of tradition Pope drew for himself—from
Waller to Denham and then to Dryden—we should link Pope to
that coalescence of the metaphysical and cavalier lines in the
seventeenth century as traced from Donne and Jonson through
Carew and Marvell. Pope's wit, Leavis thinks, is metaphysical
but distinguished by those developments that mark the Augustan frame of mind: the emphasis on civility, morality, and so-

3. William Cookson, "Tomlinson, (Alfred) Charles," in *Contemporary Poets*,
3d ed., edited by James Vinson (New York: St. Martin's Press, 1980), p. 1544.

phistication as summed up in the polished numbers of the te-
trameter and pentameter couplet.[4]

Similarly, a significant difference between the seventeenth
and eighteenth centuries lies in the transmutation of the cultural
center from predominantly aristocratic to bourgeois society. The
satirists could indeed make fun of ingenious projectors attempt-
ing to rise on the social ladder, but Pope and Swift in doing so
spoke from the reactionary fringe of the age. It was the burgeon-
ing class of businessmen and bluestockings who were to become
the social middle of the eighteenth century. Pope wailed over
the death of metaphysics as Donne had complained a century
before that the element of fire was quite put out. But the Augustan mainstream turned to more domestic themes. As Horace
coveted the quiet pleasures of his Sabine farm, the Augustans
found their lyrics in the common labor and pleasure of a man's
brief day. Matthew Prior, in his fine poem, "A Better Answer to
Cloe Jealous," put it this way: "Let us e'en talk a little like folks
of this world." The poet had to master the Horatian mode of
simple elegance. Swift himself, who rarely countenanced the
Augustan celebration of rusticity or the pastoral life, took some
pride in making Gulliver talk like folks of this world, having read
his text to the servants of his household to be certain of its com-
prehensibility. In view of this sketch of literary history, one
might expect that Tomlinson admires the Augustan poets for
their polished phrasing, their civility, and their sophisticated
wit, for these are all qualities of his own verse. Even more at the
heart of his concerns, however, is the Augustan penchant for
humble detail. For the first time, things of this world actually
mattered to these poets, not for the sake of metaphysical comparison but for what the things are in themselves. Indeed, James
Thomson used Miltonic blank verse in his epic-length *The Seasons* because he took as his starting-point the belief that an accurate and detailed portrait of the humble affairs of nature would
reveal the harmony of the world and thereby justify anew the
ways of God to men.

Certainly, such an appreciation of the uses of humble experience would account to some degree for Tomlinson's "imitation"
of the (proto-Augustan!) poet Andrew Marvell's poem "The Pic-

4. F. R. Leavis, *Revaluation* (New York: Norton, 1963), pp. 68–100.

ture of Little T. C. in a Prospect of Flowers." Tomlinson's poem, called "The Picture of J. T. in a Prospect of Stone" (*PL*, 17–18), is composed in the triadic line that Tomlinson learned from Williams, but otherwise it is a transmutation of the type of elegant metaphysical lyric that gave rise to the urbane Augustan verse. Marvell uses a manner of description and depiction that indirectly confers praise and confers it more convincingly because of the indirection.

> See with what simplicity
> This Nimph begins her golden daies!
> In the green Grass she loves to lie,
> And there with her fair Aspect tames
> The wilder flow'rs, and gives them names:
> But only with the Roses playes;
>   And them does tell
> What Colour best becomes them, and what Smell.[5]

I suspect the poem holds a certain fascination for Tomlinson because of his interest in the psychic response to things symbolized by the process of naming.[6] By indirection, a characteristic feature of Marvell's urbanity, the poet calls on little T. C. to make those improvements in the world that it must be within her power to do: such reforming power ought ideally to be entailed in so great a degree of beauty and innocence.

> Reform the errours of the Spring;
> Make that the Tulips may have share
> Of sweetness, seeing they are fair;
> And Roses of their thorns disarm:
>   But most procure
> That Violets may a longer Age endure.[7]

In this, the emotional heart of the poem, the speaker celebrates the beauty of a little girl that is magical in part because it promises, but has not achieved, its full bloom. The pathos of such ruminations, however, becomes sweetly elegiac as one thinks on "the errours of the Spring" and the forbidden wish

5. Andrew Marvell, *Complete Poetry*, ed. George deF. Lord (New York: Modern Library, 1968), p. 37.
6. Cf. Charles Tomlinson, "Adam," *WW*, p. 8.
7. Marvell, *Complete Poetry*, p. 37.

that violets, like little girls, might have "a longer Age." If Marvell may wish (in this case, in his silences—by what he does *not* say) that a little girl playing in flowers might outlive her own brief span of innocence and beauty, Tomlinson may ask that his daughter, "emerging / from between / the stone lips / of a sheep-stile," might have "the constancy of stone." Tomlinson picks up from Marvell's silences by asking whether these wishes we conceive are for ourselves or for those for whom we would wish them.

> —How would you know
>   the gift you'd give
> was the gift
>   she'd wish to have?
>   (*PL*, 17–18)

The question is posed almost as a response to Marvell's last stanza with its assumption that precious youth and beauty are gifts of nature outside the control of men.

> Gather the Flow'rs, but spare the Buds;
> Lest Flora angry at thy crime,
> To kill her Infants in their prime,
> Do quickly make th'Example Yours;
>   And, ere we see,
> Nip in the blossome all our hopes and Thee.[8]

Tomlinson the father sees his daughter here less as an emblem of fragile budding loveliness than as a human potentiality. He transforms the metaphysical conceit into a concrete image. He finds his adult concerns for his child hinging on her concrete reactions, but he knows they will be the reactions of a child who yet lacks the lessons of experience. But how to teach, how to provide a vicarious experience? Teaching becomes the acting out, the gift, of the father's wishes, but an experimentation with received meanings for the child:

> —Gift is giving,
> gift is meaning:
>   first
>   I'd give

8. Ibid.

> then let her
> live with it
> to prove
> its quality the better and
> thus learn
> to love
> what (to begin with)
> she might spurn.
> (*PL*, 18)

Both poems express a feeling of one's longing for children who we know must butt up against experience, but whom we wish to teach such lessons of our own as might harden them against sorrow.

If Tomlinson's version ends less concretely than Marvell's, he capitalizes rather on his predecessor's theme of the uncertainty of fate, transforming the elegiac implications into almost a stoic speculation about what a father may do to bring into effect the wishes our children's helplessness brings out in us.

> —I'd have her
> understand
> the gift I gave her.
> —And so she shall
> but let her play
> her innocence away
> emerging
> as she does
> between
> her doom (unknown),
> her unmown green.
> (*PL*, 18)

What characterizes both poets is their grace and wit. Tomlinson's are not Marvell's, but they tally with Marvell's intentions in a way that is authentic to our ear. The facility of the poem as a whole and the cleverness of the rhymes of the last seven lines owe as much to the British tradition as to Williams, whose style this poem copies in apparent ways.

The eighteenth century has suffered some loss of esteem, perhaps, because of our tendency to take urbanity for shallowness and grace for insincerity. The romantics, so the argument goes, had to come to put things right. To this Leavis (and Davie following) provides a surprising counterargument. As Pope had seemed to Leavis to represent the last poet of the metaphysical line of the seventeenth century even though he was the first of the eighteenth, Wordsworth stood in the same position with regard to the eighteenth and nineteenth centuries. As Davie says, "Wordsworth's Preface to *Lyrical Ballads*, hostile as it is to eighteenth-century poetry, is yet the best introduction to that poetry."[9] Wordsworth is no less important as a poet consummating the tradition that bred him than as the Wanderer striking out in new directions.

With poems like "Eden" and "Adam" (*WW*), and many others besides, the Augustan Tomlinson gives way to the Wordsworthian. He has mentioned that Eden is one of the few symbols that he uses in his poetry,[10] and it strikes me that "Eden" for Tomlinson is a contemporary counterpart to that apprehension of an "active power" in nature of which Wordsworth documents his discovery in *The Prelude*. Wordsworth's study of epistemology (primarily the associationism of David Hartley, a popularizer of John Locke) provided creative stimulus to his own reflections about the relation of poetic creation to the divine creation of this universe, fulfilling both an eighteenth-century fascination with natural theology and giving particular expression to Sir Philip Sidney's notion that poetry becomes a second creation (and the poet, by implication, a newer god). For Wordsworth, to be a man was, as Addison has said, to be a philosopher, but to be a philosopher was also to be a poet:

> How exquisitely the individual Mind
> (And the progressive powers perhaps no less
> Of the whole species) to the external World
> Is fitted:—and how exquisitely, too—
> Theme this but little heard of men—
> The external World is fitted to the Mind;

9. Donald Davie, ed. *The Last Augustans: Longer Poems of the Later Eighteenth Century* (London: Heinemann, 1958), p. xxxii.

10. *P N Review* 5, no. 1 (1977): 37. He says, "Eden crops up . . . as if one were always trying to restore one's sense of somewhere already inhabited but never properly seen."

And the creation (by no lower name
Can it be called) which they with blended might
Accomplish:—this is our high argument.[11]

The associationism of Wordsworth's poetry (not without controversy even today) gave Blake, as he said, "a bowel complaint
which nearly killed him."[12] And Arnold settled the matter, he
believed, once and for all by declaring that "Wordsworthians
. . . lay far too much stress upon what they call his philosophy.
His poetry is the reality, his philosophy . . . is the illusion."[13]
Nevertheless, Wordsworth took his philosophy seriously enough
that one can scarcely accept the poetry without at least crediting
the decided impulse of its creation. Tomlinson, as one in the tradition of Wordsworth, tacitly acknowledges his predecessor's
concerns by giving his own version of Wordsworth's themes.
"Eden" seems to recall these opening lines of *The Prelude*:

Oh there is blessing in this gentle breeze,
A visitant that while it fans my cheek
Doth seem half-conscious of the joy it brings
From the green fields, and from yon azure sky.
Whate'er its mission, the soft breeze can come
To none more grateful than to me; escaped
From the vast city, where I long had pined
A discontented sojourner: now free,
Free as a bird to settle where I will.[14]

Tomlinson's response in "Eden" is not a denial of Wordsworth's
faith that the inspiring breeze comes upon him in the open fields
and craggy cliffs of nature, but it poses a more balanced account
of the ebb and flow of nature's creative stimulus:

11. William Wordsworth, "Preface" to *The Excursion*, in *Poetical Works*, ed.
Thomas Hutchinson (London: Oxford University Press, 1904), p. 590.
12. M. H. Abrams, *Natural Supernaturalism* (New York: Norton, 1972), p. 25.
Abrams cites his sources as follows: "Henry Crabb Robinson, letter to Dorothy
Wordsworth, February 1826, in *Blake, Coleridge, Wordsworth, Lamb*, etc., edited
by Edith J. Morley (Manchester, 1922), p. 15; and *H. C. Robinson on Books and their
Writers*, I, 327. See also Blake's marginal annotations on Wordsworth's *Poems* of
1815 and on the Prospectus, in *The Poetry and Prose of William Blake*, edited by
David Erdman and Harold Bloom (New York, 1965), pp. 654–56."
13. *Poetry and Criticism of Matthew Arnold*, ed. A. Dwight Culler (Boston:
Houghton Mifflin, 1961), p. 341.
14. Wordsworth, *Poetical Works*, p. 495.

Is given one, and the clairvoyant gift
Withdrawn, "Tell us," we say
    "The way to Eden," but lost in the meagre
Streets of our dispossession, where
    Shall we turn, when shall we put down
This insurrection of sorry roofs? Despair
    Of Eden is given, too: we earn
Neither its loss nor having. There is no
    Bridge but the thread of patience, no way
But the will to wish back Eden, this leaning
    To stand against the persuasions of a wind
That rings with its meaninglessness where
                    it sang its meaning.
                         (WW, 7–8)

Tomlinson provides here a corrective on Wordsworth. The ebb
and flow of meaning in nature is not sinister for Tomlinson—he
tells of no snakes in his Garden. Nature is "inspirational" to us
only in fits and starts. As something other, nature is no less the
whole whose parts we must bring into relation with each other
in order that we may bring it into relation with us. But it is the
philosophical dilemma of reducing nature to the limited frame of
our conception that provides a theme running throughout Tomlinson's work. His poem "Adam" illustrates how the instinctive
way we reduce nature by naming is finally a kind of inspired but
delimiting "madness."

Adam, on such a morning, named the beasts:
    It was before the sin. It is again.
An openwork world of lights and ledges
    Stretches to the eyes' lip its cup:
Flower-maned beasts, beasts of the cloud,
    Beasts of the unseen, green beasts
Crowd forward to be named.
                         (WW, 8)

What Tomlinson has imagined here is our condition as observers
of the world, where, if we observe carefully, divesting our
minds of its own idols, our vision is as before the "Fall." The
"[f]lower-maned beasts, beasts of the cloud, / Beasts of the un-

seen, green beasts" are the phantasmagoria of nature that do not become arranged in our ken until they have names.

> Are we the lords or limits
> Of this teeming horde? We bring
> To a kind of birth all we can name
> And, named, it echoes in us our being.
>
> (*WW*, 8)

It is a "kind of birth," this naming, a framing of conception that gives us the sense of our identities as distinct from that which we name. To follow out the analogy, naming, conceptualizing, objectifying becomes that dominion which the Lord gave Adam over all the creatures of the earth.

> Adam, on such a morning, knew
> The perpetuity of Eden, drew from the words
> Of that long naming, his sense of its continuance
> And of its source. . . .
>
> (*WW*, 8)

Adam inferred "The perpetuity of Eden" as a consequence of "that long naming," an inference of "continuance" and "source" because naming is a cause of his coming to know. The idea of "continuance" and "constancy" comes up repeatedly in Tomlinson's work. It was the "constancy of stone" that he wished for his daughter, and, indeed, there is usually something special about stone in Tomlinson's poems as symbolic of what is epistemologically graspable in a whole of flux (not that flux is to be feared, only that the constant gives us a point of stability from which to see the unstable).[15]

Nevertheless, mind is not nature, and "naming" becomes a kind of "unmaking" of the things in themselves. Adam learns from the process of naming a truth that he can only express through "murmuring in wordless words": the truth is that naming becomes an implicit denial of the virtue of paradise.

> "When you deny
> The virtue of this place, then you
> Will blame the wind or the wide air,

15. Cf. Charles Tomlinson, "The Flood," *F*, pp. 50–52. "It was the night of the flood first took away / My trust in stone" (*F*, 50).

Whatever cannot be mastered with a name,
    Mouther and unmaker, madman, Adam."
                            (*WW*, 8)

What is "this place"? It is Eden, but the reader is now being
forced to interpret what "Eden" means, which cannot be done
except by naming once again. It is the real, the objective, the
other-than-mind over which names and concepts give us some
mastery. But this "mastery" we also sense is a domestication,
where the things mastered by names become other than what
they would naturally be. The "wind" and "the wide air" receive
the things-in-themselves into the wildness beyond human enclosing. Our pigeonholing of things denies the "virtue of this
place," and the dilemma of our uncertainties gives way to a
blaming of something in things themselves that is ineffable and
mysterious. Yet mind is what we have. We recognize that sense
data do not organize themselves into intelligibility; it is consciousness that plots sense data on fields of awareness. There is
an impasse between substance and knowledge, and though consciousness bridges the distance by fiat, it also knows the cost of
its intrepidity. As Tomlinson writes in the third poem of "Four
Kantian Lyrics":

                We cannot pitch
    our paradise in such a changeful
    nameless place and our encounters
    with it. An insufficiency of earth
    denies our constancy.[16]
                            (*PL*, 21)

Tomlinson's Adam is like the poet in Shakespeare's Theseus's
dictum, who gives "to aery nothing a local habitation and a
name." Whereas Theseus accepted that sense data faithfully
record a solid world from which a poet's imagination could be
judged for mad, our poet sees the sense data and the solid world
as part of imagination's realm.

Tomlinson's epistemological concerns are kin to matters
brought up by Wordsworth, tied to the problems of language
and naming. Wordsworth's goal in the Preface to *Lyrical Ballads*

16. For a recent return to this theme of the insufficiency of earth, see "Ritor-
nello" (*F*, 33).

was to clarify why the essence of the poetical creation is distinct from the accouterments of poetic practice through the ages. Though he discussed the application of meter and rhyme—and he gave his approval to the uses of each—his primary intention was to define poetry as distinct from these things and as much exceeding them as the soul the body.

Wordsworth's plan to retain "the language of men" was somehow important to attaining his aim of writing good poetry. How is language "like the folks of this world" so near the essence of the poetic occupation? Proper diction is more an attendant condition than an efficient cause of poetry *per se*, but what Wordsworth was trying to avoid is the stultifying habit of relying on a dead vocabulary and on ready-made phrases. Accordingly, to seek to write in the language of men is to subject one's creations to the scrutiny of a public consciousness. Not that a wide public need necessarily understand any or all of a poet's makings, but the strength of his passions and his thoughts ought to be harnessed in a shared language rather than in the jargon of a trade or esoteric concern.

One feature of Wordsworth's ideas about poetic language is liable to misunderstanding, a misunderstanding that has an exact analogue in Tomlinson. Whereas Wordsworth claimed to present the passions or thoughts of his soul in the language of men, he claimed that the poet has a greater ability to feel or to understand things than the ordinary individual. But what is the use of the language of men if the poet must necessarily outstrip the men whose language he must use? More to the point, what does Wordsworth mean to imply when he says that the poet has

> an ability of conjuring up in himself passions, which are indeed far from being the same as those produced by real events, yet . . . do more nearly resemble the passions produced by real events, than anything which, from the motions of their own minds·merely, other men are accustomed to feel in themselves.[17]

Wordsworth was striving to bring into relation what we might simply call the "real" and the "ideal." "Poetry is the image of man and nature," he says.[18] The operative word here is "image."

17. William Wordsworth, "Preface," in *English Romantic Writers*, ed. David Perkins (New York: Harcourt, Brace, and World, 1967), pp. 324–25.
18. Ibid., p. 325.

The Poet writes under one restriction only, namely, the necessity of giving immediate pleasure to a human Being possessed of that information which may be expected from him . . . as a Man. Except this one restriction, there is no object standing between the Poet and the image of things.[19]

In other words, even though the poet takes command of the presentation of transcendent truths that a non-poet cannot understand, the nature of these truths and of men is such that when the poet presents them in their vividness, they may become understood potentially by all men alike. The "image," then, is an element caught between the ideal and the real, partaking of both jointly and joining the lower to the higher.

Charles Tomlinson has been working out in his own idiom the program for authenticating and articulating the imagination that Wordsworth prescribed for himself. In "The Art of Poetry" Tomlinson writes,

> At first, the mind feels bruised.
> The light makes white holes through the black foliage
> Or mist hides everything that is not itself.
>
> But how shall one say so?—
> The fact being, that when the truth is not good enough
> We exaggerate. Proportions
>
> Matter. It is difficult to get them right.
> There must be nothing
> Superfluous, nothing which is not elegant
> And nothing which is if it is merely that.
>
> (N, 14)

If we think the truth of phenomena falls short, our trouble with poetry is a problem with our own consciousness. Our exaggerations are as much a distortion as the artificial elegances that Wordsworth castigated in the Preface to *Lyrical Ballads*. Nevertheless, consciousness has its special claims, too. The mind must discern a realness transcending the mere particular, as the poet stresses in his poem, "Against Portraits":

19. Ibid.

if there must be
an art of portraiture,
let it show us ourselves as we
break from the image of what we are:

the animation of speech, and then
the eyes eluding
that which, once spoken,
seems too specific, too concluding:

or, entering a sudden slant
of brightness, between dark and gold,
a face half-hesitant,
face at a threshold.

                                                (WrW, 47)

"Face at a threshold" is a perfect image to grasp the idea of an essence transcending the particular. Tomlinson's ability as a poet to exploit the intermediary character of art as it seeks to interpret the imagination—itself intermediate between sense and thought—is an inheritance from Wordsworth and Ruskin.

Ruskin serves more as an example of the poetic-philosophic mind championed by Wordsworth than as a contributor to the expression of the theory behind the fusion. His passion for nature haunted him, not, as Wordsworth put it, *like* a passion but *as* a passion ("the point is to define how it *differs* from other passions,—what sort of human, pre-eminently human, feeling it is that loves a stone for a stone's sake, and a cloud for a cloud's").[20] His habit of viewing distinct disciplines as interrelated—aesthetics and morality, history and religion—was a reason why R. G. Collingwood regarded Ruskin as one of the preeminent minds of his time, though Ruskin himself never stated his first principles in a philosophical way.[21] Kenneth Clark called his "intellectual chaos" the chief aid in Ruskin's study of art.

> In art it led him to reject theories of beauty founded on taste or rules of proportion. He saw that these concepts were only abstractions, made up of an amalgam of lesser faculties . . . and . . . his

20. Kenneth Clark, ed. *Ruskin Today* (Harmondsworth: Penguin, 1964), p. 22.
21. R. G. Collingwood, *Essays in the Philosophy of Art*, ed. Alan Donagan (Bloomington: Indiana University Press, 1964), pp. 5–41.

sense of the wholeness of man allowed him to recognize that these two elements in art, which writers on aesthetics had docketed away, to their satisfaction, in the department of sensation, are equally connected with man's moral and imaginative life.[22]

Ruskin's peculiar tendency to see nature as personally relevant to his care for it as an appreciative percipient accounts for his passion for the physical universe and his pains over its intricate details.

This attention to particular detail and his desire to let nature establish its own rules of interpretation—indeed, its own poetic and aesthetic—constitutes a direct legacy to Tomlinson. In "Frondes Agrestes: On Re-reading Ruskin," Tomlinson ends the poem with a reference recalling the nature-haunted Ruskin, with his passion for clouds or his equal passion to preserve art's grasp of even the smallest details in a blade of grass.

> Sublimity is. One awaits its passing,
> Organ voice dissolving among cloud rack.
> The climber returns. He brings
> Sword-shaped, its narrowing strip
> Fluted and green, the single grass-blade, or
> Gathered up into its own translucence
> Where there is no shade save colour, the unsymbolic
>   rose.[23]

> (*SIB*, 31)

These last two lines probably draw on Ruskin's enigmatic pronouncement that "colour is . . . the type of love"; and perhaps there is a hint of elegy in the poem since Ruskin embodied nature with such a providence as made him believe that the predominance of color at the opening and close of day showed "the waiting of love about the birth and death of man."[24] Some critics miss the gemlike compression of emotion in some of Tomlinson's lyrics, yet it is his cryptic restraint, instanced again in poems like "At Stoke" and "In Memoriam Thomas Hardy," that moves one exactly because in Tomlinson's poems the emotions are exactly focused.

Ruskin said that the first of the forms of dangerous error

22. Clark, *Ruskin Today*, p. xviii.
23. Cf. Ibid., pp. 102–3.
24. Ibid., pp. 155–56.

comes "when the men of facts despise design." And the "second form of error is when the men of design despise facts."[25] This balance of fact and design seems the prototype of Tomlinson's preoccupation with Eden as the supplier of forms, Eden which, when it withdraws, leaves only existences and no essences. Indeed, I would argue that the paradox fueling the bulk of his poetry has to do with the relations between sight (the faculty) as form-imposing and seeing (the activity) as form-informing. In other words, the relations and contraries between the objects of sense (fact) and the interpretive capacity of imagination (design) energize Tomlinson's poetry because imagination and sense, working in tandem, are the marks of healthy consciousness.

25. Ibid., p. 147.

Paul Mariani

5. Tomlinson's Use of the Williams Triad

In an issue of *The Review* a few years back, there was a cartoon of the English poet Charles Tomlinson sporting a Mexican sombrero and poncho, obviously looking stiff and a bit uncomfortable in such foreign garb.[1] He has been made to look there very much like the English tourist on holiday in New Mexico. It is, of course, of the very nature of cartoons to flatten out and exaggerate in order to make their point. The point here is that Tomlinson reversed what had been, until his generation (with a few notable exceptions), the acceptable manner of things: New World neophytes settling, like James, Pound, and Eliot, in London as the most natural place to learn their craft. Instead, Tomlinson has come to the New World in search of becoming, at least in terms of his craft, more "Americanized." This exchange has proved to be, however, a somewhat risky affair. We have, for measure, the earlier examples—and only partial successes—of Lawrence and Auden, who also attempted to export American homemade goods, and Tomlinson, with a great deal of good will, seems to have grafted the new onto the old stock only imperfectly.

Nonetheless, Tomlinson may yet prove to be—for he is just fifty—"the most considerable British poet to have made his way since the Second World War," as Calvin Bedient has described him.[2] If a term like "considerable" tends to wobble, however,

---

Paul Mariani is Professor of English at the University of Massachusetts, Amherst. He is the author of *William Carlos Williams: A New World Naked, A Usable Past: Essays in Modern & Contemporary Literature*, three books of poetry, and the forthcoming *Tumults & Lamentations: A Life of John Berryman*. "Tomlinson's Use of the Williams Triad" was originally published in part in *Contemporary Literature* 18 (1977): 405–15.

1. Tomlinson, "State of Poetry," p. 49.
2. Bedient, *Eight Contemporary Poets*, p. 1.

Tomlinson is, truly, a prodigious observer—of nature, of arti-fact—possessed of the painter's acute eye for design that we particularly associate with the Ruskin of *Modern Painters* and with Hopkins in his journals. For twenty years Tomlinson has set himself squarely against the English voices we evoke most readily when we consider poetry written in Great Britain since Dylan Thomas's death in a New York hospital in 1953. This dif-ference was most marked in the fifties, when Tomlinson spoke out repeatedly against the rhetorical resonances of New Apoca-lyptics like Thomas and Barker as well as against the prevalent *Kulturbolschevismus*, the "common style" of poets like Larkin and Amis. These latter two Movement writers, made very much aware of an England greatly diminished in grandeur, of an is-land nation besieged by the cries of nationalism at its own doors and reminded daily of its drab industrial sprawl and its blighted pastoral landscapes, had become by the late fifties the recog-nized spokesmen of Tomlinson's generation. To further isolate and make himself even more "unseasonable" (the term is Bed-ient's), Tomlinson turned his back on what he considered other excesses: those associated with the Liverpool scene and the Beatles, as well as those being championed by the British critic A. Alvarez in the sixties, the American confessionals.[3]

Constitutionally, Tomlinson is quiet, reflective, meditative, a poet in some ways like Larkin, who also distrusts excesses of any kind: apocalyptic moments, trombone finales. He is a poet of true intellectual powers, a classicist, really, whose natural affinities seem closer to the late Augustans, and to Donald Davie and Yvor Winters in our own time. This essential reserve, how-ever, this kind of latter-day poetic Toryism, has—at least in my reading of the poetry—acted as a weakness as well as a strength. When Tomlinson was still in his mid-twenties and looking hard for suitable models, he began to read seriously and to champion several of the American modernists, including, most notably, Stevens, Pound, Marianne Moore, and Williams—figures, as he has called them, of energetic contemplation. Some of these in-fluences are readily apparent in any reading of Tomlinson's po-etry, and anyone who has even thumbed through *The Necklace*

3. See A. Alvarez's anthology, *The New Poetry* (Harmondsworth, England: Penguin Books, 1962), which leads off with four Americans: Lowell, Berryman, Sexton, and Plath, all of whom but the first were suicides. See, too, his introduc-tion to the volume, defending his selections.

(1955) will feel that he has entered into a strange, still, imagistic world that looks very much like the world of Stevens's "Thirteen Ways of Looking at a Blackbird." For lines like the following are consciously playing with the contours and the rhythms of Stevens's "The Snow Man":

> when the truth is not good enough
> We exaggerate. Proportions

> Matter. It is difficult to get them right.
> There must be nothing
> Superfluous, nothing which is not elegant
> And nothing which is if it is merely that.
>
> ("The Art of Poetry," *N*, 14)

Thus, about a dozen years ago, Tomlinson exported a product as recognizably "American" as the variously called staggered tercet, three-ply step-down line, or triple-decker, which we associate with Williams's late phase. Williams first used the staggered tercet in the "Descent" passage in *Paterson II* and perfected it in such classic pieces as "Asphodel, That Greeny Flower," "The Ivy Crown," and "To Daphne and Virginia." We know by now, of course, that Williams himself had the examples of Mayakovsky and of Pound's translations of Guido Cavalcanti's *Donna mi priegha* as models for the staggered tercet, but it was Williams who, for us, made the form his own.[4] Making it his "own" should not, of course, be construed to mean that no other poet can use it but that it has its own internal structures, its own poetic logic, which cannot be indefinitely reworked and still be expected to function as a form.[5]

Tomlinson, in a gesture amounting to homage, attempted in *A Peopled Landscape* (published in 1973, the year Williams died) to adapt Williams's tercets and make them his own. Hayden Carruth, however, reviewing Tomlinson's volume for *Poetry*, was particularly upset that anyone, much less an Englishman, should have tried to use this form.[6] Carruth misses the point, for

---

4. See Donald Davie's argument for this connection in his *Ezra Pound: Poet as Sculptor* (New York: Oxford University Press, 1964), pp. 112ff.

5. Among those who have used the staggered tercets successfully, I might mention Robert Pack and John Malcolm Brinnin.

6. Carruth, "Abstruse Considerations," p. 243. See also Robert Duncan, "A Critical Difference of View," *Stony Brook* 3–4 (1969): 360–63.

Williams's aim was to extend the limits of the poetic line and to pass it on as part of a heritage springing out of his own experience with the American language, formalized into a variable pattern. The fact that Tomlinson experimented with the pattern only in this one volume and in his contemporaneous book of translations from Machado suggests that he had achieved only a modest success and was, at best, only moderately satisfied with his results.[7]

It is not really surprising that Tomlinson should have tried this form, for it is Williams's poems written in staggered tercets, with their meditative pace, their sense of ceremony, and even, in Tomlinson's sense, their civility that have most appealed to the British. In fact, if one were pressed to point to the one poem that most Englishmen might "safely" enjoy—in a country where Williams's works have met with only mild success, and then only since the poet's death—that poem would be "Asphodel." Certainly, the few reviewers who even deigned to notice Williams in the sixties when his work finally found a British publisher pointed to the grace, to the "traditional" qualities of this late poem. Finally, they said, this American had come round to their way of thinking. He had ceased his long, weary search for an American language and American forms and had entered at last into the venerable English meditative tradition. In short, they were still not hearing Williams's distinctive voice, nor had they managed to chart his particular homefront strategies.

Admittedly, Williams's staggered tercets look easy to imitate. What makes the form distinctive, however, is the masterful sense of open-ended meditation, of mellow rambling counterpointed sharply against a grid of hesitancies, so that we get the sense of a mind quietly but desperately seeking the fiction of an inner peace. This, decidedly, is not Tomlinson's own cast of mind: his intellectual powers are sharper, colder, more disciplined, more self-evidently in control of the utterance. There is in much of Tomlinson's work the sense of a finely controlled desire for the formal means necessary to modify his own poetic line, a means he does not seem to have been able to find among his own British contemporaries; so that he has turned to the older generation of American poets. When, however, he used a

7. Or perhaps blank verse was the basic staple to which he would, by testing and circuitous perambulation, return, which may come to the same thing.

form as distinctive as the staggered tercet, what he wanted was a "propriety of cadence," a measure he could adapt to reinforce, to shore up, what with hindsight looks like a conservative pastoral vision. The result is that these step-down lines feel peculiarly artificial when measured against Williams's best poems in the mode.

Compare, for example, Williams's "Address:" from *Journey to Love* (1955) with Tomlinson's "The Picture of J.T. in a Prospect of Stone" from *A Peopled Landscape*. Both poems use the staggered tercet, and both are addresses of sorts: Williams's to his younger son, Paul, then in his late thirties, and Tomlinson's to his young daughter. Consider, too, that Williams was in his early seventies, near the end of his career when he wrote his poem, and that Tomlinson was only in his mid-thirties and at the beginning of his career when he sketched his "Picture." Moreover, a man gives advice to another man, even a son thirty years his junior, with more deference and tentativeness than when he is addressing, even indirectly, a little girl. Still, a close comparison of how each poet uses the step-down line should be instructive.

The voice we hear in Williams's "Address:" is tentative, uncertain, the syntax itself reflecting the sense of a man who feels he must say something but is uncertain of exactly what it is he must say. Williams begins the poem with an address seemingly directed not so much toward his son as to a look "approaching" despair he has caught in his son's eyes. It is a look he knows well, he admits, for he has seen it reflected "in the mirror," has seen it, too, in other men and women. Apologetic, hesitant at this intrusion on his son's privacy, he still knows he must say something, however haltingly, as hesitancy shifts to hesitancy, verbal qualifiers extending out from the main trunk:

> To a look in my son's eyes—
>   I hope he did not see
>   that I was looking—
> that I have seen
>   often enough
>   in the mirror,
> a male look
>   approaching despair—
>   there is a female look

> to match it
> no need to speak of that. . . .[8]

How much is confessed here, and yet how much is left un-stated! What, for example, does Williams mean by that "female look" of despair? That he has seen it in the eyes of his own wife? In the eyes of his son's wife? The "meaning" here reduces to this: "To a look in my son's eyes . . . [a look] that I have seen . . . in the mirror." The rest is an attempt, a purposely failing at-tempt, to say what he cannot adequately say, or will not say. That inadequacy, that pressure felt along the line itself of a man forcing an unwilling self to get said what must be said as he ap-proaches death, that pressure of words pushing fitfully forward in starts, qualifiers, asides, is the exact opposite of the kind of rhetorical assurance and formal control we will find in Tomlin-son's poetry.

The look he sees there in his son's eyes, Williams says, is like the look that Bobby Burns must often have had in his youth, a look that "threw him / into the arms / of women."[9] It is an oblique confession of the poet-father to the son, a confession of unhappiness in which father and son, and presumably men of all ages, have shared. Men act like this—with abandon—to for-get their despair, Williams explains to his son,

> not defiantly,
> but with full acceptance
> of his lot
> as a man. . . .[10]

For all his excesses, whatever they were, Burns's wife forgave him—as, presumably, Floss has forgiven Williams, or as his son's wife will forgive his son—when he was

> too drunk
> with Scotch
> or the love of other women
> to notice
> what he was doing.[11]

---

8. William Carlos Williams, "Address:" in *Journey to Love* (New York: Random House, 1955), p. 30.
9. Ibid.
10. Ibid., pp. 30–31.
11. Ibid., p. 31.

Yet there is nothing that can erase that look: not war, not even money. What does remain, however, is a kind of difficult integrity such as that which Williams insists Burns (and Williams himself) maintained. For while Burns wrote some of his most beautiful songs for other women, they were "never for sale."

Williams begins by addressing his son, opens the field of the poem to include himself—and by extension other men, other women—and finally focuses on the figure of Burns, another singer and married lover like Williams. So the poem ends with a kind of oblique confession, in which one senses that, despite the feeling of openness and frankness, more has been left unsaid than said. It is the integrity to one's sense of oneself, finally, that Williams stops on—"stops on" rather than "stands on" because the sense of an ending here is tentative, with the tentativeness and momentary resolution of a person in the act of addressing another in what must be an ongoing process. Williams's conclusion is unsure of its own conclusiveness. In short, the strength of Williams's staggered tercets seems to lie, paradoxically, in their tentativeness, in their apparently artless vulnerability.

Once we understand the inner tension of the staggered tercets—the way the syntax gropes across the line breaks with a stumbling prosaic grace—then the line can indeed be used by other poets. Tomlinson's whole sensibility, however, his entire intellectual constitution, is foreign to this kind of utterance. I can think of no major British poet—except for Hopkins in certain moments of intense private stress—who would not feel embarrassed and uneasy with the kind of voice I have described in the Williams poem.

Tomlinson himself has told us what he was looking for in the staggered tercets in his "Letter to Dr. Williams," published in *Spectrum* in 1957, where he praises Williams for his

> propriety of cadence
> that will pass
> into the common idiom
> like the space
> of Juan Gris
> and Picasso. . . .[12]

12. Tomlinson, "Letter to Dr. Williams," *Spectrum* 1 (Fall 1957): 59.

It is a form with its analogue in the spatial angularity and fragmentation of cubism, a form "invented to be of use" for the "rearticulation / of inarticulate facts."[13] Here, in fact, the young Englishman himself makes it clear that his own intentions are no doubt different from Williams's—since propriety of cadence does not alone adequately describe the staggered tercet—but that the form itself is flexible enough to allow other voices to fit into it. And yet, one may ask, how far can one stretch or contract even a variable measure before it loses its elasticity and becomes brittle?

At Hugh Kenner's suggestion, Tomlinson began a correspondence with Williams in December 1957, shortly after he wrote his poetic "Letter" to Williams in staggered tercets.[14] He was out, he said, to be the second Englishman—the first being D. H. Lawrence—to read Williams correctly. Since part of that reading focused on the ability to use Williams's step-down lines, it is interesting to watch Tomlinson's changing attitude toward them. At first, Tomlinson is aware only of what he calls his own "technical incompetence" in trying to use what is, he admits, Williams's own form. He recognizes, too, that part of the difficulty resides in his being an Englishman, raised on a different tradition, a different kind of cadence. But by mid-1960, having a dozen or so poems in the step-down line, he is convinced that the line will work just as well for an Englishman as for an American, and that the secret lies in reading the foot as a breath unit, as Olson had said ten years earlier in his "Projective Verse" essay. The real matrix for Tomlinson shifts from Williams to the Wordsworthian meditative line, and the proof Tomlinson needs is in reading Wordsworth's blank verse lines as already containing the triple cadences of the three-ply variable foot. For Tomlinson, therefore, the aim must be to marry the iamb to the variable foot. In other words, as he hears them, the staggered tercets resolve themselves back into the traditional iambic pentameter; they are ultimately variations on the blank verse line. For this reason Tomlinson uses the three-ply line in his translations from Machado (1963), since, for him, the standard iambic measure

13. Ibid.
14. Tomlinson's letters to Williams are now among the unpublished Williams papers in the American Collection at Yale.

can and does play nicely "across and into the movement of the variable foot." And there is the crux: whether or not Williams's staggered tercets are essentially blank verse lines filed under another name.

Recall for a moment how for many years Williams himself inveighed against the old, inherited English forms, those forms for which he used the term "sonnet" as his metonymical signature. But, he warned, there were other, more pernicious influences, such as the all-pervasive blank verse line (the trouble was that when you used it, as Stevens's practice had shown, you felt compelled to say something important) and within that line the tyranny which the iambic measure imposed.[15] So, for example, in the forties Williams pointed repeatedly to the young Auden, Tomlinson's precursor by twenty years, as the figure of the Englishman who had come to the New World in search of a new line. In his lecture "The Poem as a Field of Action" (1948), Williams insisted that Auden had come to America because England could no longer supply him with the poetic means he needed were he to continue to develop as a poet.[16] And though Williams was kinder to Tomlinson, praising his 1958 volume, *Seeing Is Believing*, for its division of the "line according to a new measure learned, perhaps, from a new world,"[17] there were no examples of the staggered tercet.

Anyone who has read even cursorily Tomlinson's eight books of poetry knows that there is indeed in his lines a propriety of cadence that belongs very much to the older English tradition: to Pope, Dr. Johnson, and especially Wordsworth, a measure that remains constant whatever the American influences on his poetry. Along the way, Tomlinson has listened to Pound, for example, especially the Pound of the Chinese cantos and the Con-

15. Cf., for example, Williams's open letter to Kay Boyle, meant for inclusion in *Contact* (1932) but not printed until *The Selected Letters of William Carlos Williams*, ed. John Thirlwall (New York: McDowell, Obolensky, 1957), p. 129–36; Williams's review of Wallace Stevens's *The Man with the Blue Guitar and Other Poems*, in *New Republic* (17 November 1937), p. 50; and *A Garland for William Carlos Williams*, ed. Paul Mariani, in *Massachusetts Review* 14, 1 (1973): *passim*. Hopkins, too, felt the same metrical claustrophobia seventy years earlier, seeing it as analogous to the tyranny imposed on melody by the bar.

16. "The Poem as a Field of Action," in *The Selected Essays of William Carlos Williams*, ed. William Carlos Williams. (New York: Random House, 1954), pp. 287–88.

17. Williams, "Seeing Is Believing," p. 189.

fucian translations. He has listened to "the syllabics and delicate cutglass chimings of Marianne Moore"; has listened, too, to the meditative patterns in Stevens. And he has listened, of course, to Williams. But Williams becomes strangely muted, a pensive Wordsworthian, finally, if we hear only Tomlinson's proprieties of cadence and not a voice twisting its slow way to its fitful conclusions, discovering flashes of resolution in the very process of the poem's unfolding.

Thus, Tomlinson's "Picture of J.T. in a Prospect of Stone" is much more sure of itself, much firmer than, say, "Asphodel." Its very title, recalling Andrew Marvell's "The Picture of Little T.C. in a Prospect of Flowers," points to the poem's real allegiances, and its ceremony of address, its playful balancings between lightness and seriousness—so much like the image of light playing off stone that is a favorite of Tomlinson's—suggest the Yeats of a poem like "A Prayer for My Daughter" more than Williams. The mode here in Tomlinson is dialogic, the poet asking and assuredly answering his own questions in a version of genial catechesis, as he muses over the kind of gift he would wish for his little daughter. What the eye sees, of course, is the shape of the staggered tercets, but what strikes the ear are the older verse forms deeply embedded in the new, more flexible lines:

> to prove
> its quality the better and
> thus learn
> to love
> what (to begin with)
> she might spurn.
> (*PL*, 18)

The lines will not stay in this unstable solution (though the *prove-love* rhyme keeps the line slightly askew) but must rearrange themselves into heroic couplets such as Marvell might have given us:

> to prove
> its quality the better and thus learn
> to love what (to begin with) she might spurn.

Again, examine the final eight lines of the poem, with their syntactical and metrical regularity—

>   —And so she shall
>   but let her play
>   her innocence away
>   emerging
>   as she does
>   between
>   her doom (unknown),
>   her unmown green.
>   (*PL*, 18)

—and another pattern of loose octosyllabic couplets may be
revealed:

> And so she shall but let her play
> her innocence away
> emerging as she does between
> her doom (unknown), her unmown green.

The eight lines contain three rhyme sets—*play-away; between-
green; unknown-unmown*. In addition, the sense of an ending is
contained within the limits of that final, balanced sentence, with
its nice analogue between his daughter's intimation of mortality
and the long lovely years still ahead of her, as the poet captures
her in this frozen moment stepping lightly across

>   a sheep-stile
>   that divides
>   village graves
>   and village green? . . .
>   (*PL*, 17)

There is in this pastoral a good deal of wry humor, the play of
the intellect across an idea that we associate with an older, van-
ished world order: a world of ceremony, remnants of which
Yeats found in Renaissance Italy and even in eighteenth-century
Dublin, and traces of which Tomlinson, in his turn, finds now in
Yeats, as he himself confronts a world that is destroying its architectural forms and aging monuments to the past at an alarm-
ing rate. But Tomlinson's short-lived experimentation with the

Williams triad may, in the long run, have helped him to loosen his own rhythms and to return to a blank verse mode now notable for its delicate suspension, its phrasal modification, its hesitating stresses. Paradoxically, then, it may well be Tomlinson's contact with American free verse that has helped him to "hear" the voices of his own English fathers—Marvell and Pope and Wordsworth—more clearly. Surely, such poems as the beautiful "Swimming Chenango Lake" are new and different from either his own work or from Williams's because he has acknowledged the presence of Williams and his fellow American poets.

Addendum, 1977

If Tomlinson's appropriation of the staggered tercet has been only partially successful, he has succeeded in taking over and making his own the short, slipped line that we also associate with Williams and that other fine American poet and one-time objectivist: George Oppen. He has in fact managed to appropriate the short, jagged line, with its tonal hesitations and its play of phrasal unit against linear segmentation, and to have made it as much his own as Creeley in another way has made that pattern register *his* linguistic preoccupations. I mean specifically the kind of lines using either isostanzaic patterns or irregular paragraphs that we find in Williams as early as *Al Que Quiere!* and as late as *Pictures from Brueghel*, and that we find Tomlinson using with assured mastery in the *American Scenes* volume, among others. Consider, for example, the phrasal modulations, the line control, the finely tuned sense of the comic in the exquisitely told anecdotes of "Mr. Brodsky" and "Chief Standing Water." That mode obviously fits comfortably on Tomlinson, for he has continued to wear it, shaping it to his own specific needs. He employs this form masterfully in one of the most harrowing poems I have come across in a long while. "Underground" is too long to quote effectively here, and its sinuous continuities do not easily admit of dismemberment, even for scrutiny's sake. Ostensibly, this is a poem about one of those nameless characters one is bound to come up against if one rides the subway, tube, metro, or underground long enough. In this case we find ourselves staring at a tall woman, face toward the wall, as she sings and dances to herself, indifferent to the crowd of specta-

tors that has assembled to watch her, the poet among them.
Even when she finally gets on the train, she continues to stand,
face toward the door, singing snatches of improvised blues in
among her choked incoherencies. The observer, drawn by this
figure, moves toward a comprehension that he is witnessing
here a radical metonymic signature for the human condition and
perhaps even more specifically for the orphic poet—that curious
anomaly—and strains to get a glimpse of her face, of that which
will identify and individualize her. But he cannot, can do nothing more than watch her beat time on the closed door panes of
the subway car, where "the metal frame / masking the rest of
her," helps reduce her to a voice raised in distracted song, a
flexed mouth "fulminating its song / into the tunnel" (*RC*, 282).

But the most characteristic signature in Tomlinson is the exquisite modulation and clarity of observed detail he achieves
when he works the blank verse line, adding as he does so to the
manifold possibilities of that line as it continues to swerve in its
downward trajectory from Wordsworth, Hardy, Auden, and
Wallace Stevens. Consider, for example, the sensitive registra-
tion of phrasing in two pieces like "The Witnesses" and "Hill
Walk," the latter of which ends with these shimmering, trem-
ulous lines evoking a delicate memory of Provençal landscapes
and ruined (Albigensian?) fortifications in early spring:

> We contemplated no assault, no easy victory:
> Fragility seemed sufficiency that day
>   Where we sat by the abyss, and saw each hill
> Crowned with its habitations and its crumbled stronghold
>   In the scents of inconstant April, in its cold.
>
> <div align="right">(<i>WI</i>, 27)</div>

Or consider the sharp brilliance of a poem like "Swimming
Chenango Lake," which manages to move beyond the limits of
mediation into something like a ritualistic participation with the
nonhuman other, the primal element, a "naked" reality. I do not
see how any but a very few of those at the convocation exercises
at Colgate in May 1968, before whom Tomlinson first addressed
this poem, could have fully grasped the poem's ontological pre-
cisions, regardless of how many times they themselves may
have swum Chenango Lake. For this is a profound meditation
on the limits of human knowledge that, in its ritualistic un-

folding, directs us in almost Ignatian fashion (compare, for example, Roland Barthes's reading of the *Spiritual Exercises* in *Sade/Fourier/Loyola*) from description to meditation to participation to realization.

Tomlinson's two footnotes to this poem suggest his abiding interest in the significance and centrality of ceremony as a way of encountering and of controlling our immersions into reality itself. His first note quotes from Levi-Strauss's *The Savage Mind* the passage on the Hako, a Pawnee tripartite ceremony and invocation for the crossing of a stream (call these the moment of entrance, the movement into, and the immersion), activities that correspond to Tomlinson's tripartite poetic ritual of meditation on the waterscapes of the lake as the swimmer prepares to enter the water (it is morning, autumn, winter is not far off), entrance (a frog-like scissors stroke across the water's surface, skin to skin), and his own loss of self-identity as he immerses himself totally in that interior cold.

However, his second footnote reinforcing what the poem participates in, there are necessary limits to any such entrance. Evoking a Hopi ritual of passage from youth into manhood, Tomlinson quietly insists on the limitations of all metaphor ("the spirits [finally] remove their masks and the child sees that those he had taken for gods are only metaphors for gods: they are his uncles and kinsmen," *PI*, n.p.). Now, as the poem approaches its own terminus, Tomlinson produces the illusion of having transcended the necessary limits of language itself. For a moment we can feel that almost nameless element, that interior, inhuman cold, which is both merciless and "yet shows a kind of mercy," sustaining the observer-become-participant. The ceremony of the poem, then, enacts a baptism of *un*-naming, where self is thrown back on a pre-onomastic self, where the counters giving us the name "Chenango" in a language is irrevocably lost as those people who so named it begin to be construed now in another way. For it is by the body itself, as it scissors through the water, de-creating the patterns observed in its untouched surfaces, it is the body, immersed now in this alien element, this other-not-oneself, that must frame in an a-linguistic series of gestures a meaning all across this "all but penetrable surface" (*WW*, 3).

In the poem's final lines, we, like the observer, having emerged from that element, are made freshly aware that, though there is a pattern of correspondences or at least of geometrical equivalents touching self and other—perhaps a chiming between man and what we used to call nature (for Tomlinson has always rejected the notion of the autonomous imagination, opting for perception as a variation on a theme rather than as a pure fantasia), what he makes us realize, finally, is that all images are accidents (in an Aristotelian sense), that reality does not move, necessarily, toward the human observer for its validation. The truth seems to be that reality is constantly going elsewhere, "incessantly shaping" itself according to its own necessities. All *we* may do is learn how to participate—humbly and quietly—in that reality. The consolation is that, as we embrace it, it embraces us in its turn. For Tomlinson, then, the poem is, as he says, a rite, an initiatory ceremony, capable of bringing us into a closer relationship with our world. One of the most profound ironies in this profound poem, then, is the self-reflexive realization that even the metaphor of water as reality is only an approximation, since *no* metaphor can embrace that which we can only *call* reality.

It is here, then, in this kind of quiet, intensive meditative framework, in a tradition beginning with Wordsworth and running through the English tradition to our own time, that Tomlinson's poetic voice seems most comfortably at home with itself. Like Odysseus and Apollonius of Tyana—other travelers to distant and wild places—he too has come to understand in some deeply rooted sense that it must be the long look homeward that finally points the real way in.

J. E. Chamberlin

6. Unclenching the Mind

There is a point at which poetry is absurd. With this, only the most zealous should disagree. There is usually a much more interesting disagreement, however, about where that point occurs. In an important way, poetry begins in absurdity, with the verbal and epistemological nonsense of metaphor, for example; or with the endless puzzlement of paradoxes turning around universals and particulars, seeings and sayings, discontents and satisfactions. It is this initial absurdity that modern poetry has especially flaunted, and that in turn exhilarates its readers, for reasons that are subtle and evasive. As well, there is a complex absurdity about the ends and effects of poetry, when the ordering that it achieves is contradicted by the excitement that it arouses, or when the wonder of its imaginative celebration is realized in a moment of precise thought and carefully directed feeling. Or poetry may possibly be most essentially about its own impossibility, communicating the incommunicable with a debonair defiance. Finally, and by no means inconsequentially, the poetry of any age becomes absurd when its affectations cease to engage and start to irritate or isolate the imaginative attention of its readers. Yeats's red-rose bordered hem, Eliot's pierrotic despair, Williams's red wheelbarrow—they are all very well for a while, but perhaps they cannot forever bear the burden of having so much depend on them. And yet they have, at the same time, a perennial appeal, and something in us says that it was worth giving in to them or being taken in by the very absurdity that we now disclaim. The decorous and the frivolous change places, the trivial and the essential symbols alternate,

---

J. E. Chamberlin is Professor of English at the University of Toronto. He is the author of numerous articles and reviews of Tominson's poetry. His books include *Ripe Was the Drowsy Hour: The Age of Oscar Wilde* and *The Harrowing of Eden: White Attitudes Towards North American Natives.*

the sweet unreason of verse is delicious and distasteful by turns. Poetry is constantly renewing itself both by and from its absurdity; and we tend to approach recent poetry unsure of its illogic, cautious of its aberrations, wary of its excesses, yet knowing at the same time that these qualities may confirm its poetic authenticity even as they raise questions about its significance. Authenticity and significance are terms from another time, of course; but whatever the terms, we sense that the complicity required of us by poetry is a serious sort of thing, and that we do not want to commit ourselves to an imaginative conspiracy, that is, to a particular kind of absurdity, which is either trivial or false.

Charles Tomlinson plays to our unease, committing himself to the absurdities to which poetry inclines, and so engaging not only our quizzical attention but also our nervous confidence. It is a dangerous game, however, for among other things Tomlinson risks being taken too earnestly, treated as a custodian of permanent poetic values, and so becoming trivially accepted as orthodox before he has ever been seriously considered as absurd. Also, since he eschews Johnsonian invention in favor of Coleridgean intrigue, he is perhaps too easily isolated as not greatly original. Nonetheless, he is never far from the places where poetry finds its power and purpose, and he has a genius for discovering its causes and effects. More specifically, although Tomlinson neither begins nor ends in absurdity, he is often centered there, in the paradoxes with which great poetry has always been preoccupied—paradoxes about the self and the other; about presences and absences; about taking and being taken; about losing and finding; the fortuitous and the deliberate; about the sacred mysteries of grace and the secular mysteries of civility; and about becoming simultaneously plausible and inane. But because all this is so central, and because Tomlinson surrounds this cluster of paradoxes with clever and distracting poetic entertainment, it is easy to feel comfortably at ease, agreeably intimidated by the charming effects, fascinated by the thoughts and feelings that the poetry provides and that critics are always anxious to translate.

Tomlinson writes a kind of poetry, sometimes a kind of comedy of manners, discriminating necessary and sufficient conditions in the natural and human worlds and in their various surroundings. He writes of the murders of Trotsky and Marat, the picturesque effects of moonlight and early morning light, the proprieties of the fox and the badger and the hedgehog, the conventions of the southwestern American and the English midland industrial deserts—and he writes of them all with a similar instinct for their perversely decorous conventions. What Tomlinson finally achieves is a poetry in which the absurdities of art become confused with those of life; and the point at which these absurdities excite or exhaust our interest becomes the point at which life is perceived as instinct with order or charged with energy on the one hand, or as ridiculously sterile or dangerously chaotic on the other. The poetry in which this confusion of life and art is present is a poetry that is, surprisingly, less than fully committed to its own authority and its own apparent energies, reveling in "a time of loomings, then a chime of lapses" ("In the Intensity of Final Light," S, 28). Furthermore, the confusion of life and art that informs such poetry conveys its own need, as well as its own uncertainties about any need, for boundaries. Tomlinson talks about natural pieties and daily discontents at the same time and (what is far more disconcerting) in the same way. He confirms a poetic attitude that relishes surprising beginnings and anticipated ends, and then he deliberately shuffles them to produce not a nice reversal but a quirky juxtaposition. He toys with the pathetic fallacies by means of which life and poetry find a place, yet he retains a sure sense of the capricious character, of the intentional "likes and links" of the worlds in which the imagination finds satisfaction.

> Meshed in meaning
> by what is natural
> we are discontented
> for what is more,
> until the thread
> of an instrument pursue
> a more than common meaning.
> ("Ode to Arnold Schoenberg," PL, 51)

Eden and the new Jerusalem, the country and the city, provide models of decorum and value for these worlds, not surprisingly; the surprise is often the accommodations to reality that Tomlinson's imagination accepts, with a disarming candor and with a candid admission that he has, after all, only been able to reach a temporary truce between the ideal and the real, as between the concrete and the abstract, or the material and the spiritual. Thus, in mock anguish, he laments a "Misprint":

> "Meeting" was what
> I had intended:
> "melting" ended
> an argument that
> should have led
> out (as it were)
> into a clearing, an
> amphitheatre
> civic or sylvan
> where what could not be
> encompassed stood
> firmly encompassing
> column on column, tree on tree
> in their clear ring:
> there I had hoped to come
> into my true
> if transitory kingdom. . . .
>
> (S, 40)

Or, in convincing despair, he celebrates the allotment of one John Maydew "the ineradicable / peasant in the dispossessed / and half-tamed Englishman" (PL, 8), finding in the minimal salvations of imaginative understanding an antidote to the numbing obsessions of "a low, newspaper, humdrum, lawsuit country," as Byron once called England. Tomlinson is notorious for his Yeatsian disdain for petty compromise and parochial diversion; his genuine outrage is compelling and not given to easy reconciliations. Certainly, he has been a determined (though not entirely successful) critical force in the past quarter century in opposing the suburban compromise between tradition and conspicuous consumption that he perceives in the work of many poets of his time.

Yet Tomlinson's poetry itself, like his punctuation and his phrasing, is paradoxically conditioned by an almost comically diplomatic hesitation: by the tentative pause, the hovering uncertainty; by an exquisite poise, sometimes becoming a sternly delicate pose, embodying the natural virtues of the forest and the sky as well as the human sanctities of the town and the historical moment. It is this poise, this pause, this sense of the possible that provide for Tomlinson an analogue to the silence, the wonder at the heart of the paradoxes that he celebrates. Tomlinson's poems are informed by what he calls "hesitant distinctions [that] flare into certainties" ("Of Beginning Light," *WrW*, 26) and then collapse or collect into possibilities:

> the red fox
> Caught where it patrols its cruel Eden,
> Sets at a counter-pause
> The track of thought, as mounting the unsteady
> Wall of crumbled ragstone, it halts its progress,
> A clear momentary silhouette, before it
> Dips and disappears into wordlessness.
> ("Movements, V," *WrW*, 53)

Tomlinson often compares the hesitations that condition his poetry with a kind of truce; but it is a truce "at the end of an unending war" ("Urlicht," *WrW*, 31) between essential incompatibles, incompatibles such as accident and design, in the transposition of which the artist finds what Tomlinson, referring to Paul Klee, calls his "discovery in the act of making" (*BW*, 20).

He writes with exquisite sensitivity about "a just-on-the-brink-of-snow feel" ("In Winter Woods: Snow Sequence," *AS*, 14), and he translates the distances of time and space, and the expectations of the English landscape and of the American desert, into a moment of perception that is as certain as dream and as vulnerable as fact.

> And it seems as if a wind
> had flung wide a door
> above an abyss, where all
> the kingdoms of possibilities shone
> like sandgrains crystalline in the mind's own sun.
> ("A Sense of Distance," *WW*, 29)

In "The Way of a World," the title poem of a volume in which Adam and Prometheus share lodgings, Tomlinson centers the images of a gull and the whirling seed of the ash tree with the

sweep of the tree's boughs in what he calls a "counterpoise"—
the word itself centers the poem.

> [T]he bird,
> The seed, the windlines drawn in the sidelong
>   Sweep of leaves and branches that only
> The black and supple boughs restrained—
>   All would have joined in the weightless anarchy
> Of air, but for that counterpoise. All rose
>   Clear in the memory now, though memory did not
>   choose
> Or value it first: it came
>   With its worth. . . .
>
>   (WW, 14)

In turn, this is an item of other balances, between the mind and
the memory, between "the weightless anarchy of air" and the
laws that govern "the shape of change," between a world of
mechanistic forces and a world of teleological design:

>   we grasp
> The way of a world in the seed, the gull
>   Swayed toiling against the two
> Gravities that root and uproot the trees.
>   (WW, 14)

Several things occur in these final lines in the poem. For one, the
reader is included, as the "I" of the poem changes to "we." The
temptation is to read this as a rather glib transition from particular image to general statement, to which the poet gives a credi-
bility that it may or may not deserve by implying its universal
acceptance. It is this kind of device, to be sure; but it also marks
a change in the nature of the poetic remark, as the paradoxes
and ambivalences, the imaginative hovering, which the poem
exemplifies are brought together in a statement that locates the
poem in a delicate balance by stabilizing (rather more than by
isolating) its meaning. The elements are typical of Tomlinson:
the ambiguity in the "two gravities," for example, that refer to
the profundities of mind and memory as much as to the forces
with and against which the trees live and die, and between
which the gull and the seed find their way. Complicating this
pattern is a deft interlacing of the dualities of seed and gull, tree

and seed, the two gravities, the "I" and "we" of the poem. The insistence on grasping, seizing, and holding the image and its meaning conveys one of Tomlinson's central perplexities. At the same time he sets up the ambivalent juxtaposition of "swayed" and "toiling," words that work quite differently but together embody the orderings and the energies, the drift and the purpose, which picks up the word "again" in the relaxed paradox involving the mind and the memory, losing and finding, with which the poem opens—as the poet speaks of "having mislaid it, and then / Found again in a changed mind / The image of a gull," as well as "the ash-key, borne-by whirling / On the same surge of air" (*WW*, 14). This poet's mind is particular and universal at once, and like the flame with which it is compared in another poem,

> Reaches for knowledge as the flame for hold—
>   For shapes and discoveries beyond itself. A slow
> Crescendo of crepitations through burning music,
>   It mines in its element, shines-out its ores.
>   ("Flame," *PL*, 37)

Here Tomlinson conveys, albeit in a mildly forced way, his view of the progression of poetry from individual to shared perception, from invitation to collaboration and complicity, from "mine" to "ours," and in doing so he also conveys his sense of the paradox in which heightened individuality corresponds to greater generality, and in which in the darkness of the self is discovered a light for others.

Like many of Tomlinson's poems, "The Way of a World" states its paradoxes quite openly. In the volumes from the fifties and the sixties, especially, we find a particularly deliberate display, a stating of "calmness within the wind, warmth in cold" ("Winter Encounters," *SIB*, 2), of "a presence which does not present itself" ("Cézanne at Aix," *SIB*, 34), of the artist who "lies for the improvement of truth" ("A Meditation on John Constable," *SIB*, 30), of a "dislocation where each is located" ("Stone Walls," *SIB*, 43), of "the mercilessness that yet shows a kind of mercy" ("Swimming Chenango Lake," *WW*, 4), and so forth. Sometimes this is awkwardly arresting, as in the final lines of "The Atlantic":

> That which we were,
> Confronted by all that we are not,
> Grasps in subservience its replenishment.
>
> (*SIB*, 1)

And sometimes, as in his earliest book (*Relations and Contraries*), it begins and ends in a strenuously worked conceit. But at its best we have such fine effects as the celebration of a polyphony of sound and light "At Wells," where the movements, voices, falling flights "take and hold" the "unmoving vault" that has received them,

> and their time
> its space
> sustain
> in a single element the chord of grace.
>
> (*PL*, 32)

Here the complementary designs of time and space and the complementary energies of giving and taking are held in place by a perception that offers its achievement in an ostentatiously metaphorical form. Tomlinson is often praised for the accuracy and aptness of his descriptions; but his finest effects are more often flagrantly conjured up than simply displayed. Yet Tomlinson is one of those conjurors who depends on our knowing that it is all a sleight of hand, even—or especially—when we cannot avoid being held in the spell of the illusion. In this, there is something confidently theatrical about Tomlinson's poetry; and we are prepared both to engage and to suspend our disbelief in the presentation of the thoughts and feelings of his poems in the same way as we accept what occurs on stage as both true and not true, both artificial and natural, both virtual and actual. I like the transparent admissions of these poems, their candid display of the elements of artifice on which they depend. But they do encourage a tacit feeling of superiority in the reader, a superiority to the contraries and contradictions that the poems present, and finally a superiority to the poems themselves, as the thoughts and feelings of which they consist are carefully explicated, like the pictures in a tapestry, in terms that draw us away from the arbitrary illusions of the work itself and separate us from those splendid contradictions of mimesis and poesis, of imitation and creation, which in their awkwardly intractable juxtaposition sustain the compelling mystery of the work of art. And so, wanting more, and feeling that there is more to want, we turn to discussions of influences on Tomlinson—Wordsworth and Coleridge and Stevens and Williams, say; or to an examination of the ideas that either can be detached from the poetic forms or can be seen to be embodied in the forms, so that the poetry comes more and more to be read as being about poetic processes. Like many readers of poetry, I am easily persuaded; but it does not do Tomlinson much credit; and more importantly, it provides an impoverished version of what his poetry offers. His poems, both early and late, offer to hold us in their spell, to keep us from conclusion, to create in us an evangelical patience for some revelation that, when it comes, will be more a suspicion than a certainty; and when it is gone, it will leave conviction without proof. The poems create an illusion of control, present a facade of what Tomlinson refers to as "providential reasoning"; which is why I suggested that Tomlinson is a comfortable poet. But at the center these poems take seriously those paradoxical conditions on which art depends and on which human beings depend for a vision of life that incudes both I and you, both style and substance, both nature and nurture (or habit). And these conditions, these paradoxes, once said, cannot be unsaid, except by being said again, like Prometheus's curse. There is a fatal quality, with which all of us are familiar, in the essential achievements of poetry; a sudden crystallization of thought and feeling, which are crystallized for us and for a moment only, but also never return to solution. It is this fatality that Tomlinson's poetry conveys, not just by means of striking images or unnerving sensations but by locating itself where poetry begins and ends, where it is both most probable and most vulnerable. Impressions and expressions, mirrorings and makings, desires and regrets, questions and answers—these are the complementary items, and they each map the locus of a point; where they intersect is where the poem finds its center. The most compelling thing about Tomlinson may be that this center is in the poem, and not off the page somewhere. Tomlinson does not write poems that refer to unease, or muddled thought, or incoherent feeling; neither does he write poems that are themselves uneasy, or muddled, or incoherent. Somehow, in ways that are disconcerting, he creates the conditions of unease without the frustration, the terms of confused thought and feeling without the confusion. He establishes uncertainty as a condition, rather than merely as a subject, of the poem. Beginning with the poems in *The Necklace* (1955), he becomes compulsive about the need for "definition," but he does so mainly as an admission that the urge to abstraction is a necessary defense against the incoherences and uncertainties of space and time.

> Reality is to be sought, not in concrete,
> But in space made articulate:
> The shore, for instance,
> Spreading between wall and wall;
> The sea-voice
> Tearing the silence from the silence.
> ("Aesthetic," *N*, 1)

Tomlinson deliberately flaunts the limits of his poetry, encouraging our wonder whether, as in the music of Chopin, "all is either technique heightened to sorcery or nothing but notes" ("Small Action Poem," *AS*, 62).

One way in which he creates these conditions of uncertainty is shifting between voices and moods in the course of defining a particularly telling image, so that its definition is ultimately dependent on a suspension between imperatives, interrogatives and affirmatives, perhaps; or between human and natural insistences; or between voices from within and those from without. We are, like the conjuror's crowd, never sure what to watch carefully, never confident about the efficient cause of it all, much less about any final cause. "Tramontana at Lerici," for example, which is usually read as an announcement of Tomlinson's rejection in *Seeing Is Believing* of a bewildering subjectivity in favor of a precisely clarified apprehension, achieves its effect by an ambiguous dependence on the categories that it would presumably reject: romantic mistakings of the virtual for the actual (in this case, and with a deliberate humor, the glass falling for the imitation of glass falling); sentimental anticipations of cruelty in lace, climate in constitutions. The cold and the dark together are presented as the suspended embodiment of that which does not succumb to subjective conspiracies, but the very sharpness of the dramatic effect of the growing chill and the gathering dark diminishes the separateness they apparently represent. The mood is too powerfully conveyed, the mind too intrigued, to accept as mindless and callous that which compels them. Most tauntingly, we are not sure whether the mockery that we sense in the poem is associated with the "I," the "you," or the increasingly prominent "one" of the poem; and, if the latter, we are not sure whether this undermines the poem's polemic. The hovering uncertainty in this is not, though it is easily confused with, a discreetly ironic poise, a genteel confusion about whether one is serious or not. Rather, it is the condition of being both serious and trivial, both sincere and insincere, both clever and naive— all at the same time. The paradoxes here are hardly novel; but they are, in a manner that is typical of Tomlinson, inseparable from the poem's way of being a poem and conveying its meaning. Furthermore, this manner creates a humor for which Tomlinson is seldom given credit, a humor having in it a gentle understanding that there is a point at which reading poetry is absurd—the point at which one can say, and expect something of the pity that has just been conjured up, that "one is ignored by so much cold suspended in so much night" (*SIB*, 18). Who but an egotistical fool would expect something different? Who, as the poet has suggested, but politicians and romantics? Who but this poet, speaking this poem, indulging at the same time as he is disclaiming his own pathetically fallacious relationship to nature?

Tomlinson's humor is worth emphasizing. In part, it derives from his deliciously anticipated inclination to get it quite wrong: to go with the mind when he should trust the eye; to ask for silence so that he can be heard, and then say nothing, because he has nothing to say; to provide two meanings for something that is meaningless. More broadly, however, the humor of his poetry resides in its translation of the classical and romantic virtues of symmetry and spontaneity into the modern conditions of inertia and stupidity, or of acceptance and aplomb. Together, these paradoxically convey the stability and the sincerity that he obviously cherishes, but in a way that captures the central qualities of the natural and the human as well as the central characteristics of poetry, its dubious use of relationships and emotions to achieve a clarity and a validity for which it can offer no explanation. Tomlinson finds an affinity with that which defies the human imagination: with Lukenbac, yesterday's driver of the Tlacolula bus, writing "I flew for the Fuehrer" up in Gothic to announce his own affinity with all exiles, all those who can never be other than an affront, all those (like the poet) who can only write up oddly defiant words in an outmoded script. The analogies are not encouraging:

As we swing
out of the market square
a goat on a string
being led by someone
stops, stands and while
the bus passes by
into history, turns
on the succession of windows
its narrow stare, looking
like Lukenbac in exile.
("On the Tlacolula Bus," *AS*, 49)

Into exile . . . picking up the marginal rhymes of the southwest. The way in is also the way out. "Is it patience or anger most renders the will keen? / This is a daily discontent. This is the way in" ("The Way In," *WI*, 4). Tomlinson knows, and creates his comedy out of the knowledge, that exiles are a joke—like Adam, first and last exile, who knew (on behalf of all poets, solipsistically denying their own soliloquies),

The perpetuity of Eden, drew from the words
        Of that long naming, his sense of its continuance
And of its source—beyond the curse of the bitten apple—
        Murmuring in wordless words: "When you deny
The virtue of this place, then you
        Will blame the wind or the wide air,
Whatever cannot be mastered with a name,
        Mouther and unmaker, madman, Adam."
                    ("Adam," *WW*, 8)

There is an indication of some of the changes in Tomlinson's poetry when we turn to more recent poems such as "To See the Heron." Here as well there is a determination, as a modern poet of manners might join with a modern nature poet in saying, to respect the heron; and there is a continuation of the commitment to the notion that seeing is believing and that faith in either can be absurd. But the amusing paradoxes that create the possibility of the poem are at the center of the poem's method in a rather different way this time. First of all, the question in the infinitive, which is also an affirmation, creates the feeling of incompleteness that the poem both affirms and contradicts. This is especially revealed in the final lines:

> risen
> it is darkening now
> against the sullen sky blue,
> so let it go
> unaccompanied save by the thought
> that this is autumn and the stream
> whose course its eye is travelling
> the source of fish: to see the heron
> hang wondering where
> to stoop, to alight and strike.
>
> (S, 30–31)

Here the splendidly achieved hesitation of "hang wondering where" is only apparently resolved by "to stoop, to alight and strike," since the ambivalence of "to see the heron," repeated in this final phrase, holds its own. But there are more complex ambivalences: in the juxtaposition of stoop, with its connotations of giving assistance, with the murderous strike, though this is itself countered by an echo of lighting a fire, or setting off

> that blaze
> where ranks of autumn trees
> are waiting just for this
> raised torch, this touch,
> this leisurely sideways
> wandering ascension to unite
> their various brightnesses, their fire-
> music as a voice might
> riding sound. . . .
>
> (S, 30)

Furthermore, we are invited to compare "leisurely sideways / wandering ascension" with "hang wondering where"; the wandering and the wondering logic of the poem is its central charm, and also its central meaning. Tomlinson's poems are not about what they seem at first to be about. Neither are they about what the next clever critic discovers. Rather, they enact an acknowledgment of critical temptations, a greeting between the orthodoxies of reality and those of the imagination, a truce between being about anything and our desire to have them be about something. The elements of the truce are the mind's desire to find meaning and the spirit's need for nourishment that is before or beyond meaning. Tomlinson's poems, insofar as they are about things, are about the mind's acknowledgment of the spirit's needs and about the spirit's recognition of the mind's desires. The mind, on the one hand, sees possibility ("Skull-shapes," *WW*, 52), but also the possibility of its own defeat ("Nature Poem," *S*, 29), knowing that "the light of the mind is poorer / than beginning light" ("Of Beginning Light," *WrW*, 25) and not very good illumination anyway, though perhaps sufficient for intermittent illustration. The spirit, on the other hand, seeks to "unclench / the mind" ("A Given Grace," *AS*, 12) but knows that it can only do so by resigning both hope and despair and by trusting that most unlikely virtue—tact. Eden is a place not of innocence but of imaginative propriety, of appropriate patience, of sudden rightnesses—of artistic tact and lively discretion.

The emotions that give life to the poems are therefore embodied in the needs and the desires of the mind and the spirit. In saying this, I am not suggesting that there is anything especially cloistered about the range of feeling in Tomlinson's poetry: he is enough of a romantic to believe that the mind's desires for meaning are often satisfied by the senses; and his is a sufficiently classical sensibility to realize that the spirit is sustained by order and decency. But there is a tone in Tomlinson's poetry that speaks of the mind and the spirit, a tone that has echoes of evangelical sermonizing, of being called on to witness. In this, his poetry is profoundly Keatsian, intending to be "a friend to man," helping us to live our lives, celebrating the wonder and the wretchedness of the world. Yet, unlike Keats, Tomlinson sees from the

pulpit that the health of the spirit is threatened not by the pleasures of the flesh but by the enticements of the mind; and he
intimates that the mind's clarity is jeopardized not by obscurity
but by impatience. There is a kind of purity of motive the poet
can claim that will often mitigate the insidiously hasty determin-
ism associated with thinking and feeling in time and place; but
Tomlinson knows that a complication of motives will often exhil-
arate the spirit more refreshingly and suspend the fretful intelligence more discreetly.

So his poems celebrate an interdependence that is not dialectically satisfying but awkward—an uneasy truce, a treaty that
will surely be broken, a reconciling of elements that have neither
the nice irreconcilability that the romantics adored nor the fine
agreements that classical art embraced, but that relish their im-
pertinent and arbitrary stubbornness. Tomlinson celebrates all
this in conditions of picturesque extremity—deserts, oceans,
ruins, desolate landscapes peopled with a tentative human presence, intimating the shapes of absence. In "Arizona Desert," for
example,

> to be,
> is to sound
> patience deviously
> and follow
> like the irregular corn
> the water underground.
>
> Villages
> from mud and stone
> parch back
> to the dust they humanize
> and mean
> marriage, a loving lease
> on sand, sun, rock and
> Hopi
> means peace.
>   (*AS*, 22–23)

Tomlinson goes far, in poems such as "Juliet's Garden," to make
of this awkwardness an ingenuous strategy, and to invest it with
the sanctity of a kind of negatively naive capability, a type of
longing—as Tomlinson suggests elsewhere, quoting Kafka—"to

catch a glimpse of things as they may have been before they show themselves to me" (*BW*, 20),

> flowers merely grew,
> showing no knowledge of her:
> stones hunching their hardnesses
> against her not being there:
>
> . . . .
>
> such presences could only
> rouse her fears,
> ignoring and perfuming
> this voluntary death of hers:
>
>
> and so she came rushing back
> into her garden then,
> her new-found lack
> the measure of all Eden.
> ("Juliet's Garden," *WrW*, 46)

But here, though the poem is certainly accomplished, there is a tidiness that is not Tomlinson's major achievement. He is, above all, a poet of the ill-fitting, the aberrant, the unmatched, the intractably awkward, the insistently questioning—all presented in the language and form of nineteenth-century philosophical (and political) accommodation, of marriages of opposites, but not succumbing to the tense calm of which such marriages have often been the emblem. Tomlinson is becoming more confident in his explication of the absurd comedy that seems to inform life and death, and that is exemplified in the paradoxes by which the existence and meaning of each is conveyed, and in the poised sensibility of which they are both cause and effect. The hesitations of his poems convey comic indecision rather more than they prepare for a moment of insight, and they suggest a coy appeal for confidence rather more than an artless humility. But they are still structured by the most compelling of antiphonies, by a balancing between the mind's desire and a fortuitous grace, between invention and discovery, between choosing and being chosen. And they candidly display the poet's shuffling search for authority.

I took a tree for a guide—I mean
 Gazing sideways, I had chosen idly
Over walls, fields and other trees,
 This single elm, or it had chosen me. . . .
("Tree," S, 50)

 Tomlinson often locates this ambivalence and intimates a kind of authority in dreams, to be sure, where they are much at home; but he also builds up a complex pattern of ambivalence through his shifting between a rhetoric of active holding (or withholding) and one of passive waiting (or leaving). Often, too, he employs the ambiguity of reflections to convey this, as the mirror and the lamp become one in the contemplations of the poet, or the window and the door open out and keep out at the same time. He situates his poems, and his readers, on the verge of the perceptive insight or of the impossible fantasy, poised between vision and prophecy, description and prescription. An early poem, ambiguously entitled "Reflections," outlines this with a somewhat uncertain rigor. It is not one of Tomlinson's best poems, but its clumsiness is in a way typical, for as the poet develops the specific complexities of mirrorings, reflections, truths, and lies in later and better poems, we are still presented with the same kind of deliberately surreal flaunting of the absurdities of poetry—of its traditions, its diction, its inviting images, and its forbidding meanings.

The river's mirrorings remake a world
 Green to the cliff-tops, hanging
Wood by wood, towards its counterpart:
 Green gathers there as no green could
That water did not densen. Yet why should mind
 So eagerly swim down and through
Such towering dimness? Because that world seems true?
 And yet it could not, if it were,
Suspend more solid castles in the air.
 Machicolations, look-outs for mind's eye
Feed and free it with mere virtuality
 Where the images elude us. For they are true enough
Set wide with invitation where they lie
 Those liquid thresholds, that inverted sky

Gripped beneath rockseams by the valley verdure,
   Lost to reflection as the car bends by.
                        ("Below Tintern," *S*, 26)

The illusions of reflections become the elusive images to
which the mind attaches itself—images that are, in turn, lost to
the reflections of the mind in its eagerness or its eccentricity.
And the poem, reveling in its own shades and nuances,

   bring[s] the mind half way to its defeat,
Eluding and exceeding the place it guesses.
                   ("Nature Poem," *S*, 29)

Tomlinson keeps us in suspense, in what he calls a "place of perpetual threshold" ("Departure," *S*, 20), wondering whether he
is being devious or straightforward, obscure or transparent,
mindful of an available logic or committed to a mindlessness in
nature.

   The promenade, the plage, the paysage
   all met somewhere
   in the reflection of a reflection
   in midair. . . .
   ("Le Rendez-Vous des Paysages," *WrW*, 8)

Tomlinson's windows and doors, which are among his favorite conjurings, are often as tentatively suspended:

   space
   window
   that looks into itself

   a facing
   both and
   every way

   colon
   between green apple:
   and vase of green.
     ("Poem," *WrW*, 31)

And, just as they have been instrumental in his "decalco-manic" painting, they become in his poems temptingly emblematic of poetic processes:

> The beginnings have to be invented: thus the pictograph is an outline, which nature, as the poet said, does not have. And the ends? The ends are windows opening above that which lay unperceived until the wall of the house was completed at that point, over that sea.
> ("A Process," *WW*, 55)

Doors, in turn, are "both frame and monument" ("The Door," *AS*, 8); and the volume *American Scenes* in particular develops the illusions of poets such as Eliot and Williams, of the door to experience (and to the past as well as to the future) that

> is open now
>   that before
>   was neither
> open
>   nor was it there.
> ("Small Action Poem," *AS*, 62)

The images in Tomlinson's poetry, therefore, are often first of all arrestingly confusing and then surprisingly coherent. It is in this conjunction of effects, of the confusing and the coherent, that Tomlinson's uniqueness lies; for it is a conjunction of causes as well as of effects, as the final cause of the poem is deliberately juxtaposed with the efficient cause, and both are juggled with circus aplomb within the poem itself. All the while, the poet tries to effect a reconciliation between the apparently antagonistic elements of his poem, as the magician does between what is obviously impossible and what is demonstrably possible. What the poet needs is a complicity, first between the mind and its object—each unknowable, unknowing and unknown without the other—and then between the poem and its reader. That this complicity is absurd simply heightens its charm; that it is necessary reduces the absurdity to the level of the sacred; that it is sufficient elevates it into the realm of the mundane. In this respect, it is little wonder that Tomlinson emphasizes the achievements of his poetry not as an enclosing of meanings but as a hovering over the qualities of experience, of life and art.

Snow brings into view the far hills:
    The winter sun feels for their surfaces:
Of the little we know of them, full half
    Is in the rushing out to greet them, the restraint
(Unfelt till then) melted at the look
    That gathers them in, to a meeting of expectations
With appearances. And what appears
    Where the slant-sided lit arena opens
Plane above plane, comes as neither
    Question nor reply, but a glance
Of fire, sizing our ignorance up,
    As the image seizes on us, and we grasp
For the ground that it delineates in a flight
    Of distances, suddenly stilled: the cold
Hills drawing us to a reciprocation,
    Ask words of us, answering images
To their range, their heights, held
    By the sun and the snow, between pause and change.
                   ("Appearance," *WrW*, 32)

Here we have in profile the elements of Tomlinson's poetry: the hovering moment, almost caricatured in its generously nervous hesitation; the comically inappropriate question matched with the surprisingly right answer; the ambivalent conjunction of grasping and being seized, of holding and withholding and being held for, as he says in "Swimming Chenango Lake," of being "between grasp and grasping, free" (*WW*, 3); the confidently assured manner conveying a disturbing and uneasy amalgam of sense and nonsense, of sensitive emotional insight and crudely clever thought, of fine intelligence and dramatic exaggeration.

Watching the mistlines flow slowly in
    And fill the land's declivities that lay
Unseen until that indistinctness
    Had acknowledged them, the eye
Grasps, at a glance, the mind's own
    Food and substance, shape after shape
Emerging where all shapes drown.
                ("Mistlines," *WrW*, 50)

Tomlinson's poems deliberately entertain the origins of poetry—in riddle, in narrative, in celebration or lament or, as he has argued, in a ceremony of initiation, a way into the mysteries of life as well as art (*The Poem as Initiation*). But what his poems do even more deliberately is seek out the contradictions of poetry: rational thought, feeling predicated on a kind of emotionally gratifying logic, silence. And he delineates the touchstones of poetry, as they are (or are not) redeemable in translation—for Tomlinson is a gifted and determined translator. Finally, he demands a passivity, a hesitancy to commit the understanding, a suspension of imaginative anxiety, a kind of genial confidence. We are to relax into acquiescence; instead of the logical grammar of prose, we have the absurd grammar of poetry—a bewildering teleology without a telos, concentrating on that which determines the indeterminate. His ultimate focus is, therefore, on what he perceives as the intersecting conditions of poetry: the decorum of meaning and the value of sound, intersecting in the silence of wonder.

> Silence. The man defined
> The quality, ate at his separate table
> Silent, not because silence was enjoined
> But was his nature. It shut him round
> Even at outdoor tasks, his speech
> Following upon a pause, as though
> A hesitance to comply had checked it—
> Yet comply he did, and willingly:
> Pause and silence: both
> Were essential graces, a reticence
> Of the blood, whose calm concealed
> The tutelary of that upland field.
> ("The Hand at Callow Hill Farm," *PL*, 16)

Few poets display a more transparent respect for the sanctities of life and death than Tomlinson. His secret may be his knowledge that both are the stuff of prose and that poetry simply fills the gaps in the story—celebrating a special moment here, recapitulating an event there, reflecting on circumstances everywhere, stopping with a poignant anxiety on the point of awareness, and always centered in the paradoxes by which poetry, no less than life and death, confirms meaning and being.

And he knows that poetry is all that makes it worth the while, that poetry maps the only "just geography" ("The Farmer's Wife," *PL*, 14), a geography both equitable and minimal. Just so, "solid vacancies" of poetry both "orphan and father" us ("On Water," *WrW*, 3). Or words to that effect. "Admiration," suggested the great English book designer and illustrator Charles Ricketts, "is the essence of all art—it is that which makes us wish in childhood, when power is not yet, and before experience has shut the gates, for larger flowers." The folly of this wish is the folly that Tomlinson both exemplifies and encourages, both supplies as a given grace and demands as his due, as the due of poetry.

Kathleen O'Gorman

7. Space, Time, and Ritual in Tomlinson's Poetry

> One might show, for example, that aesthetic perception too opens up a new spatiality, that the picture as a work of art is not the space which it inhabits as a physical thing and as a colored canvas . . . that the dance evolves in an aimless and unorientated space, that it is a suspension of our history. . . .
>
> Merleau-Ponty, *Phenomenology of Perception*

In their most traditional aspects, space and time are important frames of reference for Charles Tomlinson. The farm at Hinton Blewett, a bridge in Venice, the historical allusions of "Prometheus" and of "Assassin" all bring the particular, a sense of rootedness, of solidity to the poems in which they appear. This particularity of reference—in space as in time—localizes and explores the relationship between perceiver and perceived, but does so always with respect to the "mutuality of the relation"[1] realized. Yet Tomlinson's poetry transcends the limits of the particular, so that notions of space and time become involved in a different way as the reader apprehends his own inherence in a world. Space and time become part of man's immediate awareness, his bodily presence in the world, not mere cognitive structures imposed on experience to define reality. Such immediacy in a work of art compels the reader's response to the rhythms of the interplay of verbal and visual textures with modulations of tone and meaning in a poem.

Tomlinson repeatedly affirms this concept of art. He begins

Kathleen O'Gorman, Assistant Professor of English at Illinois Wesleyan University, has written on Tomlinson, David Jones, Geoffrey Hill, and Samuel Beckett. She is currently coediting a series of books, *Twentieth-Century British Literature*. "Space, Time, and Ritual in Tomlinson's Poetry" was originally published in *Sagetrieb* 2 (Summer-Fall 1983): 85–98.

1. Grogan, "Way of His World," p. 486.

The Necklace with the poem "Aesthetic," the first two lines of which read, "Reality is to be sought, not in concrete, / But in space made articulate" (*N*, 1). He begins *A Peopled Landscape* with "A Prelude":

> I want the cries of my geese
> To echo in space, and the land
> They fly above to be astir beneath
> The agreement of its forms.
>
> (*PL*, 1)

In the next poem of the same volume, "Return to Hinton," Tomlinson states, "Our language is our land" (*PL*, 4). "Aesthetic" and "Return to Hinton" state more directly what "A Prelude" presents metaphorically: the idea that in poetry, language can create a reality different from that of everyday life. Michael Hamburger says as much when he asserts that metaphor "lends itself to . . . transferences from one order of reality to another,"[2] and Harvey Gross, in his *Sound and Form in Modern Poetry*, phrases it most succinctly: "The articulations of sound in temporal sequences, rhythms, and meters, present us with 'aesthetic surface'; it is this surface which our perception immediately engages."[3] Poetic form itself, then, the structure and texture of words in relation to each other and to the reader, creates verbal "space," as, simultaneously, sound and silence, movement, stress, and tension become "felt time, musical 'duration.'"[4] Tomlinson shows a clear grasp of this in his own discussions of the poetic process as well as in his poetry itself:

> Rhythm, as it is felt in the act of writing, signifies the creation of a continuum, an imaginary space within which words and memories, the given and the possible, can be felt as co-present, held over against each other, yet constantly crossing one another's paths. As the mind attends to the pulsation of the growing poem, it is as if it enters and shares this created space, which, filled by the invitations of movement and sound, seems at once landscape and music, perhaps more music than landscape.[5]

2. Michael Hamburger, *The Truth of Poetry: Tensions in Modern Poetry from Baudelaire to the 1960s* (Harmondsworth: Penguin, 1972), p. 96.

3. Harvey Gross, *Sound and Form in Modern Poetry: A Study of Prosody from Thomas Hardy to Robert Lowell* (Ann Arbor: University of Michigan Press, 1973), p. 23.

4. Ibid., p. 16.

5. Tomlinson, "Not in Sequence," p. 53.

In creating "imaginary space" through a temporal continuum of sounds, the poet thus creates a new center of experience in relation to which man is defined and which is itself defined by that relationship. The lived experience of a poem—including the "felt time" and "imaginary space" it creates as well as the visual, aural, and intellectual content it embodies—becomes for the reader a different order of reality, an experience of space and time analogous to, but not identical with, his everyday experiences of extension and duration.

Tomlinson clarifies his own grasp of the significance of the aesthetic center of experience that space and time create in a poem when he defines a poem as a rite of initiation. He states that a poem constitutes a "dwelling on the inner rhythms of events" (*PI*, n.p.) that establishes a relationship between reader and poem, perceiver and perceived, occurring outside of ordinary spatial extension and temporal duration. In Tomlinson's control of language especially, with his use of rhythmic structures as expressive forms, one is continually aware of the appeal of his poetry to a level of cognition different from the intellectual. Tomlinson's sense of the structures of sound in appealing immediately to the pre-reflective faculties, coupled with his awareness of the lived experience of the body as the primary locus of meaning, leads him to conceive of the function of poetry in terms of ritual, the experience of reading a poem, a "rite of passage" (*PI*, n.p.). Tomlinson elaborates in his address to the Phi Beta Kappa Society of Colgate University:

> The poem, in itself, is a ceremony of initiation. . . . It is a rite of passage through a terrain which, when we look back over it, has been flashed up into consciousness in a way we should scarcely have foreseen. (*PI*, n.p.)

From the start, then, for Tomlinson, the notion of rite or ritual necessarily involves the ideas of space and time: the rite of passage is "through a terrain," our awareness is a "looking back" through time and space, and even the notion of "a way we should scarcely have foreseen" binds together visual perceptions of space with an abstract concept of time. As Merleau-Ponty states, "Spatial outlines are also temporal: elsewhere is always something we have seen or might see."[6] Tomlinson de-

6. Maurice Merleau-Ponty, *Phenomenology of Perception*, trans. Colin Smith (London: Routledge and Kegan Paul, 1976), p. 329.

scribes the manner in which a poem compels the reader to "pause over the stages of the act" that it describes/embodies—again using terminology that refers to space and time to detail the workings of the poem as a rite—and concludes with an acknowledgment of the limits of ceremony, of ritual. To define poetry in such a way is to see that the poem has a power of its own, a capacity to engage the reader in a meaningful process, an immediate relationship. In the case of Tomlinson's poetry especially, such a definition provides yet a different sense of the structure of experience through which man can comprehend the nature of that relationship.

To try to isolate the notions of space, time, and ritual, to try to dissect a work of art or a theory of aesthetics in terms of any one of these elements assumes an identity for each completely independent of the others. Such an assumption is false, as it relegates the terms "space," "time," and "ritual" to the realm of abstract formulation, and does not account for their embodied presence in man's lived experience of the world. As Merleau-Ponty asserts, and as Tomlinson agrees, our awareness of the world occurs at a pre-reflective level; in trying to conceptualize that awareness, "analytic thought . . . seeks in the mind the guarantee of a unity [of time and of space] which is already there when we perceive.[7] The philosopher continually reminds us that space and time are a part of our "primordial encounter with being . . . [that] being is synonymous with being situated."[8] Merleau-Ponty joins the ideas of space and time with that of ritual in his discussion of the rhythms of existence inherent in perception,[9] pointing out that perception "ratifies and renews in us a 'prehistory,'"[10] or a unity of the flux of spatial/temporal existence that is realized in the lived body, independent of any abstract notions of space and time. The correlation between this and Tomlinson's notions of space, time, and ritual is clear, par-

7. Maurice Merleau-Ponty, "Indirect Language and the Voices of Silence," in his *Signs*, trans. Richard C. McCleary (Evanston: Northwestern University Press, 1964), p. 69.

8. Merleau-Ponty, *Phenomenology of Perception*, p. 252. Merleau-Ponty devotes most of *Phenomenology of Perception* to the notions of space and time and refers to them also in "Indirect Language and the Voices of Silence," as well as in most of his other writings. He consistently emphasizes the importance of their radical embodiment in the lived being.

9. Ibid., p. 213.

10. Ibid., p. 240.

ticularly in Tomlinson's emphasis on the poem's "dwelling on the inner rhythms of events." Works such as "Poem" (*RC*, 263), "Eight Observations on the Nature of Eternity" (*N*, 4), "Distinctions" (*SIB*, 8), "Ode to Arnold Schoenberg" (*PL*, 50), "Wind" (*AS*, 7), and "Swimming Chenango Lake" (*WW*, 3) suggest the complex relationship between time and space that the rite of the poem compels.[11] They affirm, as do most of Tomlinson's poems, the concept of the body as the primary locus of meaning in the aesthetic experience. As philosopher and poet would have it, the actual impulses of meaning in a work of art, together with the visual and intellectual content, effect the transference from one order of reality to another. The "aesthetic surface which our perception immediately engages"[12] initiates the reader into the way of a world in which

> We bring
> To a kind of birth all we can name
> And, named, it echoes in us our being.
> ("Adam," *WW*, 8)

Tomlinson makes real the ritualistic presence of the poem most clearly in those works whose subject matter itself concerns specific rites—those that mark the passage from a lower to a higher status, and those that mark recurrent events.[13] Rites of initiation almost always designate an elevation in status, while those celebrating the "rhythmic forms of nature—the day, a season, the life of a blossom—"[14] constitute cyclical rites. Tomlinson's poetry considers ritual in both its forms and renders that which is considered in a rite of initiation of its own. Poems like "Prelude" (*PL*, 1), "Harvest Festival" (*PL*, 16), "The Matachines" (*WW*, 25), and "Before the Dance" (*WW*, 27) celebrate the cyclical events of nature, while "A Death in the Desert" (*AS*, 23) and "Swimming Chenango Lake" (*WW*, 3) restore the proper relation between the passage of individuals from one state of being to

---

11. See Grogan, "Way of His World," pp. 480–82, for a more complete discussion of the embodiment of Merleau-Ponty's ideas in "Swimming Chenango Lake."

12. Gross, *Sound and Form*, p. 23.

13. Victor W. Turner, *The Ritual Process: Structure and Anti-Structure* (Chicago: Aldine, 1969), p. 167.

14. Robert Haas, "Listening and Making," *Antaeus* 40–41 (Winter-Spring 1981): 498.

another and mark the eternal recurrences of nature.[15] A closer examination of several of these poems indicates the way in which Tomlinson views the ritual process and establishes the concept of space and time "indefinitely recoverable, indefinitely repeatable"[16] that is the space and time of every ritual.

"Return to Hinton" (*PL*, 1) incorporates both forms of ritual in a number of different ways. The speaker of the poem alludes throughout to rites of initiation marking various individuals' passages from one important stage of life to another, and he surveys the farm and its inhabitants—their past and present—with reference to recurrent natural and religious cycles. The occasion of his return is the death of someone's father, and the visit calls to mind the idea of the mother as a bride (the speaker notices "The Bridal March" on the piano)—both instances of transitions that are marked by ceremonial rites of passage. He associates the traditional color, "white," with the Bridal March and contrasts that with the "widow's silk" and the "blackened bellies" of the kettles in the kitchen. The speaker refers twice to doors and in both cases sees them in their ceremonial role as points of passage or transition, again symbolically from one stage of life to another.[17] The kitchen door is the first one considered, and this becomes the threshold between two different worlds:

> The television box
> is one,
>   the mullions and flagged floor
>   of the kitchen
> through an open door
>   witness a second
>   world in which
> beside the hob
>   the enormous kettles'
>   blackened bellies ride—
> as much the token of an order as
>   the burnished brass.

15. Turner points out that the aim of a particular ritual is always the "restoration of the right relation." See Turner, *The Ritual Process*, p. 18.

16. Mircea Eliade, *The Sacred and the Profane: The Nature of Religion*, trans. Willard R. Trask (New York: Harcourt, Brace, and World, 1959), p. 69.

17. Arnold van Gennep, *The Rites of Passage*, trans. Monika B. Vizedom and Gabrielle L. Caffee (Chicago: University of Chicago Press, 1960), pp. 20–25, 57–67.

           You live
    between the two. . . .
                    (*PL*, 2)

The ambiguous "between the two" can designate the point between the world of the television and that of the kitchen or between the worlds betokened by the blackened bellies and the burnished brass. It can indicate, also, the distinction between "a world (English and rural) that is stridently contrasted to the world of the U.S. whence the poet has returned."[18] In any case, the open door allows for passage from one to the other. Appropriately, the second mention of a door refers to the widow's closing her door on despair, "as the gravestones tell [her] to" (*PL*, 3). Door is used metaphorically in this instance to indicate the finality of the widow's acceptance of her husband's death, having "given / grief its due" (*PL*, 3) and signifies also the woman's passage into a new order herself. It simultaneously reinforces the finality of the passage of her husband from life to death. The gravestones then serve as the literal reminder of that passage, the physical counterpart to the metaphysical reality.

The passage of the individuals from one state of being to another—the woman, from bride to widow, her husband, from life to death—takes place within a context of cyclical forms, religious and natural. The Bible, Genesis, prayer, and "chapel gospel" are specifically mentioned, and the phrase "'God / saw the light / that it was good'" (*PL*, 1) works in several ways to underscore the ritualistic nature of the occasion. In quoting the passage, Tomlinson suggests the familiarity the family has with the Bible, "whose cadences became a part of one,"[19] but he also chooses a phrase that is repeated over and over in the Bible to suggest the ritualistic repetitions in the story of creation. The ellipsis between "light" and "that" draws further attention to that repetition and to the implied endless recurrence of it in all of creation.

In addition to the religious references, the seasons, the cycles of fertility of the land, the passing on of land from one generation to another, and the return of the speaker to Hinton Blewett betoken an order beyond the immediate. The patterns of repeti-

18. Donald Davie, Letter of 6 January 1982 to the author.
19. Brenda Tomlinson, Letter of 19 March 1981 to the author.

tion in nature and in human lives move events beyond our everyday notions of space and time and allow for the lived experience of extension and duration, felt time and rhythmic cognition.

Just as the structure of a ritual compels the participants to "pause over the stages of the act" (*PI*, n.p.), the occasion of the speaker's return compels him to meditate on the death of a man and its place in the rhythms of human experience, personal and impersonal. But the cadences of which that death is a measure are realized as well in the texture of the poem itself, so that the ritual process described becomes also the process rendered. The three-step line in which the poem is written forces the reader to pause over the stages of the act that is the poem, as does the repetition of words such as "death," "land," "door," and "certainty" coupled with the interplay of assonance and alliteration in lines like "express / won readiness / in a worn dress." The oppositions of life and death, suggested in the white and black of the woman's clothes, find counterparts in other oppositions referred to in the poem as well: poverty and prosperity, certain and uncertain enemies, past and future. Of the poem's subject matter, its visual suspense, the verbal and aural texture, and the juxtapositions of opposites, it might easily be said, "It is through them and with them that we take this grip on significance" (*PI*, n.p.), that the reader establishes relationship. In responding to the contours and measures of the poem, we grasp the way of a world; and the locus of meaning, as in all ritual, is in the lived experience of the body participating in the rite.

Equally complex in evoking the function of ritual and equally compelling in poetic force and aesthetic achievement is Tomlinson's poem "The Matachines" (*WW*, 25). Ritual works in "The Matachines" again on several different levels simultaneously: it defines the nature of the event that the poem treats, and it determines how the reader relates to the poem. The title refers to "a / dance of / multiform confusions" (*WW*, 26) whose purpose even the Indians performing the ceremony no longer understand.[20] In "The Matachines," Tomlinson embodies the tensions between a

20. Frank Waters, *Masked Gods: Navajo and Pueblo Ceremonialism* (Chicago: Swallow Press, 1950), pp. 272–73. I am most grateful to Brenda Tomlinson (personal letter of 19 March 1981) for directing me to this book, which was of importance to her husband in the early 1960s. Waters's explanation of the dance known as "The Matachines" corresponds precisely to Tomlinson's rendering of it and understanding of it in his poem "The Matachines." The poem is published

number of different elements. Catholic ceremonies and person-
ages are set against those of the American Indians (references to
Saint Anthony of Padua, the Holy Virgin, a church with altar
and crucifix, juxtaposed to the masked figures participating in
the dance). The war between the Moors and the Spanish Chris-
tians is alluded to with references to the morris—"the Moor-
ish dance"—"the way the Moors / were beaten in Spain," the
daughter of the Moroccan emperor, again set in opposition to
the Christian references. The Spanish and the Indians of Mexico are similarly related (Cortez, the Malinche, Montezuma);
male and female (the bull betrayed by the girl, the lines of men
through which they dance); sexual indulgence and sexual absti-
nence (the Indian mistress and the Holy Virgin); the past and
the present (the confused events of a number of different histories made present in the dance). The tensions are realized in the
poem in the evocation of the girl dancing, in the ritual that
brings them all together. But the ritual of the poem, in addition
to that described by it, constitutes an equally compelling encounter, a profoundly evocative center of experience.

Just as observer and dance create the encounter described,
reader and poem mutually determine the aesthetic achievement
of the experience of the reading. The suspended syntax, which
only comes to rest in the final line of the poem, creates immediately a sense of anticipation that involves the reader with the
poem in his attempt to resolve the verbal complexities. Tomlinson's frequent use of colons, semicolons, and dashes serves a
similar function, visually as well as grammatically compelling a
movement forward, and the shorter lines that continually leave
an idea or a phrase incomplete do the same. The patterned repetition of key words and phrases—"the saint," "the Moors," "be-
trayal," "the dance," among others—echoes the recurrent ritual
of the dance. This repetition becomes especially important at
the beginning and the end of the poem. The first line, "Where,
but here," is repeated as the ninth line, and a variation of it,
"where, / but in this / place" occurs nine lines after that. What
begins as a question and establishes itself in the ear and mind of
the reader echoes as a resolution in the phrase "we are here"
(line 80), which signals the approaching conclusion of the poem

---

in a limited edition by San Marcos Press, 1968, and is included among the "Western Pieces" that comprise the second section of *The Way of a World*.

and which later ends it. Beginning and end unite in a verbal cycle that renews itself and the aesthetic experience in every reading, just as the performance of the dance reactualizes the events it commemorates. The repetition of the lines that follow "we are here" signifies an important change in the participants' perception of their performance and further complicates the patterns of meaning and sound that give the poem its ritualistic effect:

> we are here
> whatever we
> do or
> mean in this
> dance
> of the bull
> and the betrayal:
> whatever we
> do we mean
> as praise, praise
> to the saint
> and the occasion. . . .
>   (*WW*, 26–27)

The change from "whatever we / do or / mean in this" to "whatever we / do we mean / as praise, praise" radically alters the participants' sense of the dance, the reader's response to the poem. The vagueness of the first proposition is reinforced with the emphasis on the conjunction "or" ending line 82 and on the demonstrative pronoun "this" ending line 83. That vagueness disappears completely when the lines are repeated in slightly altered form. Those who participate in the "dance of / multiform confusions" give it meaning themselves, and the decisiveness of that act is underscored with the repetition of the word *praise* twice in one line. The lines "It is / done" also provide a tone of resolve toward the end of the poem, without sacrificing the tensions of the language and of the historical and religious events to which they refer. The declaration, "It is / done," follows the reference to the crucifix, calling to mind the last words of Christ; yet it establishes simultaneously that the ceremony of the dance is finished. Again the mutual oppositions assert themselves— Christian and Indian, especially—in a masterful articulation of the relationship that defines them and that measures the ritualistic experience of the dance, the aesthetic experience of the poem. With the last line, "we are here," the poem comes full circle, and "here"—at a church, at an Indian ceremony, in the present—signifies as well all that has taken place outside this particular church, in repetitions of this ceremony throughout the whole history of the Indians, in a time measured, not in hours or days, but rather in the rhythms of the seasons, in the pulses of a ritual dance.

Those pulses are transformed into impulses of meaning in "Before the Dance" (*WW*, 27) and enrich the aesthetic surface to which the reader responds by making real the feeling of anticipation that it describes. "Before the Dance" details the sense of apprehension before a Navajo dance begins, acknowledging that

> the waiting
> for the Indian
> is half the dance,
> and so they wait
> giving a quality
> to the moment
> by their refusal
> to measure it.
> (*WW*, 27)

This suspense is made real in the visual suspense of the short lines and, again visually, in the repeated use of the colon throughout, signaling that more follows to complete the meaning of what has come before. The ellipsis at the end of the poem sustains the feeling of expectation created visually throughout and subtly embodies the content in the form. The "beginning / drum," mentioned only at the end of the poem, with the ellipsis following, again reinforces the anticipation described earlier in the piece. The language of this poem too creates a continuum of sound with repetitions of several key words: "wait" recurs three times, "the dance," three times, and "the moment," three, while "begin," "the wind," and "the movement" are used twice each. The phrase "the moment / is expansible" occurs twice, and the effect of that repetition is particularly important. In its initial use, the phrase indicates the transformation of all sense of time that accompanies the ritual of waiting for the dance. The phrase recurs, however, separated into two phrases, each in parentheses: "(the moment)" and "(is expansible)." In its second occurrence, it is divided by a line of the poem: "on the earth floor." The passage reads,

> they wait, sitting
> (the moment)
> on the earth floor
> (is expansible)
> saying very little.
>   (*WW*, 28)

The effect is threefold. The parentheses and the double interruption of syntax give the reader the sense that he has heard the phrase elsewhere, without putting undue emphasis on that fact. The appeal, clearly, is to the pre-reflective level of cognition. Equally important, however, is the integration of the phrase into the passage in alternating lines. "They wait, sitting / on the earth floor / saying very little" describes the actual appearance of the people waiting for the dance to begin. The separation of subject and subject complement—"the moment" separated from "is expansible"—reinforces visually the notion of time that the statement describes. In addition, interrupting the parenthetical phrases with the prepositional phrase "on the earth floor" creates the effect of grammatical wholeness, with "on the earth floor" modifying "moment." This links the concept of time with the Indians' bodily presence on the earth and emphasizes subtly the notion of lived time in which the participants and the reader are both involved. As the poem proceeds, the moment it describes becomes expansible for the reader, and time and space take on qualities that distinguish them from ordinary temporal duration and spatial extension. The ritual time and space described become, for the reader, those which he experiences in the process of the reading. The poem itself, in its capacity to make real that which it describes, joins Merleau-Ponty's notion of the rhythms of existence inherent in all perception with generally accepted notions of the power of ritual to reactualize the time and presence that it celebrates.

This is not to suggest, however, that those poems concerned

with the ritual process *per se* are the only ones in which "restoration of the right relation"[21] between man and the world occurs. It is a measure of Tomlinson's achievement that his poetry consistently renews the process of our encounter with the world, and does so regardless of the subject matter. In those poems that are not specifically about ritual, the actual rite of the poem is just as easily understood. That rite consists of the transference from one order of reality to another through the aesthetic experience; from the images and references of the poem, from its visual and aural structures, as well as from the temporal and spatial reality it creates with the reader, the meaning emerges. One has only to examine briefly such poems as "Venice" (*N*, 1), "Arizona Desert" (*AS*, 22), and "Paring the Apple" (*SIB*, 23) to sense how the commonplace becomes a part of that transference, a part of the order of reality created in the interaction between reader and poem.

We are made to dwell on the inner rhythms of the event of a city's coming into being in "Venice," as the poem creates the verbal time and space in which "the houses assemble in tight cubes" (*N*, 1). Ordinary time and space are displaced from the start as the abrupt, single-syllable "cut" effects the perceptual upset it describes. Tomlinson's use of three-stress and four-stress lines throughout the rest of the poem continues to measure the event in "felt time," and the controlled unfolding of meaning and sound creates an aesthetic surface that continually renews and reveals the perceptual change that it effects, the transition from one order of reality to another. Perceiver and perceived, reader and poem, are both revealed in the process, as the cadences that determine the space and time of the poem become a part of the reader, re-define him at a pre-reflective level.

In "Arizona Desert" (*AS*, 22), the reader is compelled to pause over the stages of the act of seeing that the poem describes, in a time and place in which

> to be,
> is to sound
> patience deviously
> and follow

21. Turner, *Ritual Process*, p. 18.

like the irregular corn
the water underground.
           (*AS*, 22)

The sound patterns of "Arizona Desert" are as complex as those of "Nine Variations in a Chinese Winter Setting" (*N*, 2–3), and the irregular vowel and consonant patterns become the verbal counterparts to the course of "water underground" to which the poem refers. The images of this poem are particularly arresting: "layers / of flaked and broken bone / unclench into petals, / into eyelids of limestone" (*AS*, 22), "A dead snake / pulsates" (*AS*, 22), and "Villages / from mud and stone / parch back / to the dust they humanize" (*AS*, 22). As the sound patterns move the reader forward, the images and syntax slow progress, so that together form and content work to determine the pace at which the poem takes on meaning for the reader. The reader, in perceiving the poem as an intentional unity (that is, in the phenomenologists' sense of intentionality), "sound[s] patience deviously" as he measures and weighs each poetic unit—syllable, foot, line—at a precognitive level and experiences each passage of the poem as a literal "passage" into its own particular space and time, into an order of reality grasped in his immediate experience of the poem.

There is the same immediacy in "Paring the Apple" (*SIB*, 23), and in that poem, too, the "recognition" compelled is as much the rite of the poem as it is the experience of the reader. In this work especially, the suspense of syntax undermines the reader's expectations of extension and duration, never resolving the verbal tensions it creates.

And then? Paring it slowly,
From under cool-yellow
Cold-white emerging. And . . . ?
           (*SIB*, 23)

It has been said of "Paring the Apple" that "the act [described/ embodied in the poem] becomes almost a ritualistic gesture, a manual prayer, something sacerdotal. It takes place in a space between human and inhuman."[22] Yet here we must distinguish

22. Swann, "English Opposites," p. 226.

between secular and religious notions of ritual. The secular is profoundly rooted in man's experience of the world, while the religious is a manifestation of belief in and devotion to a deity. The former has man as its central concern, the latter, god(s). It is important to understand that in Tomlinson's poetry the ritual realized is secular. Tomlinson is careful always to focus on man's relationship with the world, a relationship predicated on a profound respect for the world as it is given to the senses, as it is known through the body, and as man's relationship with it can be reactualized through language. To introduce the notion of a deity would be to shift the focus entirely. Tomlinson himself cautions us against such a mistake in "A Process": "One accords the process [of knowing the world] its reality, one does not deify it" (WW, 55). In his interview with Alan Ross, Tomlinson's response to an inquiry concerning his religious views again fixes his poetry firmly in the world of the secular:

> Place—this place—speaks to me more than the dogmas of any religion, and it speaks of very fundamental things: time, death, what we have in common with the animals, what things are like when you stop to look. . . .[23]

As Tomlinson states in an early poem of *Seeing Is Believing*, "Place is the focus" ("In Defense of Metaphysics," *SIB*, 35), and, as he continually reminds us, it is the body that places us, which is the primary locus of meaning in all experience. Only through our bodily inherence in the world can we come to know the world truly, and only in that encounter can we come to know ourselves.

Tomlinson returns to the notion of the poem as a ritual in his address at Colgate University and speaks of the limits of ceremony:

> The Hopi [Indian] removal of masks confesses the limit of ceremony, but the very act of doing so is a ceremonial act which would have been impossible without the context of those masks and the rites of which they are a part. . . . We put down the book. We put aside the mask. But it is the book and it is the mask that bring to bear the mystery and the qualities of the process of living.
>
> (*PI*, n.p.)

23. Ross and Tomlinson, "Words and Water," *London Magazine* n.s. 20 (January 1981): 37.

We should add that in Tomlinson's case it is the poetry, the reader's interaction with the aesthetic surface with which Tomlinson presents him, that brings to bear that mystery, that renews the process of living. Though that is perhaps to confess the limits of ceremony, it is to do so with full appreciation for the work of art as an object in its own right and in full acceptance of our own existence as a perpetual process of becoming.

Michael Edwards

8. Collaborations

It was in the spring of 1969, the year that saw the publication of *The Way of a World*, that Tomlinson collaborated with Octavio Paz, Jacques Roubaud, and Edoardo Sanguineti to elaborate *Renga*, a striking, multilingual long poem, in which English, Spanish, French, and Italian participate equally. Radically suggestive, it poses many questions, and in particular the question of translation, in new ways. Tomlinson and Paz then worked together on a smaller, bilingual poem, *Airborn / Hijos del Aire*, published in Mexico in 1979 and in London in 1981.

Renga is based on, and named after, an ancient Japanese poem-form, which could itself be of great interest. Usually a collective work, it consisted of a series of small segments or "links" of three lines, of respectively five, seven, and five syllables, and of two lines both of seven syllables. Each poet added the next link in turn, so as to further the whole poem but also in such a way that the new link would constitute a poem with the previous link. The completed text was therefore not one but many poems, and was susceptible of a plurality of readings. Moreover, as each link made a different poem with the links that preceded and followed it, it changed and underwent that essential process of transformation of which translation is arguably a type.

Renga adapts the Japanese form to Western poetry. It is a sequence of twenty-eight sonnets—of which the last was left unwritten—without rhyme or syllable-count, grouped in four series. Each series employs a different type of sonnet and also

---

Michael Edwards is Professor of English at the University of Warwick, England. His volumes of poetry are *To Kindle the Starling*, *Where*, *The Ballad of Mobb Conroy*, and *The Magic, Unquiet Body*. His criticism includes *Towards a Christian Poetics* and *Poetry and Possibility*. A version of this article, "Renga, Translation, and Eliot's Ghost," was originally published in *P N Review 16* 7 (1980): 24–28.

plays with the order of quatrain, tercet, or couplet by alternately inverting it, so that the lines of the Shakespearean sonnet of the third series, for example, are disposed either in the pattern 4-4-4-2 or 2-4-4-4. Each poet contributed one section to each sonnet, in a predetermined order, and then wrote in its entirety the final sonnet of the series that he had begun.

Renga translates the renga. It too is a plural work, each sonnet functioning as a simple poem while at the same time contributing to the one complex poem; and the latter offers two possible readings—the four series one after another, which is advancing page by page, or the first poem in each series followed by the second in each down to the seventh, which is the order in which the work was written. Moreover, although the sections of the sonnets don't of course form different poems with the sections that come before and after them, they do change, because of the vertiginous language-leap involved. The reader never quits a passage into the language that he enters it from, so that in the process of one's reading into and out of it, the passage alters. English-after-French, as just one instance, is not the same thing as English-before-Spanish.

In replacing the tanka, the basic five-line unit of the renga, with the sonnet, the European poets have renewed both the sonnet and the sonnet sequence. They have composed multilingual, collaborative sonnets and placed them in a multilingual, collaborative sequence; and they have given the sequence meaning by playing its structure against the structure of natural process. The twenty-eight sonnets rhyme with the twenty-eight days of the lunar month and are divided into four series or weeks of seven sonnets or days. The twenty-four participatory sonnets rhyme with the twenty-four hours of the day; the four series also suggest the four seasons. Since the poems of the second series are curtal sonnets of eleven lines, the number of lines in the four first poems, the four second poems, and so on, is near enough 52; the total number of lines in the whole poem is close to 365. Once again, translation is involved: the Japanese renga also advances, or so one gathers from Octavio Paz's introduction, through various sequences or modes, based on the passage of the season or of the hours of the day.

Renga is far from being the first European collaborative work or the first multilingual work. There have been many of the latter produced by single writers, usually in societies where more than one language has been current, and there is also the special case of macaronic, occasioned by the continued deployment of Latin for specialized uses and developed, I have suggested elsewhere, as a device for overcoming Babel burlesquely by forcing Latin and a vernacular into a comic osmosis. Eliot and Pound transferred this polyglot writing into a new cultural situation with a different linguistic consciousness. Simultaneously, the surrealists furthered collective works in a single language, as *Les champs magnétiques* of André Breton and Philippe Soupault, while Dada even produced examples of polyglot collective poems, like the German-French "Balsam cartouche" by Hans Arp and Tristan Tzara. Nevertheless, *Renga* remains the first important poem to be multinational, multilingual, and collaborative. It moves in the direction of Goethe's prophecy of a *Weltliteratur* by sounding certain trends in twentieth-century writing and combining two of its major projects: the collective authorship of the surrealists and the polyglot poetry of Pound and Eliot.

By "translating" from Japanese into no single European tongue, Tomlinson and the others have made, in the aftermath of Babel, a new language. No Volapuk, or Esperanto, or Stefan George's synthetic *lingua romana* ("las unas devorando las otras"), but a communal speech activating, and indeed intensifying, the diverse resources of each national speech. It is a kind of European, conveyed in the dominant European poem form, the sonnet, and having Europe as its reference: the poets introduce their respective countries, with Paz's America entering as the splendid object of European desire. They also introduce their literary predecessors, through quotation and allusion, calling on Baudelaire, Donne, Dante, Quevedo, and many others of the voices that have constituted the literary discourse of Europe to participate in their work. By bringing into the space of a single volume echoes from four of the national poetries within European poetry, they cause one area of the European tradition to operate in an entirely novel manner.

Renga also functions internally as a kind of serial translation. It is translation that governs the combining of the four dialects into a polyglot chorus—and "translation" in a wide band of its meanings, from the strictest to the very free. Each successive poet continues the work by translating into his own lines the language of three foreigners. Often the translation is simple: Roubaud's "livres de lierre" (books of ivy) become Paz's "libros de yedra." But far more is involved. On one occasion, for instance, a word basic to our world traverses a sonnet (the first of the second series) through each of the languages, as "terre," "terra," "tierra," and finally "earth." Whereas translation usually separates, by replacing an original with its version, here it combines, by placing all the texts together, in a slow, numerous naming. Earth also gives rise to sphere and apple (actually, by another and different process of translation), and these too diversify as "sfera-esfera-sphere" and "poma-apple."

Translation also proceeds by interlingual punning. In sonnet IV / 2, the French "poisse" of Roubaud ("makes sticky") is taken up by Tomlinson as "poises." The change is in part polemical: Tomlinson counters the verses that the Frenchman has passed him, on the grounds that what he terms "that syntax of deliquescence" is refused by "the hardness of what is real" and that, as against Roubaud's troubled experience of "air" and "smoke" that "make sticky," poise is achievable by genuine "relation." It is a moment in a running debate about the given that our "Charles Pope (a Tory anarchist)," as Sanguineti calls him, conducts with the others. It is also, however, the point where, as in the *Catullus* of the Zukofskys but within the same text, translation enters the process of burlesque. "Poises" is a kind of instant travesty—you give me a word in your language and I'll wrench it into one in mine—that unstabilizes the correspondence between two tongues and puts them into a condition of creative play. (Had Roubaud cared to bounce the word back into French he might have declared that Tomlinson's Augustanism was "poison" to him.) *Makes sticky* is a "natural" transformation of *poisse*; *poises* is an unnatural one that opens to larger possibility.

A more customary kind of pun is at work in another line of Tomlinson:

> . . . the shadow . . . spreads
> its inkstain into the wrinkles of weathered stone. . . .
> (*R*, 41)

It is the pun as well as the sun's shadow that spreads "ink" into "wrinkles" and a "stain" on "stone." (Duke Senior, one remembers, with the same linguistic appropriateness found "books" in the running "brooks.") Punning does not subvert here but, on the contrary, binds together. It partakes of that wider process of linking words by identical or similar sounds, when sense is not necessarily involved, that binds the poem as an aesthetic object, that binds the reader's experience of reading it, and that seems to bind the world to which the poem refers. The process is at times deliberately extravagant in *Renga*: perhaps it was the extra degree of linguistic self-consciousness, in that polyglot forcing-house, that led to lines like Sanguineti's "Confusa ritorni, confusione diffusa, insetto incerto," or Paz's "corales de coral en el caracol de tu oído." In Tomlinson—

> Vague, vain
> implosion, a seepage, ghoststain
> (*R*, 57)

—sense is in fact usually explicit in the play:

> The given is ground. You are bound by it
> (*R*, 69)

and he characteristically uses alliteration for different kinds of dual statement: "these lines that are life-lines, / these veins vines," "syllables in search / of marriage, meaning," and so forth.

This wordplay occurs on the inside of English, or Italian, or Spanish. *Renga*, however, offers the opportunity of doing something more. As each poet takes over, he changes the poem's language but is free to continue its sounds. If he elects to do so, he blends the sounds of his own language with those of someone else's, and thereby makes phonic connections not within a language but across languages. This is what they sound like:

> une parole préparée dans cette grotte
>
> Principi, tomba e teca . . .
> (*R*, 40)
>
>   . . . une ronde noire entrait dans l'eau
> et la nuit était une moitié de lac
>
> And love, a command no more, to each one
> the way lies clear . . .
> (*R*, 58)

nidi per le mie vespe, giardini per i miei topi morti:

je déambule parmi tes lices de patelles

(R, 70)

entre la maleza oscura, la espuma y sus profecías.)

Le même ensevelissement féroce nous sépare de la
pierre.
(R, 72)

Paz's "corales de coral en el caracol" likewise takes the hint from
Tomlinson's " . . . baptises / colours clean" (R, 85); and one conjunction of their writing contains considerable sound-play both
inside each language and from one language to the other:

. . . a self
lost in a spiral of selves, a naming:

y la espiral se despliega y se niega y al
desdecirse se dice.
(R, 94)

In all it makes a remarkable language to listen to, and one which
can only exist in a multilingual text. It is yet another kind of
translation that *Renga* has brought off, the sounding of a pentecostal language of phonological renewal.

Even when the move from language to language involves
simple separation, it implies a delight in differences, a rejoicing
in multiplicity. Already in the first sonnet, at the point where
that punning of Tomlinson occurs, English and French eye each
other, across what becomes a dizzy gap between a quatrain and
a tercet:

. . . the shadow . . . spreads
its inkstain into the wrinkles of weathered stone:

Car la pierre peut-être est une vigne. . . .
(R, 40)

It is a thorough translation from English to French, which reveals how astonishingly they diverge in their ways of building
sounds and of suggesting concretion and generality. The juxtaposition of the lines leads one, moreover, to rethink certain commonplaces about that divergence. At first glance, to Tomlinson's

English, "empirical," specificity of objects, carried in the closeness and detail of the consonants and in those persistent vowels, Roubaud replies with the Gallic "abstraction" of "la pierre . . . est une vigne." It is true that "weathered," which describes the look and feel of the stone while also placing it in time, in seasons, and in climates, proves intractable to translation: in their French and Spanish versions of *Renga*, Roubaud settles for "vieillie" and Paz for "gastada." It is true also that the French definite article, as in "la pierre," equally accompanies abstract nouns—"la force," "le calme"—and for the French may confer on stone the same intellectuality. However, "la pierre," while it certainly designates the generality of stone available to the mind, also designates this particular stone—where in the next line "ants jet out their acid"—available to sight and touch; while "stone" likewise hovers between the world as we sense it and the world as we conceive it. Moreover, if it lacks the article, so do "force" and "calm." Wouldn't one say, in fact, that English, free from the weight of any deictic, names more directly than French?—and thereby recovers, strangely, the method of Latin. It moves not less but more easily toward the substance (say) of stone, or of wind, fire, water—of force, calm, majesty, desire.

Renga comes into being, springs into words, by a form of immediate translation. As a way of composing and as a finished text it blurs the line, therefore, between translation and creation. It continues the kind of blurring relaunched for modern poetry by Pound's "Homage to Sextus Propertius" and modifies it (translates it) radically by making the process reciprocal—as if, Pound having worked on Propertius, Propertius were to work on Pound. The writing in *Renga* is fully collaborative and involves a submission to other writers without the option to pull back. The poets belong, in Paz's expression, to a "combinative system of producers of signs." Each intervenes according to a mathematical sequence, surrendering his words and his sense of life to the otherness of his partners' literary and human habits and initiatives, the chance of a collective text and the remoteness of foreign tongues. He throws into the poem, almost as one might throw dice, an idea, a passion, a quotation, a rhetorical figure, a syntactical turn, a pattern of sounds, each of which moves beyond his power, to become the temporary property of each of the others, to do with as he will.

More deeply, each poet has to undergo, so as to further the emerging work, the spirit of the renga, of which Shinkei, apparently one of its greatest exponents, said, "The art of renga is not the art of composing poems, or stanzas of a poem, but an exercise of the heart to penetrate the talent and the vision of another" (*R*, 34). To participate in a renga is to venture on a special kind of literary criticism: to enter someone else's work (a work one has helped to engender) so as to write not a study of it but a continuation. It involves writing in such a way that one is not the only one writing.

The poets hear the voice of the other, submit to it, resist it, modify it. It precedes their writing, to guide them in the presence of several masters sitting in the same room. It follows them, once they have relinquished separateness and ownership, to intrude in their writing, perhaps to flare unpredictably all across it. And it apparently continued to sound beyond the physical encounter. Tomlinson, at least, states in his preface that even the making of his own sonnet, after he had returned to England, was governed by the group experience: "One still found oneself speaking with a communal voice" (*R*, 37). The poem hints at a pentecostal speech uttered, in a justness of spiritual discipline, by oneself and by more than oneself.

Such collaborative and multipersonal writing has obvious attractions, for the writer as well as for the reader. It also throws light on more conventional literature. Any writer, after all, can feel an impersonal pleasure in viewing his own work and can admire it without vanity, as if it came from someone else. He may sense that in a way it did—that the initial prompting arrived partly out of the blue, and that the developing text was alive with surprises. And isn't this even more obviously true of the translator? All translating, we know, is or can be an "exercise of the heart." Isn't it also cooperative and bi-personal, the production of a dual text—not "my" version of "your" poem, but "our" new poem in my language?

Renga exists through external translation, from the Japanese renga, and through internal translation, from one to another of its poets. It also raises, in a novel way, the question of its own translation. For one thing, a translation has already accompanied each of its successive publications, in France, Mexico, the United States, and England; and these versions by Roubaud,

Paz, and Tomlinson differ in kind from any version that might be made by someone not involved in the original poem. They are implied in the poem, since in the process of composing *Renga* each writer was already translating for himself before continuing his partners' work, and they are not activities exterior to the poem but reworkings of it from the inside. In the absence of the others but in the presence of their texts, each poet in his translation prolongs the collaborative encounter. The others cooperate with him to produce a new work in his language; he gives them a new language in which they can speak together. Each of these versions is a new utterance, in a single tongue, of the communal voice.

Each poet, moreover, is not only translating the others: he is also translating himself. Here too *Renga* moves forward. The self-translator like Beckett or Nabokov who shifts his own text across two languages creates a different kind of space-between, or textual passage, from any other translator. Part of the interest of *Waiting for Godot* is that it is Beckett's translation of Beckett's *En attendant Godot*. Each poet translates *Renga*, however, less by turning it into another language than by restricting it to one of the languages that it already includes and in which his own lines are already written—through a process not so much of substitution as of saturation. He translates his own text by keeping it in the *same* language while placing it in a new linguistic milieu. So Tomlinson's English, for example, alters, when the reader, no longer modulating into and out of it via Spanish, French, and Italian, receives it as part of a continuously English discourse.

Since the poet is translating the whole of *Renga*, he might also consider his own text as no more unchangeable than the others' and as being free to undergo modifications. In fact, there are few examples of this, beyond some changes of punctuation and what is no doubt simply a second thought by Paz, when "la playa" becomes "una playa." Roubaud does, however, occasionally vary the typographical disposition of his lines. The beginning of the first sonnet of section two:

> Aime criaient-ils aime gravité
> des très hautes branches tout bas pesait la
> Terre aime criaient-ils dans le haut
>
> (*R*, 54)

becomes

Aime   criaient-ils aime   gravité
       des très hautes branches   tout bas pesait la
Terre   aime   criaient-ils   dans le haut.

(R, 54)

Perhaps he too is only revising his original, to match it to the typography of his verse in other poems of this section and in his final sonnet. (It is the new typography that Paz and Tomlinson translate in their versions.) One could actually imagine far greater changes in translating a work of this kind—occasioned either by the new pressures on one's own lines from lines that are no longer, having changed language, those to which one initially responded, or by the new stimulus of reliving the encounter.

Renga also disturbs the relationship of "original" to "translation." There is still an original, authoritative (or quadri-authoritative) text: one would need to look elsewhere for the overthrow of that—to the sixteenth-century Dutch poet Jan van der Noot, imitating Ronsard in a poem in French that he then translated into Dutch, or to Eliot again, publishing "Dans le restaurant" in *Ara Vos Prec* and then translating a passage from it for the "Death by Water" section of *The Waste Land*.[1] In each case the first text, rather than being the definitive original from which the secondary translation derives, is the means for the production of a text which is both definitive and translated. The effect of *Renga* is the reverse. The poem is so constituted that any translation becomes problematic. By placing four languages on the same level it disallows the relationship of a single original language to a potentially inexhaustible number of translations. A German version, say, would be inappropriate through being unilingual. By placing four writers on the same level, it disallows the relationship of a single original writer to a potentially inexhaustible number of translators. A German translator would be inappropriate through being alone. The only apt translation that one could conceive would be bizarre, and perhaps comic. Since the poem, quadrilingual and collaborative, ought to be translated on its own terms, presumably it should be approached by four translators of different nationalities to produce a quadrilingual and collaborative translation—maybe passing their translated passages each to each, in a kind of translators' renga.

1. See Leonard Forster, *The Poet's Tongues* (Otago, New Zealand: Cambridge University Press and Otago Press, 1970).

At which point the obvious thought occurs that they would be better employed composing a new renga of their own.

It also troubles the notion of "foreign." If we read the line, "—Et ô ces voix d'enfants chantant dans la coupole!" in Verlaine's "Parsifal," we are aware that it is French and perhaps that its foreignness places us in Babel. If we read the same line in *The Waste Land* its foreignness is foregrounded by the fact that it occurs in a basically English poem—Verlaine's French changes in this new context—and the awareness of Babel is far more pointed. The French-ness of Roubaud's French is similarly underlined in *Renga* by occurring among three other languages; it changes from what it would have been in a poem by Roubaud. Here, however, there is no home language from which to consider it—from which to deem it foreign—and in which to feel secure. The English of *Renga* no longer has the status it had in *The Waste Land*: all four languages being equal, English becomes one language among many (as it does, it is true, at the end of Eliot's poem) and is no less foreign than French. While intimating Pentecost, *Renga* is also sharply Babelic, since it leads us, linguistically, into exile.

And so it also poses in a new way the question of the reader. It fails to do what we take for granted from a literary work—to posit the reader's nationality—and thereby make any reader a foreigner. But it equally makes *all* readers foreigners, together. An English reader has to acknowledge that English in the space of the poem is one language among others, and that his ability to read the poem is limited at those points where, say, an Italian reader is better equipped. In the same way, therefore, that *Renga* links the poets in their separateness, each having surrendered the primacy of his language and of his writing activity, so it links readers in their separateness, each having surrendered the primacy of his language and of his reading activity.

Renga is a new kind of literary work—multinational, multilingual, collaborative poetry—written in a new language. Like all languages, it needs to be learned. One has to discover how to read a composite volume that is more than the sum of its parts; to respond to a text that has no author, but not because the author is unknown; to find the ground in a poem that deploys places, times, and other poetries as never before, by establishing literary and personal links across the presents and into the pasts of four cultures.

Appropriately, language is one of its themes. It talks about its own existence as a special tongue, and about the meeting of the four poets within itself. The self-reference enters in the fourth line—"Dream ceases: languages begin"—and persists in the last—"from east to west to north to south above below flow forth the languages."[2] The languages flow, in fact, into a final silence, since Sanguineti's sonnet that should have closed the poem remains unwritten. According to Tomlinson's preface to the Penguin edition, Sanguineti decided that his sequence was already complete: "his silence was his sonnet." Whatever the reason for it, the silence is deeply right. At the end of a work engaged, in a quite novel way, with Babel, it is the necessary muteness, a sign that the confusion has been used, ordered, and beautified but not removed. At the same time, dialectically, it gathers into itself all those many processes of linguistic re-creation that the whole poem has brought to bear. It is not empty but full with those possibilities.

Renga was clearly beneficial to Tomlinson for the developing of his own poetry. He continued to explore "the given," the there-ness of the world as at once postulated and bestowed as a gift; and to suggest the receding mystery of the observed. The world for the eyes and the mind is at one point a "frame of near-nesses" (an image from Baudelaire) leading through to only half-seen boughs, and beyond them to air, on which the boughs inscribe both their meaningful "calligraphy" and their unmean-ing "confusion" (*R*, 69). The collaborative nature of *Renga* was, after all, sharply appropriate to his concern with the relations between the self and the other: it faced him with the "contingen-cies and quiddities" of other writers' words (*R*, 47), committed him to a new kind of creative chance, and provided an original discipline.

Precisely in those terms, however, one wonders if the encoun-ter really worked for Tomlinson. He seems to have been im-pelled to state and to re-state his theme through finding himself at odds with the others, to the point, as he said in a broadcast on *Renga*, of calling attention to the real Paris outside the myth-inhabited hotel basement "in a kind of protest." He countered what he considered a language of mental essences and surreal

---

2. Actually that fourth line is "mine," since I wanted to point to the fact that the same word, Paz's "lenguajes," opens and closes the poem. Tomlinson, by a large act of transformation, translates the first instance as "the gift of tongues."

fantasia, where "objects went on disappearing," by means of a language of things, a syntax of careful deliberation, a prosody moving at accurate moments with the tradition, a citing (and glorious extending) of Pope's finely relevant line about laughing Ceres reassuming the land (R, 45). Even in replying to Paz, the one poet whom he felt to be engaging in dialogue, he found it necessary to insist on a process of "decipher[ment]" rather than "invent[ion]" (R, 79). One senses also in Paz's suspicion of the self as illusion—at one point: "caracola, amonita . . . cuarto vacío, lector" / "seashell, ammonite . . . empty room, lecteur" (R, 52, 53), he redirected Baudelaire's moral and spiritual challenge to the "hypocritical reader" toward Mallarmé's invitation to a voiding of the self by quoting the shell and empty drawingroom of the latter's "Ses purs ongles très haut dédiant leur onyx"—that this oriental aloofness about the "I" could not match Tomlinson's desire for a true and concrete self defined in response to what is beyond it.

It was a certain dissatisfaction with *Renga* on the part of both Tomlinson and Paz that led to the writing of *Airborn / Hijos del Aire*.[3] (*Renga* was expected to inspire many such collective works, by poets not necessarily involved in the original experiment, though I know of only one other.) The evident objective here was genuine collaboration. Each of the two sequences, consisting of three shared sonnets, whose sections traveled between the poets in transatlantic letters, and of a fourth unitary sonnet, is begun by one writer and concluded by the other, so that neither sequence "belongs." More decisively, the book was derived from deeply charged words, "house" and "day," chosen, moreover, among those that had been actually spoken during a stay of the Pazes at the Tomlinsons' cottage. On this warmly personal-impersonal groundwork is constructed an authentic duologue, in which the poets concur and are seen to concur, in the direction that the developing poem should take. This is apparent in the second sonnet of "House / Casa," where Paz (as I read it) accepts a nudge, almost an admonition, from Tomlin-

3. Airborn is printed bilingually in a recent re-edition in Holland, with a renga-ed Dutch translation facing, by Peter Nijmeijer for the English and by Laurens Vancrevel for the Spanish. Only in this extraneous edition does one find the primal text. Anvil Press published *Airborn / Hijos del Aire* as a book in 1981, and it appears most recently in *New Direction in Prose and Poetry* 42, ed. James Laughlin with Peter Glasgold and Frederick R. Martin (New York: New Directions, 1981).

son, for the poem to go where it does. The lines in italic are by
Paz, those in Roman by Tomlinson:

> *House that memory makes out of itself*
> *between the spaces of blank time—more thought*
> *than lived and yet more said than thought,*
> *house that lasts as long as its own sound takes:*
>
> house, you began in milk, in warmth, in eating:
> words must re-tongue your first solidities
> and thought keep fresh your fragrance of bread baking
> or drown in the stagnation of its memories:
>
> *house in which two pasts conjoin and two*
> *hands inscribe their separate histories,*
> *a murmur in search of meaning builds you*
>
> where, in a hive of words, time's honeying
> flavours and fills with momentary savour
> this mouth and mind, this citadel of cells.
>
> (*A*, 15)

In fact there is debate throughout, with Tomlinson, as here,
doing most of the steering. Yet the reader is aware not of a colli-
sion but of an interleaving, of two very different life experiences
and ways of experiencing. Doubly autobiographical, the volume
is composed, as it were, from the antiphons of friendship.

The manner in which the poems are printed also furthers this
impression of the production by two voices of a single poem.
The initial intention was presumably to print them bilingually
with a facing translation, like *Renga*: the sonnet that first appeared in the review *Prospice* was in that form. In the book, however, original and translation have been combined, so that
entirely English poems face entirely Spanish ones. The multilingual effect of *Renga* has been sacrificed in favor of securing an
effect of cooperation, where either Tomlinson joins with Paz to
speak Spanish or Paz with Tomlinson to speak English.

Since the English and Spanish versions have the same status
in the book, they alter even more than *Renga* the relationship of
"original" to "translation." They are not internal prolongations
of the poem: they are the poem. They are the two facets of the

original work—the two *versions*, precisely, of a work only existing in forms that are both creative and derived. By a simple move, Tomlinson and Paz have devised yet another new kind of text.

This means, of course, that any changes wrought by translation cause the one poem's two phases to differ. In the first tercet of the sonnet quoted above, Paz writes,

> *casa en la conjunción de dos pasados*
> *y de dos escrituras, construída*
> *por un murmullo en busca de sentido*
> (*A*, 14)

and one sees that Tomlinson has drawn Paz's contribution toward his own. "Two hands" inscribing are more intimately human than two unfleshed "writings," and those hands inscribe in addition the real times and places of two "histories," albeit "separate." In this novel structure, any variations of emphasis, any seizings of possibility, rather than being those of a secondary translation, enter the work itself.

Like *Renga*, *Airborn / Hijos del Aire* is still preoccupied with its own existence, with "lines," "rhyme," "syllables." Its two themes are eventually transposed by metaphor into the work they generate, "the poem's single day . . . this house of vocables" ("Día / Day," *A*, 29). Perhaps this was natural, given that the book's underlying theme is memory, and the negotiation with memory for meaning, habitation, a present: the poems are the "now" where all converges. It does prompt one to ask, nevertheless, if it is possible to write collaborative poetry that is not taken up with itself; and also if Western writers, when working together, are capable of a poetry truly impersonal. Does collaborative writing give scope for this or, on the contrary, make each writer not less but more conscious of himself? The hope, I take it, would be, if not the origination of a common "we" transcending the "I's" of the individual poets, at least a sense in the reader of poets so concentrated on their theme, so attentive to the voice of the poem, as to be caught, so to speak, unawares. And there is another difficulty: the unwontedness of cooperative works inclines one in reading them to consider the poets too directly, as, in this case, the immediately present Charles Tomlinson and Octavio Paz, and so to mishear, to miss hearing, their poem. It is a problem, one realizes, also for readers.

Donald Wesling

9. Process and Closure in Tomlinson's Prose Poems

The prose poem has not been favored by English poets, perhaps because of the prestige and unquestioned greatness of their national tradition of line and rhyme. Those who with Charles Tomlinson have experimented with the prose poem, like Roy Fisher and Geoffrey Hill, have been a shade more internationalist in outlook, open to certain formal possibilities from France and America. Tomlinson himself has written only eight prose poems, all of them grouped in the section called "Processes" in *The Way of a World* (1969).[1] The longish and very fine text titled "Prose Poem," from *The Shaft* (1978), is in lines and rhymes and makes such a unique, separate case—teasingly defining prose as a subject matter and not as a kind of notational style—that I reserve it for last. My brief for the eight poems called "Processes" is that Tomlinson, admiring chance effects but not abandon, experiments with extreme caution, refusing to be drawn toward the form's anarchic possibilities. The difference between his themes and methods in the prose poems and in his

---

Donald Wesling has written books on Wordsworth, on John Muir, and on questions of poetic form. He is chair of the Literature Department at the University of California, San Diego.

1. For his *Selected Poems 1951–1974* (London: Oxford University Press, 1978), Tomlinson has chosen only two of his eight prose poems, "Autumn" and "Skull-shapes." Apparently the prose poems do not stand very large in his personal canon. A related group of texts seem to me slightly too relaxed to call prose poems—they belong in the uncertain territory between the prose poem and one of its many cousins, the journal entry. In this group are "Image and Chance: From a Notebook," *In Black and White: The Graphics of Charles Tomlinson*, introduction by Octavio Paz (Cheadle, Cheshire: Carcanet New Press, 1975), pp. 21–22; "Sight and Flight," *The Christian Science Monitor*, 29 August 1977, 25; "Chimayó, from a New Mexico Journal," *Perfect Bound*, edited by Peter Robinson and Richard Hammersley (Cambridge, 1978), pp. 63–65; "The Near and the Far," *F*, pp. 18–19.

other poems is minimal, though by no means trivial. That difference could not fail to be significant to someone who, both poet and graphic artist, has spent upward of thirty-five years practicing the sister arts of *line*.

A reading of Tomlinson's prose poems—texts in that hermaphroditic and avant-garde format—must serve in the end to reinforce one's belief that he is after all a traditional poet. He is traditional in the way of the painter Constable, whom he admires, accepting the evidences of perception, loving the world's physical presences, and trusting that the artist's materials (word, pigment) can graph what's seen and felt. The notation of the work of art would be, for him, accurate to the way of a world, and also public; no accuracy but one that is communicable. The hygiene of "deconstruction" is not unknown to him, with its privileging of ideas of absence, indeterminacy, the text as a "galaxy of signifiers" (Roland Barthes), but Tomlinson is after all British, midlands British—incorrigibly perception-based, an artist who watches climate and landscape with the kind of charged perception that, he once said (quoting Kafka), catches a glimpse of things as they may have been before they show themselves to the observer. Tomlinson's attraction to notions of absence and chance, to the deconstructing and dispersing maneuvers of the international avant-garde, is always chastened by his fact-noticing Englishness.

For this reason we often see him in dialogue with Stéphane Mallarmé, the strong deconstructive poet whose works precede by generations the philosophical deconstruction of Martin Heidegger, Jacques Derrida, and Paul de Man. There is an "Homage and Valediction" to Mallarmé, along with Laforgue and Eliot, in the six-part poem "Antecedents" in *Seeing Is Believing* (1960); and the title of one of Tomlinson's drawings of a seashell, dated 11 October 1968, is "Débat avec Mallarmé." More to the point here, the first and to my mind the most considerable of his prose poems in the Processes section is "Oppositions: debate with Mallarmé":

> The poet must rescue etymology from among the footnotes, thus moving up into the body of the text, "*cipher*: the Sanskrit word *sunya* derived from the root *svi*, to swell."
>
> To cipher is to turn the thought word into flesh. And hence "the body of the text" derives its substance.

The master who disappeared, taking with him into the echo-chamber the ptyx which the Styx must replenish, has left the room so empty you would take it for fullness.

Solitude charges the house. If all is mist beyond it, the island of daily objects within becomes clarified.

Mistlines flow slowly in, filling the land's declivity that lay unseen until that indistinctness had acknowledged them.

If the skull is a memento mori, it is also a room, whose contained space is wordlessly resonant with the steps that might cross it, to command the vista out of its empty eyes.

Nakedness can appear as the vestment of space that separates four walls, the flesh as certain then and as transitory as the world it shares.

The mind is a hunter of forms, binding itself, in a world that must decay, to present substance.

Skull and shell, both are helmeted, both reconcile vacancy with its opposite. *Abolis bibelots d'inanité sonore.* Intimate presences of silent plenitude.

(*WW,* 49)

There are nine verset-like parts, six of them fully equivalent to a single sentence. The third and the ninth versets refer to Mallarmé, to whose sonnet, "Ses purs ongles très haut dédiant leur onyx," Tomlinson's poem is a reply. Mallarmé there conjures an empty room (second quatrain);

> nul ptyx,
> Aboli bibelot d'inanité sonore
> (Car le Maître est alle puiser des pleurs au Styx
> Avec ce seul objet dont le Néant s'honore.)
>   [no ptyx,
> Abolished bibelot of sounding inanity
> (For the Master is gone to draw tears from the Styx
> With this sole object which Nothingness honours.)][2]

2. Both the Mallarmé quatrain and its translation are quoted from a text Tomlinson seems to have used, *Stéphane Mallarmé: Poems,* translated by Roger Fry (New York: New Directions, by arrangement with Chatto & Windus of London, 1951), pp. 104–5. The commentary (p. 239) identifies the ptyx as possibly a shell, the meaning Tomlinson gives in his note to this poem on his own acknowledgments page; and the symbolic sense given (p. 238) for this nonce-word bears on Tomlinson's debate: "[Mallarmé] took it from the Greek word πύξ, which means a fold, the rhyme being the place where the verse folds back. But 'ptyx,' a word almost entirely without sense, yet capable of such rich rhyme, represents

For Tomlinson, who was drawing skulls and shells in profusion at just this time of his debate-poem in 1968–1969, such hollow objects are, and are occasions for, reconciliations of outer and inner, presence and absence. Tomlinson's lightly joking use of converging words, *ptyx* and *Styx*, suggests another kind of reconciliation—rhyme forcing a strained semantic connection even in a prose poem, even when one of the terms is a neologism and the other an archaism.

The poem proceeds from a manifesto (versets 1–3) to instances of the union in the art-object of absence and presence (4–7), to a generalizing statement (8) and a direct rebuttal of Mallarmé's sentence fragment in French by Tomlinson's in English (9). Tomlinson arranges this argument-by-juxtaposition so as to have the last word himself, but Mallarmé's assertion of a sounding inanity, a Nothingness, is not treated by Tomlinson with irony, merely contradicted with severe insistence. The mingling of assertion and example is Tomlinson's way to defend (by speaking) the silent plenitude of such natural yet artful objects.[3] His defense of presences in the final sentence is foreshadowed by a rhetoric of body and substance in all the earlier versets, but especially, I should say, in the pun on *present* both as a transitive verb meaning "give" and as an adjective meaning "immediate" (verset 8). This doubling effect, putting into doubt etymology and phonology, would not function in a metered poem, where relative stress on first or second syllable would tell the reader how to sound and therefore how definitively to interpret the word. The prose poem preserves the several meanings and thus, in this instance, actually comprises more meaning than a metered poem.

Charles Tomlinson shows himself convinced, for this poem anyway, that the world means, means well, and means through a linguistic sign so thoroughly motivated that its cipher can "turn the thought word into flesh" (verset 2). Ferdinand de Saussure and Jacques Derrida and I might take Mallarmé's side in the debate, in order to resist Tomlinson's defiant Cratylism,

---

[Mauron thinks] 'Rhyme for Rhyme's sake'—for the pleasure of the ear, 'abolished bibelot of sounding inanity.'"

3. The word "bibelot" is singular in Mallarmé's original but plural in Tomlinson, presumably to accommodate skull, shell, oakleaf, flattened fieldmouse, frozen infusoria in a pond, daisies like "paper accents," pipe, artful objects that inhabit the eight poems in "Processes."

his hope, with its emblem the Sanskrit root, to charge the word with so much presence it actually protrudes toward the noticer. The poet seems positively to have encouraged such dissent by setting the poem up to make debating points—by pronouncing on the way of a world, his world. He does this often, too, in his line and rhyme poems, stating how the world is, but the prose poems seem to accept this argumentative, point-making approach somewhat more easily. (The exception, to my mind, is the last of the eight, "A Process," which has a higher proportion of declaration to image than "Oppositions.") Sometimes, with Tomlinson, the reader wants to resist being told how the world is; what "we" see, feel, know can be finicky, coercive to a degree; manifestoes of seeing seem to take over to persuade the reader that perception is a profound and not altogether helpless form of moral cognition. But without these continuous, really rather unobtrusive injunctions to see! feel! know! our perceptions, Tomlinson would be a landscapist pure and meek. The injunctions are part of his whole effort as a writer, and hence his admiration for Ruskin; only when the injunctions begin to outnumber the famous Tomlinsonian "instances" of charged perception on which they depend do they seem preacherly. The poem "Oppositions" is not, to my mind, coercive—rather argumentative and emphatic, in order to prepare the reader to receive the seven other poems in the section called "Processes."

These poems are processes because, like all prose poems, they foreground a structuring principle in post-romantic poetry that may tend to recede from view in verse-formats, namely, sequence itself, the reader's sense that the text is a narrative of consciousness and of grammar. The eighth and last of these is called "A Process" and states aesthetic principles of continuous change, walking boundaries to "lay claim to them, knowing all they exclude"—a process in the sense of a trial (French *procès*), a proceeding, a test of how something can be a "complication and . . . unravelling." The beginnings of such experimental works have, Tomlinson says here, "to be invented"; and the ends, he claims, are indeterminate, openings-out rather than terminations:

A process; procession; trial.
. . . .
Its perfect accompaniment would be that speech of islanders, in

> which, we are told, the sentence is never certainly brought to an end, its aim less to record with completeness the impression an event makes, than to mark its successive aspects as they catch the eye, the ear of the speaker.
>
> (*WW*, 55)

That would be the verbal equivalent of the method of decalcomania Tomlinson had begun to experiment with in the late 1960s, black gouache spread unevenly on a glossy white sheet, covered with a sheet that is then removed slowly. That was his phase of the created chance, the unpredictable, the exploratory, but Tomlinson next covered his decalcomanias with masking sheets with windows scissored in them. He wrote in a letter to Octavio Paz, "Scissors! Here was the instrument of choice. I found I could draw with scissors, reacting *with* and *against* the decalcomania."[4] As maker of prose poems and decalcomanias, Tomlinson's habit seems to have been to open his creative process to effects of chance, but always to round off the work by an explicit return to choice for the purpose of making a finished pattern.

Tomlinson's endings are not usually as forensic and emphatic as the one on "Oppositions," but he does employ syntax and allusion to create maximal closure. The prose poem entitled "Poem" has six sentences, the first of which ends on an ellipse as if incomplete:

> The muscles which move the eyeballs, we are told, derive from a musculature which once occupied the body end to end.
>
> (*WW*, 53)

And the last sentence, describing (as so often elsewhere in the prose poems and the lined poems) the interpenetration of outer and inner, perception and cognition, picks up, elaborates, and completes the first sentence:

> So that "over there" and "in here" compound a truce neither signed —a truce that, insensibly and categorically, grows to a decree, and

4. Decalcomania is described at some length by Octavio Paz in his introduction to *In Black & White*, especially pp. 10–13. The letter to Paz is quoted by Paz in *In Black and White*, pp. 12–13.

Pursuing chance deflections with pigment and syntax might help the painter/ writer achieve a higher degree of impersonality. The prose poem would be more adaptable to chance, perhaps, than the poem in verse. Plainly the convergence of painterly and writerly experimental procedures at the same time in Tomlinson's work is appropriate: different versions of a single intent.

what one hoped for and what one is, must measure themselves against those demands which the eye receives, delivering its writ on us through a musculature which occupies the body end to end.

(*WW*, 53)[5]

In between the opening supposition and the closing declaration come the confirming Tomlinsonian instances of perception, sentences so stout and fine they help the reader accept what is to be declared. ("Sunblaze as day goes, and the light blots back the scene to iris the half-shut lashes.") The poem "Autumn" deals with a seasonal truce, a moment of poise before winter wins out over life and color; that poem ends as it has proceeded, with abrupt answer rephrasing abrupt question:

> There will be a truce, but not the truce of the rime with the oak leaf, the mist with the alders, the rust with the sorrel stalk or of the flute with cold.
> It will endure? It will endure as long as the frost.

(*WW*, 50)

"Tout Entouré De Mon Regard" deals with another truce, the one between what the glance can take in and the sustaining and balancing "darkness behind you," and the closure is emphatic by means of image, not statement:

> To see, is to feel at your back this domain of a circle whose power consists in evading and refusing to be completed by you.
> It is infinity sustains you on its immeasurable palm.

(*WW*, 51)

That, as in all Tomlinson, is a secular infinity, an infinity of possible perceptions like the one the poet approves in his epigraph from Jorge Guillén, which in my rough translation reads, "And the present gives so much / That the walking foot feels / The wholeness of the world."[6] Presenced perception is the content,

---

5. There is a pun on "writ" in the passage quoted—using the French sense of process I have already mentioned. An English paraphrase might affirm that the eye is process-server to the body. This text, "Poem," and the one that is placed before it, "The Daisies," seem to me, with "Oppositions," Tomlinson's best efforts in the prose poem; but I do not linger on the former two because I have given readings of them in a chapter of my book on avant-garde prosodies, *Form As Proceeding*. Other poems quoted in this paragraph are on pp. 50, 51 of *The Way of a World*.

6. The passage from Jorge Guillén's "Perfección" is

Y tanto se da el presente
Que el pie caminante siente
La integridad del planeta.

strong closure the method of these eight prose poems—different and dovetailing expressions of an optimism that human nature and outer nature have a vital relationship before language, and, fortunately for poetry, in language.

The prose poems are the second last section in *The Way of a World*. The last section contains two lined poems, as if to assert a larger closure that will place a final bracket around the less regular prose poems. "The Chances of Rhyme" and "The End" are not only in a section called coda but also in the very process of letting

> him know
> Who reads his time by the way books go,
> Each instant will bewry his symmetries.
> ("The End," *WW*, 60)

The two poems are also rich with closural allusions and ornate effects of terminal rhyme. While diminishing art's little subendings, in theory, such poems play them for all they are worth. So we may find a special caution in Tomlinson's writing and deployment of his prose poems. Though his sentences are ingenious and eventful, he refuses to explore the furthest limits of English sentence structure. Though his narratives of consciousness are exploratory, especially in their instance-packed middles, he is not a poet of the irrational leap, the dream-logic that flashes unrelated images in sequence. His attitude is teacherly or lawyerly, not bardic; his rhythms are typically choppy, with short paragraphs and abrupt turns.

A certain uneasiness with the rhapsodic possibility of the form is hinted like a countercurrent in one of the prose poems, "Skullshapes," when Tomlinson writes,

> The skull of nature is recess and volume. The skull of art—of possibility—is recess, volume and also lines—lines of containment, lines of extension.
>
> (*WW*, 52)

Perhaps containment is slightly preferred to extension? In lines of verse the containment is more certain, or at least more obvious.

Thus the assumptions of "Prose Poem" (*S*, 19), Tomlinson's sendup or skirting of the whole issue, are not entirely playful. The poem, written a decade after the "Processes" section, is a philosophical narrative of opening a century-old apothecary's jar. This story the poet has set out in thirty-nine lines with admirably unpredictable rhymes:

> What had to be done
> If we were to undo it, was to pass
>   A silk cord round the collar of glass
> And rub it warm—but this friction
>   Must be swift enough not to conduct its heat
> Inside—the best protection against which
>   (Only a third hand can ensure this feat)
> Is a cube of ice on top of the stopper.
>
> ("Prose Poem," *S*, 19)

The jar is presented from the poem's beginning as an example of an unresolved issue in aesthetics: in what sense are the useful arts art? In the poem, this is transposed into a question about prose and poetry: can prose be for contemplation, poetry for use, thus upsetting a traditional hierarchy? By showing the poem's first and last lines we can see how Tomlinson avoids resolving this issue by keeping the terms *use* and *contemplation* equal in value, privileging neither:

> If objects are of two kinds—those
>   That we contemplate and, the remainder, use,
> I am unsure whether its poetry or prose
>   First drew us to this jar. . . .
> · · · · · · · · · · · ·
>   There is one sole lack
> Now that jar and stopper are in right relation—
>   An identifiable aroma: what we must do
> Is to fill it with coffee, for use, scent and contemplation.
>
> (*S*, 19)[7]

The bottle on opening is put to ear and gives, the poet says, "a low, crystalline roar" that is neither seashell murmur nor emptiness, but "so full of electric imponderables, it could compare /

7. Among Tomlinson's drawings of 1968 is one dated 21 October, which shows an ordinary household corkscrew under the (mockingly?) Mallarméean title, "Ptyx utile." The apothecary bottle, in "Prose Poem," to be filled "with coffee, for use, scent and contemplation," is another such ptyx. See *In Black and White*, pl. 6.

Only with the molecular stealth when the jar / Had breathed"
(S, 19).

Here the jar is personified ("breathed") but also, giving sound, made an analogue for poetry, made worthy of contemplation, though earlier it had been presented as sealed off, a product: "Its cylinder of glass, / Perfectly seamless, has the finality and satisfaction / Of the achieved act of an artisan" (S, 19). Plainly Tomlinson admires objects, including poems, that deconstruct the opposition between using and contemplating, artisan-work and poetic art.[8] His title-term, "Prose Poem," and the beginning and ending of the poem keep the uncertainty from being resolved on one side or the other.

However, there is provocation in giving this title to a poem in this format, as if the poet is faintly parodying those others, including his own earlier self, who might reserve the term for a specific formal procedure, a notation of justified margins (though with an aura, it may be, of a nonlogical sequence of images). If my earlier readings are correct, this poem's disjunction between title and format is the obverse procedure from the processes in *The Way of a World*, where prose poems follow the narrative of consciousness of emphatic closure one usually sees in the line-and-rhyme tradition in English lyric. We may conclude that line-and-rhyme, or verse as such, has no special privilege for Tomlinson, and no special subject-matter; his works share in the era's stylistic pluralism and its democracy of subject. What he privileges, instead, is "the finality and satisfaction / Of the achieved art of an artisan." Accordingly he has written few prose poems and those of maximal closure. His experiments are done with carefully polished and calibrated instruments.

8. Very likely I would not have noticed the artisanal values in Tomlinson if Donald Davie had not already done so. See Davie's important poem, "To a Brother in the Mystery," *Collected Poems 1950–1972* (London: Routledge & Kegan Paul, 1972), pp. 106–8; and the note on the poem, p. 301.

Overview

Michael Edwards

10. The Poetry of Charles Tomlinson

The important, sometimes major poet who is denied early recognition is classic to our century. The case of Charles Tomlinson is at this moment the most disturbing, since what must surely be the inevitable acceptance of his status has not yet occurred. On the contrary. The most powerful poetry now being published by an Englishman, to my knowledge, is still, generally speaking, shrugged off.

It is true that enthusiastic, and *distinguishing*, commendations have appeared, from poets and critics as demanding of attention as, for instance, William Carlos Williams, Richard Wilbur, Hugh Kenner, and Donald Davie. Indeed, a compilation could be made of passages from reviews—suggesting that he is the young English poet who most combines ambition with imagination, that he is the "most original and accomplished of all our post-war poets," even that *Seeing Is Believing* is "the most important book of verse by a new writer since *Harmonium* or *Observations*"— which would appear to constitute a veritable triumph. Yet these have been isolated celebrations. The bulk of comment is against him (at least in this country); critical interest is directed elsewhere; he is habitually excluded from the company of poets through whom English verse is thought to be developing.

The reviews of his latest book, *The Way of a World*, confirm one's sense of his rejection. They were slow to appear, and nearly all those I have seen were cool or aggressive and suffered from that general unwillingness to *read* the book in hand, that failure to analyze and to distinguish achievements and limitations, which makes most reviewing so unsatisfactory at the present moment.

Michael Edwards is Professor of English at the University of Warwick, England. "The Poetry of Charles Tomlinson" was originally published in *Agenda* 9, 2–3 (1971): 127–41.

It is time for those who admire Tomlinson to state their reasons and to examine his poetry in depth. With four full-length volumes and two books of translations, he has now created a considerable body of work, finely detailed and massively coherent. This is an attempt to show the rewards of exploring it closely.

*   *   *

Tomlinson's poetry is a negotiation with space and time. It is a continually repeated attempt, by meeting an uncontrollable world of spatial complexity and temporal flux, to create a dwelling for human imagination and human passion. The negotiations focus on an encounter between the poem's narrator, or a second- or third-person projection of him, and a natural scene bodied against his eye, his mind, and his will; or on the establishment of wider meaning and larger poise through social convergence; or on certain buildings, usually "not ancient but old," which harbor space and time in a richness of relation.

"Swimming Chenango Lake," the first poem in *The Way of a World*, is perhaps the finest enactment of natural encounter. The swimmer first "reads" the scene—characteristically at the approach of winter, the season of maximum affront to one's sense of life—and perceives unity and correspondence, "a consistency, the grain of the pulsating flow" (*WW*, 3). He then, according to the pattern that Tomlinson has established for several poems of this kind, acts powerfully on his observation and reflection—"he scissors the waterscape apart / And sways it to tatters" (*WW*, 3). In the give and take of the encounter, in grasping and being grasped by the lake's coldness, he enters his body's "inheritance," "making a where / In water" (*WW*, 3). The waters then escape his mind—his "questions"—as they slip from his body, reducing him to a recognition of his "solitariness," "unnaming" him by this "baptism." Yet out of this moral and epistemological humility, by confronting the element with his humanity he learns and accepts its profound ambivalence:

> Human, he fronts it and, human, he draws back
> > From the interior cold, the mercilessness
> That yet shows a kind of mercy sustaining him.
>
> > > > > (*WW*, 4)

After the steadily held, basically four-stress lines that have carried so far the close observing and the deliberate acting, the final lines embody in their lengthier rhythms the wider, ungovernable movements of the lake, "The going-elsewhere of ripples incessantly shaping" (WW, 4). "Shaping," the last word of the poem, organic and metaphysically buoyant, balances the first word, "Winter."

"Swimming Chenango Lake" is a deeply perfect disproof of certain charges commonly leveled against Tomlinson. He is accused of lacking feeling, of coldly reporting the minutiae of things, of committing himself to the poem only as an observer, of being incapable of claiming the reader through more than adequate imagery. (It is temporarily unfortunate, in fact, that he is known to be a painter, since this facilitates slipping the adjective "painterly" into descriptions of his writing; and once the word has stuck we are stuck with the idea, along with its implied limitations.) Yet the pressure behind the poems is manifold, and richly human. Insofar as there is recording, it is often the recording of what *Seeing Is Believing* calls "delight." The sensuousness of "Chenango," while it lacks the colorful gladness of many other pieces, merges easily, and with no heaviness of obtrusive intention, with the swimmer's probing for meaning:

> Winter will bar the swimmer soon.
>   He reads the water's autumnal hesitations
> A wealth of ways: it is jarred,
>   It is astir already despite its steadiness,
> Where the first leaves at the first
>   Tremor of the morning air have dropped
> Anticipating him, launching their imprints
>   Outwards in eccentric, overlapping circles.
> (WW, 3)

The mental and physical sense of the scene blend in "bar"; the ambivalence of the lake's "meaning" emerges through the recovered cliché, "a wealth of ways"; in "jarred" there is the pleasure of exact (and unpedantic) natural knowledge. The poem's complex of feeling, finally, concentrates toward the end in a sudden and strongly controlled deepening, played through an image, easy and expansive, compellingly beautiful:

> The image he has torn
> Flows-to behind him, healing itself,
> Lifting and lengthening, splayed like the feathers
> Down an immense wing whose darkening spread
> Shadows his solitariness: alone, he is unnamed
> By this baptism, where only Chenango bears a name
> In a lost language he begins to construe. . . .
>
> (*WW*, 3)

Less numerous than the poems where an individual consciousness encounters the external world, those that rehearse a similar posed relation to space and time through the achievement of a *social* and natural bond center typically on a communal rooting within the shifting solidities of the English countryside. The experience of living in America has also quickened a corresponding interest in the survivals of cohesive primitive cultures. Navajo Indians, in "Before the Dance" (*WW*, 27–28), wait for the dance that will bind them to time and space, despite the "aridity" of the landscape—one notes the characteristic fundamental hardness to be reckoned with—which they "wear" on their faces. The form repeats a basic maneuver of Tomlinson's poetry in exacting a Symbolist awakening to a sudden, privileged moment of heightened perception and profounder being. Yet their dance recalls less the dance of Symbolism than that of the Renaissance-Augustan tradition. The Navajos awake not to a fragile and necessarily momentary illumination but to a pattern of ritual dance that gathers the tribe and discovers the pattern of the elements, "'the movement / with the wind / of the Orient and / the moment against / the wind / of the Occident'" (*WW*, 28). The poem makes use of the very short lines first developed in *A Peopled Landscape*, which draw the eye and the mind swiftly down the page, for a new, reverberating terseness that drives to the powerful and human-metaphored climax:

> to wake
> in the clangour of the pulse of time
> at the beginning
> drum. . . .
>
> (*WW*, 28)

Yet the poetry is equally aware of the loss of concord, of the loosening of ties. One recalls that Tomlinson was writing in the fifties; several of his poems belong to the literature of that period concerned—as *Look Back in Anger*, *Lucky Jim*, Larkin's "Church Going"—with the disruption and drift of society and belief. It is in this context that his "building" poems establish their thickly textured sense of loss or their difficult faith.

Tomlinson's poetry of buildings derives in part from Yeats's poems on great houses. Nevertheless, the harmonies that he perceives grounded on rooted building and rooted ways of life, and the emotional tone of his searching for them and declaring of them, differ widely from the world and manner of Yeats. Although for Yeats "contact with the soil" is the dream as much of the beggar-man as of the noble; although "traditional sanctity and loveliness" are written in "the book of the people"; although the favored company is one essentially of artists—the vision remains aristocratic, the allegiances to peasant and to artist find their natural fulcrum in "a rich man's flowering lawns," old terraces, urns, old marble heads, great rooms, escutcheoned doors. Tomlinson does on occasion capture something of the Yeatsian haughtiness, and reproduce Yeatsian vocabulary; but his more characteristic poems explore humbler dwellings. Many of them are farms; the Hall at Stowey has a door that aimed at a "civil elegance" but hit in fact a "sturdier compromise" (*SIB*, 40); the town of Delft is correspondingly "staid," and as "a staid but dancing town" (*SIB*, 26) it points the social and emotional tempering of the dancing metaphor after the "dance-like glory" of Yeats's Coole Park. Tomlinson's houses merge for a greater identity not with famous ancestry and famous guests but with their few inhabitants; not with great gardens and feudal dependencies but with orchards, cow-sheds, farmed land. The plain solidities of "four unheraldic sheep-dogs" keeping the kitchen floor has replaced Juno's peacocks. The fundamental union is between the pent fertilities of the earth and of human dwellings; it is packed into this clenched metaphor for the door at Stowey: "clumped from the arching-point / And swathing down, like a fist of wheat" (*SIB*, 41). The lines recall—no doubt unconsciously but not without point—Péguy's image for one of the towers of Chartres cathedral: "*C'est l'épi le plus dur qui soit jamais monté / Vers un ciel de clémence et de sérénité.*"

Against the enemies of local habitation, rich in the awareness of continuities with the neighborhood and with the past,
Tomlinson pits firstly—like Yeats—a style of acute response.
But whereas Yeats resists dissolution with a resonant passion,
a powerful syntax, a high-toned magniloquence, Tomlinson's
verse is steady and precise, holding close to the threatened realities with a warmly felt and detailed exploration of their presence.

He opposes essentially to the fading and the dismantling an
Augustan poise. Tomlinson has a firm sense of eighteenth-
century equilibrium, very different from Yeats's mythologizing
of the same period. "At Holwell Farm," one of the really beautiful things in *Seeing Is Believing*, establishes the Edenic "meaning" of the place through something of the manners of Augustan thought and language. It opens like this:

> It is a quality of air, a temperate sharpness
>   Causes an autumn fire to burn compact,
> To cast from a shapely and unrifted core
>   Its steady brightness. A kindred flame
> Gathers within the stone, and such a season
>   Fosters, then frees it in a single glow. . . .
>   (*SIB*, 39)

One notes the particular tone of the adjectives "shapely" and
"kindred," at the center of the poem's directing toward harmo-
nious decorum; the syntactical speed of the last line; the frank
symbolism of "unrifted core"; the balance of physical and abstract in "temperate sharpness," "steady brightness." A series
of concrete details then converges into the poem's focal abstraction: "a pattern of utilities." The suggestions throughout of the
iambic pentameter are sealed in the final lines:

>   . . . a quality of air,
> Such as surrounds and shapes an autumn fire
>   Bringing these sharp disparities to bear.
>   (*SIB*, 39)

The hint of the rhyming couplet recalls that linguistic manifestation of Augustan order. The final verb, "to bear," concentrates
the pressure of feeling behind the abstractions—resumed, again
in balance with the physical, as "sharp disparities." The Edenic
wholeness of the site—"Rooted in more than earth to dwell / is

to discern the Eden image"—is sustained by the Augustan resolution of opposites, of the "sharp disparities" of fire and cold.

The mediation is in no sense a pedantic, abstract affair. It is
embodied by an unemphatic yet warmly imaginative responsiveness to objects, as in the quietly surprising line, "Pears by
the wall and stone as ripe as pears" (*SIB*, 39). The poem blends a
"Wordsworthian" feeling—Wordsworth is deliberately evoked
by a reference to "natural piety"—and the intellectual severity
of an earlier discipline.

There is much Augustanism in Tomlinson; yet the poetry also
declares that the comprehensive poise of the Augustan "civilities" (a favorite word, in this nature poet) is no longer available
to us, that our "tragic lack" lies precisely in our unease before
Pope's now impenetrable intelligibility (see "Le Musée Imagi-
naire," *PL*, 31–32). The recovery of Eden is a local and momentary triumph within the general dissolution, both social and
metaphysical.

Tomlinson's poems on buildings clearly partake of a tradition—less, ultimately, that of the seventeenth- and eighteenth-
century country house poem, revived by Yeats, than that of the
outcries, inside poetry, at the passing of the possibility of meaningful place since the Industrial Revolution. It can be objected
that his poetry in this area is limited and that it is not "contemporary," in that it does not face the particular problems of living
with cosmopolitan technology. But it *is* actual. (The dying of
what Lawrence called "the old England" is, of course, still with
us.) And his sense of certain rooted values is no mere repetition.
The particular sensibility that he brings to buildings, their
people, their objects, and their land, and the style and pressure
of linguistic organization by which he establishes his own personal-impersonal response are not to be found in his predecessors in what is—paradoxically—a long tradition. He provides a
new and rich awareness of possible relations (I have had space
here only to glance at them), on which our imagination may still
be enlivened.

*   *   *

From another perspective, the staking out of a world of relations and contraries involves what Tomlinson calls the negotia-

tion of "a truce in time." Time is an enemy, a cause of decay and estrangement, yet only through its acknowledgment is an assured relationship with the world possible. It is the Stevensian argument that time and change, the adversaries of life, are precisely where life resides.

The acceptance of the ubiquity of time issues in a poetry of alertly timed movement. Nearly all of Tomlinson's poems are on the move: they come into being not (as reviewers maintain) through a stilled recording of phenomena but through a delicate tracing of urgent modifications. The following is typical:

> The day veers. He would have judged
> Exactly in such a light, that strides down
> Over the quick stains of cloud-shadows
> Expunged now, by its conflagration of colour.
> ("A Meditation on John Constable," *SIB*, 30)

Their power lies often in their swiftness, their swiftness often in the delight of capturing the ephemeral. Tomlinson's poetry, like that of Antonio Machado, is a *palabra esencial en el tiempo*, an essential word in time—not poetry about time, but language poised over time and bodying time in its activity.

Outside of nature, in the domain of aesthetics and politics, Tomlinson's sense of the ineluctable all-pervasiveness of time leads him to resist, among other things, what he calls apocalypse. "Prometheus" (to which one cannot do justice by quotation—it is to be found in *The Way of a World*) is a poem beyond what is normally considered his range. It develops such earlier poems as "Farewell to Van Gogh" (*SIB*, 33), with their insistence that the factuality of the real survives artistic "frenzy," for a powerfully voiced, burlesquing assault on Symbolist and Marxist apocalypse. The Russian composer Scriabin is the target, triumphantly appropriate for having taken the dreams of such as Wagner and Mallarmé ("the trembling of the veil") to their conclusion, in the aspiration toward a cataclysmic transformation of the world via a reunion of all the arts and of all the senses; and for having coincided historically with the political cataclysm of the October Revolution. The title "Prometheus," from a tone-poem of Scriabin, brings also within the poem's irony the Promethean and apocalyptic ambition of a part of romanticism and even, perhaps, the corresponding Revolution of 1789. The apocalypse did not, of course, happen, and, insofar as something occurred in Russia, it was not a transfiguration in beauty. The Great War merely destroyed. We are still living in the trough of this desperate hope, artistic and political, starkly surviving the fact that Scriabin's "supreme and final ecstasy" did not take place, to accomplish the "Decadence," to reverse "the decline of the West," to water "the waste land." Although the particulars of the poem reach down on occasion into banality, its general burden seems to me a profound interpretation of a tract of recent art and politics and a moving suggestion of the modern world as an aftermath—not the aftermath of a happening, but of the expectation of happening. Its presence in Tomlinson's poetry ought to convince one of the *variety* of his kinds of excellence.

*   *   *

From yet another point of view, the negotiation with the world maneuvers through a passionate epistemological exploration. Epistemology accounts for one major strand of "romantic" poetry—from the romantics themselves to the present day—concerned with how we know and what we know, with the range and limits of knowledge, with the relationship between the mind and the external world. One could say that the romantic movement was, on a not unimportant level, a crisis in epistemology, and a crisis through which we are still working. An epistemological notion—though without any of the dryness which that abstraction bodes—sustains the most inflamed utterance of Blake ("Imagination is Eternity"), of Keats ("the holiness of the Heart's affections and the truth of Imagination"). It underpins the wider meditations in some of the best things of Wordsworth—"Tintern Abbey," parts of "The Prelude," "Intimations of Immortality"—and in Coleridge's Dejection Ode, as in Shelley's "A Defence of Poetry." It is fundamental in Baudelaire's "*Correspondances*," Mallarmé's "Toast *funèbre*," Rimbaud's *Les Illuminations*, Valéry's "*Le Cimetière marin*," in much of William Carlos Williams, in a great deal of Stevens. It is integral to Yeats's "The Circus Animals' Desertion," to Eliot's "The Waste Land" (from one point of view the recording of a massive epistemological debacle), to Guillén's *Cántico*.

Tomlinson's relation to this tradition is complex, since the epistemological basis of his poetry is very varied. At times, what is "bodied over against" the observer denies him, by a cold, detailed definition that evades the interpreting mind and ignores the claims of the emotions. Yet it is often precisely the quiddity of the world outside that makes possible a steady poise between the self and the non-self. The two perceptions combine in "Clouds" (*WW*, 18). "Clouds" is one of Tomlinson's finest poems, consummate proof of his ability to create sonorous and shapely melody, bodied by subtle and moving emotion, varying its pace in time to the flow of feeling. The beginning is all (untroubled) exclusion:

> How should the dreamer, on those slow
> Solidities, fix his wandering adagio,
> Seizing, bone-frail, blown
> Through the diaphanous air of their patrols,
> Shadows of fanfares, grails of melting snow?
> (*WW*, 18)

The end is the salvation from a dream world through the recognition of the sharply beautiful otherness of the real:

> Cloudshapes are destinies, and they
> Charging the atmosphere of a common day,
> Make it the place of confrontation where
> The dreamer wakes to the categorical call
> And clear cerulean trumpet of the air.
> (*WW*, 18)

On a wider scale, the poems range, through several stages, from awe at the unnameable and unknowable to a vivid Blakean celebration of the mind and its own "sun," its grasp, beyond presented facts, of "all the kingdoms of possibilities." The antithesis finds its ground in a poem called "The Hill" (*AS*, 11). "The Hill" is a mature and richly human gathering of moods before nature into a single mood deeply balanced and sustained by a calm intellectual rigor. A girl climbing a hill is both "shrunk" and "magnified" into particularity by its wide sweep; "unnamed" by the expanse she yet bestows a "name"; between nature as "hard" and nature as a "giant palm" (it is a favorite image) she shows the art of "negotiation." This pattern of antitheses culminates in a final swelling of the imagery, the emotion and the idea:

> So, do not call to her there:
> let her go on,
> whom the early sun
> is climbing up with to the hill's crown—
> she, who did not make it, yet can make
> the sun go down by coming down.
>
> (*AS*, 11)

This last stanza, of one of the most pondered of Tomlinson's poems of slow, quiet power,[1] perfectly blends a "statement" about epistemology—advanced to the point where it becomes ontology—into a warmly resonant human gesture.

*   *   *

The vision of antithesis informs the whole of Tomlinson's work and leads one into the core of his imagining. The world, and the possibility of poetry, are on the one hand a promise of "delight." Throughout, a taut describing, a detailed precision, holds a world of subtle and compelling particulars, engendering a sustained, "Tomlinsonian" vocabulary of "tessellation," "irised," "striation," "stippling"; releasing its energy often in sudden charges: "quick gold," "sunglaze," "raw fire"; grasping the matter of the real occasionally through an onomatopoeia that relishes both rhetoric and things.[2]

Yet nature is as alien as it is welcome, especially in *American Scenes*, the most searching and varied exploration of what stands against life. There is much awareness in Tomlinson's poetry of

1. The emotional urgency owes much to the address to the reader about a commonly observed third person—deriving partly, perhaps, from Stevens's "The Idea of Order at Key West."

2. An example of this is from "Reflections":

> Like liquid shadows. The ice is thin
>   Whose mirror smears them as it intercepts
> Withdrawing colours; and where the crust,
>   As if a skin livid with tautening scars,
> Whitens, cracks, it steals from these deformations
>   A style too tenuous for the image. . . .
>
> (*SIB*, 3)

disinheritance, estrangement, madness. There is much violence, and much death, both animal and human. And the poems on the death of animals—potent in their engaged but objective observing, their refusal of sensational postures—cause this savagery to question precisely the natural and artistic beauty that they are at the same time perceiving and generating.

The response is to pit one against the other, the beauty and the death, the celebration of wonder and the acknowledgment of terror. At the hub of Tomlinson's poetry there is a cluster of antithetical images, modulating each into each: light and dark, fire on dark, fire against cold, fire against snow or frost, and—the seemingly focal ones—sun-and-frost, sun-and-snow. The poetry holds the contraries. The sense of life, of rootedness, of kinship is won characteristically, in terms of the natural year, against winter itself, or against the threat of winter in autumn, the echo of winter in spring. Tomlinson's country poems, although they arise from the pastoral tradition, happen in a hard season and not in an eternal May time. Winter cold and darkness bring a hostile pressure to bear on the most convinced affirmations of natural warmth and light, balancing them into a severe wholeness.

The tragic antithesis of the physical universe sunders through to the human world. As the swimmer in "Swimming Chenango Lake" is posed between the water's "mercilessness" and its "kind of mercy," so plants, birds, and humans tread between contraries, contraries bound together often by rhyme or alliteration: ash-key and gull sway in the wind between "the two / Gravities that root and uproot the trees"; a diving cormorant's head is "pared" yet "spared" by the searching sea; a young girl emerges between "village graves" and "village green"; harvest offering of pears and apples mingle with the crown of thorns on a chancel arch in a canon of human and natural fertility and pain—of "delight and death." The vision reaches through to its conclusion in rhetoric—the oxymoron—to blend the disparities in "white darkness," "glowing obscurity," "cold fire," "frigid burning," "barrenly fertile," "fecund chill," "cruel mercy."

The most powerful stating of the antithesis is probably "The End," the last poem of *The Way of a World*. After a witty rejection of the art-work as a static autonomous world outside of time, removing the sting from pain by easing it into an aesthetic "perfec-

tion of regret," the poem moves into the continuities and the oppositions of living, into the ambivalent seasons on either side of
winter:

> Such ends are just. But let him know
>> Who reads his time by the way books go,
> Each instant will bewry his symmetries
>> And Time, climbing down from its pedestal
> Uncrown the settled vista of his loss.
>> Is it autumn or spring? It is autumn or spring.
> Before door and window, the terrible guest
>> Towers towards a famine and a feast.
>
> (*WW*, 60)

   Tomlinson's poetry of antithesis is a delving down to the fundamental commonplaces of tragedy—to the common places, indeed, of the most basic human responses to the world. "*Nous
causâmes tout d'abord de lieux communs,*" says Baudelaire of his
first meeting with Delacroix, "*c'est-à-dire des questions les plus
vastes et les plus profondes*" ("We spoke first of commonplaces,
that is to say, of the vastest and profoundest questions of all").
The conquest of commonplace (avoiding platitude, and without
enlisting the language of generality), through the exploration of
the known regions of traditional thought and feeling, seems to
be an aim of Tomlinson's poetry. (It is, of course, an Augustan
aim.) The task is particularly delicate and also particularly urgent, one would suppose, at the present time. It speaks to over-
wrought sophistication, to complicated ignorance.
   This sense of poised contraries stands at the center of his vision. It also points to the limitations of that vision when one
makes the highest demands of it—and with a poet of Tomlinson's stature only the highest demands are relevant.
   On the one hand, his poetry has not yet attained—for me (one
has to speak for oneself)—the joy that he seems to be seeking
for it, as when he commends Yeats's "abounding glittering jet"
or Nietzsche's gaiety, and quotes, as the epigraph to the first section of *The Way of a World*, lines from Jorge Guillén's jubilant
Cántico. There *is* delight in his work, but not many of the cen-
trally human joys are celebrated. There is a style for delight, but
not quite a style for the acutest or the easiest joy. This would
involve, perhaps, a keener intensity of passionate utterance

than that for which he tries, or a larger manner than that which he permits himself.

The same reservation applies to the other extreme of his poetry. Given the claims that Tomlinson's poems make for themselves, one could expect a more decisive showing of the world's darkness. Even allowing for his technique of deliberate understatement, and for the fact that his poems usually make their mark slowly, the pain of his nature lacks (for me) the absolute, final conviction; partly, perhaps, because of his insistence on local instances, which fail to generate the sense of a wider, planetary sorrow—his limitation here being a sign of one of his virtues: his refusal of the magniloquent gesture; partly because the pain is rather quickly absorbed, or partially forgotten, in the various performances of the will: physical and mental resistance, wit, humor. Of all his volumes, only *American Scenes* is consistent in its sustained focusing of anguish.

Human pain in Tomlinson's poetry, though also present, leaves a similar feeling that certain reaches of experience have only been hinted at. The few moving indications of "groundless humanity" appear unsupported, even occasional. There is even less exploration of the obscurities *within* the self. "The Cavern" (*AS*, 21), with its chill delineation of the self's "unnameable . . . home," is isolated to the point where its presence reveals essentially surrounding absence. And nowhere in Tomlinson's own poetry is there that sense of inner evil that impinges so powerfully in his translations of Tyutchev's "Italian Villa" and "Night Wind." Once again, the weakness arises from a strength, from the rejection—motivated as much morally as aesthetically—of the poetry of confessional hysteria. Yet Tyutchev himself indicates one of the ways in which the chaotic pressures within can be at least disclosed—he goes no further into actual detailed enactment—without self-regarding indulgence, and without the objective integrity of the poetic artifact being sacrificed. Given the direction of the more tormented side of Tomlinson's writing, it does not seem arbitrary to suggest that it is precisely the absence of the idea of evil—as something other than suffering only—that prevents this poetry from attaining the depths it frequently intimates.

*   *   *

Another limiting feature of Tomlinson's poetry is its dependence on the poetry of others, though this is less extensive than some critics maintain, and its damaging effects are far less acute. It is true that one is often aware, in reading his poems, of formal devices borrowed from, say, Laforgue, William Carlos Williams, or Robert Creeley; and that the moral and intellectual impulse of much of his work coincides with the "post-Symbolist" rejection (in Stevens, Williams, Valéry, Claudel, Guillén) of the private image of the Symbolists proper—projected from the footloose mind—in the name of external reality. Trust in the real otherness of the world of matter standing before the observing intelligence was partly, for that generation, an attempt to escape from solipsism, from the epistemological anguish engendered, for many French writers especially, by popular renderings of Schopenhauer and, for Stevens as for Eliot, by a central passage in Bradley. Tomlinson's "Antecedents" (*SIB*, 57–70), which advances from the Symbolist mirror, in which one sees only oneself, through the realization that "We lack nothing / But a significant sun," to the final "egress": "Sun is, because it is not you; you are / Since you are self, and self delimited / Regarding sun . . ." (*SIB*, 66), merely restates the movement charted perfectly in Guillén's *"Amanece, amanezco"* ("It dawns, I dawn"): *"heme ya libre de ensimismamiento / Mundo en resurrección es quien me salva"* ("Now here am I, free from absorption in self. World in resurrection is my salvation"). We assume—though perhaps we are wrong—that this is no longer quite our problem.

On the other hand, Tomlinson's poetry does—continually— invite one to new experiences. However secondhand some of his "ideas" may be, however many echoes one may catch of other writers, the constituted whole in which they stand resembles only tangentially the poetry of any of his predecessors. His presentation of the matter of the world is decidedly original, it is shot through with individual response, and it is, often, of a compelling urgency. To focus his relationship to post-Symbolism in this way prompts the reflection that his poetry in general extends one's mind rather than orders one's feelings, refines one's perception, and energizes one's imagination.

Indeed, to consider the quiddity of Tomlinson's poems is to realize how much they transcend the manner of post-Symbolist and Symbolist poetry, and how well he has created a world recognizably his own. It is difficult to convey this in an article, though I trust that something of his particularity has emerged. Reading through his four full-length volumes, one might note also the convincingly personal organization and pacing of scenes, the exact and dramatic handling of sudden gestures, the numerous varieties of wit, burlesque, fantastication, serious levity, the sharp eyeing of incongruity, dry, affectionate humor. There are signs throughout of a clearly stamped personality, which combines both closely elaborated finesse that is everywhere acknowledged and a strength that criticism has been slower to remark. The negative maneuver of his poetry is that the refusal of indulgence, of dissipation, is made not in the name of a "Movement" wryness but in favor of an incisive energy. And at the core of his work there is an admirably clearsighted (though relatively narrow) purpose, a taut center from which all his poems radiate, together with his persuasively finished translations,[3] and his articles and reviews.

Despite pressures in his poetry of a European-American literary movement, it seems evident also that Tomlinson is as much an "English" writer as an international one—even essentially an English writer. His syntax and line-distribution, for instance, though sophisticatedly influenced by foreign experiments, draw powerfully on a native English tradition; they manage frequently a neo-classical muscle and speed, and have, in fact, many of the virtues recommended by Donald Davie in a partial reaction *against* the language-forms of "modernism." And the matter of his poetry is largely the English countryside, which he writes about not as an urban dilettante but as someone who knows: his verse is weighted with "marl," with "crosswind," "windlines," "shale." He is as close to Constable as to Cézanne, if not closer.

Tomlinson himself indicates this ballasting of certain cosmopolitan preoccupations with the local particularities of England in his comments (in a Poetry Book Society Bulletin) on the final poem of *A Peopled Landscape*: "[E]ven in the 'Ode to Arnold Schoenberg,' which celebrates a discovery international in appli-

3. After Machado, could one hope for "Versions from Jorge Guillén," a very fine writer insufficiently attended to?

cation, namely the twelve-tone system, Gloucestershire church bells and cockcrows insist on being heard in the piece." Many of his poems are rooted, certainly, in foreign places; yet it is essentially his combination of an awareness of wider movements of art with a sense of England that constitutes his singularity. His strengths are both cosmopolitan and local; and that is a surprising balance from which we can learn a great deal.

Michael Kirkham

11. An Agnostic's Grace

The evolution of Tomlinson's poetry has been gradual, organic, involving modifications and extensions but no disavowals of his past work. There have been changes over the years, but, as Tomlinson himself said to Michael Schmidt in 1977, "The underlying continuity remains the important thing."[1]

In the late fifties, aspects of his work that caught the eye of contemporary readers were those contrasting most sharply on the one hand with the neo-romanticism of Dylan Thomas and on the other hand with the new "realism" of Philip Larkin (a marriage, rather, of "faithful and disappointing" realism with its complement, a disappointed romanticism).[2] Tomlinson was evidently neither a romantic nor a defeated, reductive realist. His earliest poems conducted a polemic against the romanticism of the forties. Early influences in the formation of his personal style were the clean line and phrasing of the American modernists—Pound, Stevens, Moore, and later Williams—and the reasoned structures, civilities, and conceptual diction of the eighteenth-century English poets. Linguistic restraint, the ordering of confusion, and the moderation of expectations, submission of the eye to the objective world and of the mind to a consciousness of natural limits: a literary regimen of chastening, corrective severity was what these poems recommended and

---

Michael Kirkham, Professor of English at the University of Toronto, has had articles on Tomlinson published in *Essays in Criticism*, *The New Pelican Guide to English Literature*, *British Poetry Since 1970*, and elsewhere. His *The Imagination of Edward Thomas* was recently published, and he is completing a book-length study of Tomlinson. A portion of this article has been published in *PN Review* 12, 2(1985): 25–26.

1. Schmidt, "Tomlinson at Fifty," p. 35.
2. See Philip Larkin, "Lines on a Young Lady's Photograph Album," *The Less Deceived: Poems* (New York: St. Martin's Press, 1960).

demonstrated. It was not, as we shall see, the complete picture. As for realism, if Larkin's theme was the disparity between reality and desire, Tomlinson's was plainly not self and its emotions at all but the reality that exceeds and includes man, the reality of nature and, it became clearer in the sixties, of history and of man's accommodations with history. He chose to measure the scope of being rather than to trace "the graph of pain"—a revealing phrase of the early seventies ("Melody," *WI*, 45). It would no doubt be nearer the truth to say that this subject matter chose him, that it also signaled his conscious repudiation of the literary milieu for which Larkin became the unofficial laureate.

Tomlinson dared to be positive, and his voice carried what was in the fifties an unfamiliar note of authority. In "A Meditation on John Constable" (*SIB*, 29–30) he commends in the painter "the labour of observation"; his own poetry has the same scrupulous respect for facts, but we are not allowed to forget that art is observation infused with "passion," that in effect "delight / Describes" ("A Meditation on John Constable," *SIB*, 30). In a later declaration this claim for art is strengthened and extended: "man / In an exterior, tutelary spirit / Of his own inheritance, speaks / To celebrate" ("Movements V," *WrW*, 52). Yet this version articulates an instinct or conviction that has informed Tomlinson's work from the beginning. Neither romantic nor realist, he combines an Augustan vigor of mind with, say, Hopkins's passionate interest in sense experience rendered in a muscular, kinaesthetic language. For Tomlinson poetry was—and is—an exploration by the senses and the mind of the world before them. Though his poetic terrain has been primarily sense experience, his aim was not—the contrast I have in mind is the early poetry of Ted Hughes—immersion in sensation, the illusion of the "thing itself," but investigation of the world perceived and of the act of perception. The bias of his interest was and has remained evaluative: not mere seeing but seeing that is believing, right seeing, is his theme. The realms of aesthetics and ethics here border on each other: accuracy of eye and ear, which lies in the proper relations of foreground to background, part to whole, usually implies also in these poems the tempering of emotion to its object and the clarity and impartiality of the judicious mind. It is, in a word, normative poetry: it seeks to define norms of sensory perception, of feeling and thinking—ultimately of human dwelling, as when, in "At Holwell Farm" (*SIB*, 39), admiration of the handsome farmhouse includes appreciation of the humanity expressed in the building of it:

> this farm
> Also a house, this house a dwelling.
> Rooted in more than earth, to dwell
> Is to discern the Eden image, to grasp
> In a given place and guard it well
> Shielded in stone.
>
> (*SIB*, 39)

The phenomenal world, the reality of place, landscape, and weather, dominates *The Necklace* (1955) and *Seeing Is Believing* (1958, 1960). It kept its central position in Tomlinson's poetry of the next decade, and indeed it is the primary concern of all his work; but it is probably true to say that the processes of time and history, which received some attention in the fifties in such poems as "On the Hall at Stowey" (*SIB*, 40–42), figure more prominently in the three volumes he published during the sixties. "John Maydew" (*PL*, 8–10) and "Up at La Serra" (*PL*, 23–27) are notable examples in *A Peopled Landscape* (1963). In *American Scenes* (1966), "The Snow Fences" (*AS*, 4–5), "Arizona Desert" (*AS*, 22–23), and "The Well" (*AS*, 47–48) are diverse treatments of man's "negotiations" with time. As well as "Prometheus" (*WW*, 4–5) and "Assassin" (*WW*, 10), poems about time, history, and revolutionary attitudes, *The Way of a World* (1969) contains "In the Fullness of Time" (*WW*, 12), Tomlinson's tribute to "the beauty of succession" and his "consent to time."

If my description of his early anti-romanticism suggests that in the fifties Tomlinson barricaded himself behind the ramparts of a defensive neo-Classicism, I have given a false impression. There was nothing defensive about it. "Moderation of expectations" was one phrase I used; but it is the poetic principle in question that might be less misleadingly defined as the measuring of expectations by the yardstick of both the actual *and* the possible. I also said, trying to avoid the limiting, doctrinaire implications of a label like "objectivism," that "he chose to measure [what cannot be measured] the scope of being." In this and the amended definition, I am suggesting that "measure" (measurement *and* moderation) is practiced in the interest of liberation, not constraint. The measuring eye in "Ponte Veneziano" (*SIB*, 4), "Stripping the vista to its depth," and in "Tramontana at Lerici" (*SIB*, 18), the mind that threatens the sentimental imprecision of "politicians and romantics" with a "clarity" and sharpness of "definition" "that could cut like steel," are also the perceiving intelligence that in the former poem "broods on the further light" and, having stripped the vista to its depth, tunnels into prospects beyond. In different versions, this image of the penetrant mind that uses keenness of sensory perception as a tool of the prospecting imagination recurs in poems of the sixties and seventies. "How it happened," the poem that closes the sequence of "Four Kantian Lyrics" (*PL*, 20–22), ends,

> no absolute of eye can tell
> the utmost, but the glance
> goes shafted from us like a well.
>
> (*PL*, 22)

This in turn looks forward to "The Well" in *American Scenes* (*AS*, 47–48) and "The Shaft" (*S*, 48), the title poem of a recent volume. The note of praise and celebration, when it is sounded, is clearer and more confident in the last gathering of the sixties, *The Way of a World*; some titles are sufficiently revealing: "Eden" (*WW*, 7),[3] "Adam" (*WW*, 8), and "Night Transfigured" (*WW*, 9). The tendency signified by these titles finds an echo, ten years later, in a title that Tomlinson also adopts as his heading for a group of poems, "In Arden" (*S*, 47). *The Shaft* (1978), where the poem appears, groups its contents into five categories. They are, though not in this order, Seasons, Histories, Perfections, In Arden, and Bagatelles. The difference between images of perfection and Arden is touched on in that poem's opening line, "Arden is not Eden, but Eden's rhyme" (*S*, 47), and elaborated in the body of the poem.

In the collections of the seventies there is much that is familiar to the reader of Tomlinson; themes are not repeated, however, but renewed, refreshed. A subsidiary theme of "Snow Signs" (*F*, 1), for example, is the complementary relationship of contraries. Snow that has retreated in thin lines and dots and, with

3. The Eden motif occurs earlier, however, in "Glass Grain" (*SIB*, 16) and "At Holwell Farm" (*SIB*, 39) quoted above.

"Touched-in contour and chalk-followed fold," "has left its own white geometry / To measure out for the eye the way / The land may lie," discovers what otherwise would be missed, "the fortuitous / Full variety a hillside spreads for us" (*F*, 1). The simplification of geometry sharpens the eye's sense of the scene's complexity, and the satisfaction of measurement, of taking mental possession by that means, enhances appreciation of what measurement leaves out, the illimitable, indefinable, unpredictable fullness and variety in what the eye sees. It is essentially the same surprising conjunction of the analytic eye-and-mind and the questing imagination illustrated in the previous paragraph from "Ponte Veneziano" (*SIB*, 4) or, to recall "A Meditation on John Constable" (*SIB*, 29–30), of observation and delight. It seems a paradox that the measuring eye and the impartial mind should serve the motive of celebration.

In "Snow Signs" (*F*, 1) a large portion of his visual experience is, so to speak, reassembled; it is not a repetition but a reordering prompted by the stimulus of new particulars. The following passage refashions and lines up into a sequence thoughts about the interaction of subject and object that have been divided among many previous poems:

> Walking, we waken these at every turn,
> Waken ourselves, so that our walking seems
>   To rouse some massive sleeper out of winter dreams
> Whose stretching startles the whole land into life,
>   As if it were us the cold, keen signs were seeking
> To pleasure and remeasure, repossess
>   With a sense in the gathered coldness of heat and
>   height.
>
>   (*F*, 1)

Looking discovers features unnoticed before; in turn the act of discovering, which is a kind of wakening or regeneration, wakens us, the onlookers, to new life. The increase of alertness and awareness is an intensification and expansion of self, as the poet's images and wordplay ("walking . . . waken") accentuate the reciprocal action. One could trace numerous connections between this and earlier poems. The "wakening" image, for instance, takes us back to the very early "Poem," the only piece to be rescued from *Relations and Contraries*, a volume of youthful experiments, for inclusion in *Collected Poems* (1985). These lines also give a less emphatic, less epigrammatic rendering of "What he saw / Discovered what he was" ("A Meditation on John Constable," *SIB*, 30). Tomlinson's language has remained unashamedly intellectual, but where the style of the Constable poem, and of *Seeing Is Believing* generally, is formal, public, and favors the sculptured symmetries of ordered thinking, that of "Snow Signs" (*F*, 1)—and this makes it representative of his later verse—is, for all its careful elaboration and intricacy of syntax, nearer to a flowing speech. It is noticeable that a lighter wordplay replaces epigram, so that, for example, "Waken ourselves" does not so much stand in logical and paradoxical antithesis to the first "waken" as modify it, absorbing the potential contrast and transferring attention to the unity—it is almost interchangeability—of perceiver and perceived.

The next stage in the sequence is that, wakening and being awakened, we therefore seem to rouse a whole landscape from its winter sleep, and a few lines later the words "transfigured" and "resurrection" appear. But the poem leaves no doubt about the meaning of those words: they convey facts, the facts at once of an objective world and of subjective response. The vocabulary of religion is used to articulate the transformations of the imagination, and imagination is not for Tomlinson, as it was for Coleridge, an intermediary between the temporal and the eternal, the human and the divine, but the faculty that brings to what the senses perceive here and now an inner sense of its contrary. What is present is thereby complemented by what is absent, the visible by the invisible (meaning only what is not apparent): fact is completed by imagination to create a *whole* composed of what is and is not immediately apprehensible. The apprehension of wholeness, wholeness of vision, is Tomlinson's delight and purpose.

What is not-self, the reality of objects, is primary in Tomlinson's thought, but it is the relationship, the interchange, between self and not-self, subject and object—especially so in his later poetry—that receives the main emphasis. The insistence in the early poetry on the irreducible otherness of objects, the stubborn separateness of facts, a sense of things that has remained integral to Tomlinson's work, was nevertheless a tactical insistence in response to the provocation of a neo-romantic subjectivist poetic. In the later poetry there is perhaps a more acute sense that the double awareness constitutes a paradox: it creates an exhilarating tension between two ways of seeing the world— as simultaneously having an independent existence and depending on the observer for its meaning. The visible world as it is presented in "At the Edge" (F, 17) seethes with various interests for itself and for what it implies that is not visible:

> Edges are centres: once you have found
> Their lines of force, the least of gossamers
> Leads and frees you, nets you a universe
> Whose iridescent weave shines true
> Because you see it, but whose centre is not you. . . .
>
> (F, 17)

The contraries of self and not-self entail others: the apparent and the hidden, the part and the whole, contraries that are in fact complementarities in that they are mutually exclusive viewpoints and yet both true. Each polarity expresses the same paradox, that the world has its center simultaneously (not alternately) inside and outside the perceiver; edges are centers for the viewer, but they do not cease to be edges too, and the world's center is not you—the netted universe is private and common, particular and general.

The double focus in Tomlinson's poetry on the thing itself and on the whole of which it is a part or a sign is reflected in the "sensuous abstraction" of the language, a quality of the French language he has said in an interview with Michael Schmidt that he envies. It is also a notable quality of Augustan verse; "Condemned to Hope's delusive mine," the first line of Johnson's "On the Death of Dr. Robert Levet," is a memorable example. "Foxes' Moon" (WI, 17–18), which studies the transformation by moonlight of quotidian existence, "England's interrupted pastoral," and assimilates the disparity between the two Englands to the incongruity of the fox's night world with the adjacent human world ("These / Are the fox hours cleansed / Of all the meanings we can use . . . "), illustrates this quality of Tomlinson's language:

> The shapes of dusk
> Take on an edge, refined

> By a drying wind and foxes bring
>   Flint hearts and sharpened senses to
> This desolation of grisaille in which the dew
>   Grows clearer, colder.
>
> (*WI*, 17)

The imagery, factual and figurative, is precisely, incisively sensuous, but even in the thought-connections that link "edge," "refined," "drying," "flint," "sharpened," and "grows clearer, colder," the control of the abstracting mind is evident; it becomes conspicuous in "this desolation of grisaille." The juxtaposition of the fact and its interpretation is more striking a few lines later:

>   they nose
>   The garbage of the yards, move through
> The *white displacement* of a daily view
>   Uninterrupted.
>
> (*WI*, 18, italics mine)

Representing the poetic search, in "Movements II" (*WrW*, 51), as a "Grasping for more than the bare facts warranted," Tomlinson might easily be naming the motivating principle in a language of "sensuous abstraction." We might link it, also, to another image in "At the Edge" (*F*, 17). Watching the movements of a wren darting in and out of its hole, "It made me," he remarks of its visible energy, "measure all the force unspied / That stirred inside that bank" (*F*, 17). The extension of the concrete into the abstract is a similar leap of imagination, spurred by the need and the will to measure the immeasurable.

Tomlinson has always worked to incorporate in one vision the near and the far, the data of sense experience and the "something else" ("Canal," *PL*, 6–7) of imagination; repeatedly his poems trace a movement outward from the known to the edges of the known and just beyond—the "glance" of his poetry "goes shafted from [him] like a well." "At the Edge" gives us that movement in the rapid transition from a web's edge to a netted "universe"; but the delight in the "unspied," the attraction of hiddenness as such ("The off-scape, the infolds, secreted / Waterholes in the boles of trees"), is, I think, a new mood, and as such it corresponds to a habit of camouflaging analogy that has become more common in his later poetry. This is difficult to illustrate without quoting extensively from a poem, so I have chosen as my example a short poem from *The Shaft*, "The Roe Deer," which follows "In Arden" and precedes the title poem and is related in theme to both:

We must anticipate the dawn one day,
Crossing the long field silently to see
The roe deer feed. Should there be snow this year
Taking their tracks, searching their colours out,
The dusk may help us to forestall their doubt
And drink the quiet of their secrecy
Before, the first light lengthening, they are gone.
One day we must anticipate the dawn.

(*S*, 47–48)

This has a *sotto voce* intimacy of tone that, though the voice is not the same, resembles in one respect the voice of Frost or of Edward Thomas: an undemonstrative quietness of manner that, as in their verse, is the medium chosen to convey intimations of "other meaning"[4] than the surface one. It is as though the lowness of the voice makes audible the faint murmuring of an undervoice, which augments the overt text with a covert significance. The coexistence of the two levels can be shown best by a modified paraphrase of the poem. The roe deer partake of a secret life; to "drink the quiet of their secrecy," we must follow tracks leading in the twilight to a hidden, pre-dawn pristineness of which the deer are part and to which, in their exquisite sensitivity and alertness and delicacy of movement, they alone are privy; as, barred from Eden itself, Adam in nature's Arden "tastes [the] replenishings" of Eden's waters in springs brought underground. We must make our approach as silent as they and it are silent. We can resolve to enjoy this secret life only at a remove: the silence is easily broken, the deer easily scared away, and "they are gone" at "first light" with a quiet suddenness that suggests hallucination, as if they have no daylight existence. One could probe further and speculate whether "their doubt"— an oddly human word for animal wariness—is a transposition

4. Wallace Stevens, "Effects of Analogy," in his *The Necessary Angel: Essays on Reality and the Imagination* (1942; reprint, New York: Random House, 1952), pp. 105–30.

of a doubt felt by the poet and responsible for his hesitancy of approach to the Eden source; but I have gone far enough into the poem to bring out the reticent suggestiveness of this kind of latent analogy.

It is customary in discussions of Tomlinson's work to distinguish the poems of sense experience—poems that direct attention to the natural world, to life in space—from the poems of human experience, which concentrate on the processes of time and history. The division exists, though it would be more accurate to say of the latter group that the poems are more *overtly* concerned with the human world than those of the former; for the poems that explore the perceptual world and the act of perception have human implications. "Inanimate or human, / The distinction fails," Tomlinson was able to demonstrate in "Winter Encounters" (*SIB*, 2), a poem of the fifties; in the early seventies, "The Witnesses" (*WI*, 26), with its picture of "hillside woods" in summer as an "aerial city," produces the same fusion of the natural and the human. The poems I have examined so far belong, if one employs the conventional distinction, to the first category: they are primarily studies of nature and the world of perception, only indirectly or metaphorically of the human world. Yet, despite the obvious differences enshrined in the classification, there is no clear boundary between the two groups; indeed they resemble each other more than they differ, or what they have in common is of more significance than what separates them. Just as it is more important to stress continuity than change in Tomlinson's development, so it is potentially more illuminating to notice the homogeneity of his work than to distinguish its parts. His preoccupation with encounters—for example, encounters between self and not-self, the human and the nonhuman—is as characteristic of the one group as of the other.

Thus "Mackinnon's Boat" (*WrW*, 3–5), which scrutinizes the work of two fishermen (not forgetting the dog) on a typical day's fishing, describing not only the sea itself and the light with the precise "sensuous abstraction" we should expect but also the journey out to the site, the hauling in of the catch, the disentangling of unwanted "Crabs, urchins, dogfish, and star," the rhythms of each task, is about "the daily dealings" of man with the nonhuman "underworld." The two environments are mutually repellent: the "flailing / Seashapes pincered to the baits" die in the air, "their breath all at once grown rare / In an atmosphere they had not known existed" (*WrW*, 4); as for the dog, a solipsistic landlubber, the sea is virtually nonexistent—"he stays / Curled round on himself: his world / Ignores this waste of the in-between, / Air and rock . . . " (*WrW*, 4). Only man negotiates the territory "in-between." The poem highlights on the one hand the encounter, the transaction, and on the other hand the absolute discreteness of the two realities and in particular the impenetrable otherness, inconceivable to the human mind, of the sea-world. This sea gives back not even a ragged, twisted *image* of the boat: "Black, today / The waters will have nothing to do with the shaping / Or unshaping of human things. . . . The visible sea / Remains a sullen frontier to / Its *unimaginable* fathoms" (*WrW*, 4, 5, italics mine).

Although the theme is familiar, among the "human poems" "Mackinnon's Boat" is in several respects a new venture. The length itself, ninety-eight lines, is unusual and makes possible an unusual expansiveness of treatment; comparison with "On the Hall at Stowey" (*SIB*, 40–42) would reveal in the more leisurely narrative of the later poem a greater readiness to let facts be their uninterpreted selves. The poem also extends the conception of not-self to include along with objects the impersonal world of labor. In their work the fishermen are anonymous, their anonymity corresponding to, and joining while it lasts, a reality that bears no human imprint; "making a time / Where no day has a name, the smells / Of diesel, salt, and tobacco mingle" —human purpose and pleasure, that is to say, mingle, in a temporary, evanescent blend of smells, with the salt that "at last must outsavour name and time / In the alternation of the forgetful waters" (*WrW*, 5). Serving a purpose beyond themselves, they are—like the separate stages in their rapid undoing, re-tying and new-baiting of the traps (and like a Tomlinson poem)—"The disparate links of [a] concerted action." Remembering the careful use of the word "articulate" in the early "Aesthetic" (*N*, 1), we might adapt its statement to this context: "Reality is to be sought, not in concrete / But in [the wholeness of] space made articulate" in its parts. The self-annulment of physical labor is also a release from self into a common world. And when "Their anonymity, for a spell, / Is at an end," each one is "Free to be himself more / Sharing the rest that comes of labour," their cooperation in the impersonal task both reinvigorating their individual freedoms and renewing the human bond. The *wholeness* of this world is presented as an interdependence of realities that are unassimilably separate; the *wholesomeness* of occupying the territory between them comes of an "alternation," reproducing the ebb and flow of "the forgetful waters," of action and inaction, of journeying out from self and the human domain and returning to them.

Another new development is an adoption of the standards of wholesome living—life lived according to a proportionate, whole view of reality—to the judgment of further reaches of human action, notably in those poems Tomlinson has called "Histories" (*S*, 3–16). The most striking examples are portraits, at dramatic moments of their lives, of Charlotte Corday, assassin of Marat, and Danton, characters who played decisive parts in the French Revolution. (This kind of poem and its moral standards were anticipated in "Assassin" [*WW*, 10–11], the assassin there being Mercader, the murderer of Trotsky.) An enemy of tyranny, the selfless heroine who gave her life for others, who delivered "a faultless blow," and who at her trial and execution exhibited a "composure none could fault," Charlotte Corday had, and is represented by the poet as having, impressive "strength." Yet in terms of the poem's (Yeatsian and Lawrencian) morality, her faults ran deep: she had made a voluntary contraction of her full humanity and subjected it to an *idea*. When she came to murder "her tyrant," she saw not the man, who had "a mildness in him, even," but a Julius Caesar. She was "A girl whose reading made a heroine—/ Her book was Plutarch, her republic Rome" ("Charlotte Corday," *S*, 3). She not only had lopped her feelings to fit her "whole / Intent" (a cramped wholeness!) but also, in her single-mindedness, had no clear whole view of the political situation, the outcome of which she had wished to determine—"How should she know / The Terror still to come?" (*S*, 3). Tomlinson points to the conflict in her between idealism (that is, possession by idea and ideal) and a full human responsiveness and awareness by means of one telling detail that recalls "Assassin." Unlike Mercader, she is that paradox, "a daggered Virtue," "innocence" directing a murderous "intent," one who, imitating the supreme sacrifice of Christ, also "believed her death would raise up France"; but, as Mercader's prepared impassivity was not proof against the sound of Trotsky's rustling papers and his animal death-cry, so the poet conjectures that her "composure" was almost breached by an unforeseen human incidental, the cry with which Catherine Marat at the trial "broke off her testimony."

"For Danton" (S, 6–7) passes the same judgment on its protagonist. Danton has invested the whole of himself in the partial satisfaction of enjoying "perfect power"—partial because in the pursuit of political power he has forfeited the "contrary perfection," receptiveness of the senses, the power of "seeings, savourings." This diagnosis of his moral sickness is inherent in the figure-ground composition of the picture: his egoism—he "thinks that he and not the river advances"—is set against the background of moral "consequence" acted out, metaphorically, in the inexorable progress of the river, an image for time and fate. The snatched pleasure of the river's "music," as he listens from the bridge's parapet, is set against "other sounds" of "past and future wrong." This proportionate way of seeing moments in a life is the human counterpart to an aesthetic of perception demonstrated everywhere in Tomlinson's poetry, but nowhere more explicitly than in "Poem," the earliest piece in *Selected Poems*. Describing the sound of horses' hooves in the early morning air, it ends,

> Though space is soundless, yet creates
> From very soundlessness a ground
> To counterstress the lilting hoof fall as it breaks.
>
> (*SP*, 1)

The implied standard in "For Danton" is a rounded life—the satisfaction of contrary impulses and their subordination to a sense of the whole of which they are part. The rounded life is also a full life, which needs for the realization of its possibilities a certain length of years. Early in his life, before leaving for the metropolis, Danton had made a choice between powers and is pictured at the end of his career paying a last visit to his birthplace. He had "Returned to this: to river, town and plain, / Walked in the fields and knew what power he'd lost," seeking, too late, to reverse that choice and to give to his unnurtured senses now "a life he has *no time* / To live" (S, 7, italics mine). Like Charlotte Corday, he has sacrificed fullness of humanity to the partiality of a conceived ambition; his will to power requiring the death of a king and her idealism requiring the assassination of Marat, their motives lie closer together than their respective histories and personalities would lead us to suspect. In both, the sacrifice of fullness requires that they voluntarily or involuntarily cut short their own lives. Of Charlotte Corday, as she approaches the scaffold, the poet asks, "What unlived life would struggle up against / Death died in the possession of such strength?" (S, 4). "Unlived life," in its double meaning, is Danton's tragedy too: on the one hand are tracts of personality uncultivated, of experience unexplored, on the other hand is deprival of time needed for cultivation and exploration. Time is important; life needs to be lived *out*: with quantity—a certain *number* of years—a certain quality of life is hardly to be achieved. "Ripeness is all" would outweigh for Tomlinson any persuasion to sacrifice.

I have been illustrating in Tomlinson's recent work the process of refocusing, modifying, and extending an already existing poetic world. Let me at this point gather together signs in the late sixties and the seventies of a slight shift in mood and approach, to which references have been scattered in the preceding paragraphs. Cumulatively they suggest that an attitude of *agnosticism* has become more prominent (agnosticism in its general sense, without specific reference to the question of religious belief, though, as we have seen in "Snow Signs," it includes that). I have the impression that those words of reservation and circumspection characteristic of Tomlinson's approach to metaphor, "as if" and "seems," are a little more insistent; it is as though they are meant to draw attention to the aspect of illusion in the workings of imagination. The technique of implication rather than application of thought is one expression of this more pressing sense of the fictionality of poetry. In "At the Edge" I noted the delight shown in things hidden, in what cannot be *known* directly or with certainty. I would add that this corresponds to the poet's growing preoccupation with what cannot be *said* singly, firmly, unambiguously, and with how to say it. It is the theme of "Nature Poem" (S, 29). The creative confusions of perception, "this sound / Of water that is sound of leaves," nature's "stirrings and comminglings . . . recall / The way a poem flows":

No single reading renders up complete
Their shifting text—a poem, too, in this,
They bring the mind half way to its defeat,
Eluding and exceeding the place it guesses,
Among these overlappings, half-lights, depths,
The currents of this air, these hiddennesses.

(S, 29)

The poet's consciousness of the obscurities and "half-lights" of experience (that elude the "guesses" of the interpreting mind and mock its rage for order and finality), which consequently tempers this aspiration to as much certainty as is reasonable with a readiness to advance hesitantly and tentatively, is, I think, related to a moderation, in such poems as "Charlotte Corday" and "For Danton," of an earlier habitual severity of judgment. "We must have some comradeship with imperfection," says George Eliot in *Daniel Deronda*,[5] a fastidious and judicious moralist; Tomlinson displays his comradeship in the same measure as the novelist's—only *some* comradeship, so much and no more; like her, he also has an interest in "perfections." A comparison of "Charlotte Corday" with the earlier "Assassin" would reveal an equal moral penetration, but a greater empathy enters into its delineation of human imperfection. We feel it in the question about her "unlived life." The question in the opening lines of "For Danton" has a similar quality: "Who is the man that stands against this bridge / And thinks that he and not the river advances?" (S, 6). A tone reflecting not pity but mild wonderment accompanies the firm passing of judgment. These two historical portraits only moderate their strictness: Tomlinson has not changed his colors. In the weighing of compassion and justice he is still as far from that strain of political thinking that originates in Rousseau's discussions of compassion as F. R. Leavis shows himself to be in *Nor Shall My Sword: Discourses on Pluralism, Compassion and Social Hope*.[6]

The poems in *Seeing Is Believing* have the same manner of terse authority as their title: the tone is positive, the disciplined eye and mind take command. The poems are distinguished by their

5. George Eliot, *Daniel Deronda*, edited by Graham Handley (London: Oxford University Press, 1984), p. 633.
6. (New York: Barnes and Noble, 1972).

sensory and mental clarity, by their strictness of moral discrimination, and generally by the strenuous clearing of a ground of certainty in a world of lax behavior, disordered emotion, and confused understanding. A good deal of this remains in Tomlinson's later work, but it has been modified to make a place for uncertainties and confusions. In the Arden of "in-between" in which we live—the seasons of time and nature housing memories or hopes of a timeless Eden—"the contraries / Of this place are contrarily unclear: / A haze beats back the summer sheen / Into a chiaroscuro of the heat" ("In Arden," S, 47). For it is where the real and the possible interpenetrate and distinctions blur; "the depths of Arden's springs," supplied by underground streams from their source in Eden, "convey echoic waters— voices / Of the place that rises through this place" (S, 47). "In Arden," on the one hand, finds a reason for celebration in this rich confusion of what is there with what is not there, the confusion of the real with the imagined. "A Self-Portrait: David" (S, 6), on the other hand, concerned to express the same sense of double reality (to the extent of using the same form of words), is cautionary: "This is the face behind my face," expressing a truth that "puts by / The mind's imperious geometry";

> distrust
> Whatever I may do unless it show
> A startled truth as in these eyes' misgivings,
> These lips that, closed, confess "I do not know."
> (S, 6)

Celebratory or cautionary, the deepest place in these poems is where there is not finality but an open question. "In the Balance" (S, 34) sets the finality of a winter landscape after a snowfall—its photographic immobility and clarity of definition— against the questions it raises and the doubts it leaves in the observer's mind: "Will it thicken or thaw, this rawness menacing? / The sky stirs: the sky refused to say" (S, 34). The sky is poised between fixity and change:

> Brought to a sway, the whole day hesitates
> Through the sky of afternoon, and you beneath,
> As if questions of weather were of life and death.
> (S, 34)

"The whole day hesitates"—I think we may extract a little extra meaning out of "whole": wholeness is composed of *shifting* parts, nature is a "shifting text." If wholeness is always unpredictably rearranging itself or induces that expectation, then "you beneath," the speculative mind, must copy that hesitancy in sensitive attunement to the nature of things; and this holds true, too, for "questions . . . of life and death." Nature—likewise the nature poem—is, as we have seen, a "shifting text"; its shades and secrets "bring the mind half way to its defeat, / Eluding and exceeding the place it guesses"; and if "they ask to be / Written into a permanence," that is to say, "not stilled"—"a poem flows," its permanence is not fixity—"but given pulse and voice." A poem, in this view, has the changing permanence of life renewed with each new reading. The aim, then, is "not to seize the point of things"—an early statement of his position ("Kantian Lyrics I," *PL*, 20)—but to catch the fugitive hint of Eden from the stream of time. He uses this image, without making it as overtly metaphorical as I have made it, in "Departure" (*S*, 20), when he reminds his recent guests of the "stream / Which bestows a flowing benediction and a name / On our house of stone" and adds:

> it is here
> That I like best, where the waters disappear
> Under the bridge-arch, shelving through coolness,
> Thought, halted at an image of perfection
> Between gloom and gold, in momentary
> Stay, place of perpetual threshold,
> Before all flashes out again and on
> Tasseling and torn, reflecting nothing but sun.
>
> (*S*, 20)

As it is a "place of perpetual threshold" for the stream, so for the contemplating mind it is a threshold between the known and the imagined.

The mind must practice a delicate hovering of attention to catch its images, but it is only a "*momentary* stay against confusion" (to complete the quotation from Frost), and the image is willingly relinquished, allowed to dissolve in the rush of waters. The poet balances appreciation of the mind's reflection, the

stilled image, and enjoyment of the stream's flash of movement—"reflecting nothing but the sun." The stream bestows on
the house two things, as separate and as inseparable as a baptism and a christening: "a *flowing* benediction" and an *unchang-
ing* name, as fixed and permanent as the stone of which the
house is built. The certainty of stone receives its benediction
from the *living* flow of water. The clumsily sensitive movement
of the stream is in immediate contrast with that of the jet which
carries his guests to their destination, the trail of which "is scor-
ing the zenith / Somewhere"; the language of water, "pushing /
Over a fall, to sidle a rock or two / Before it was through the confine," feeling its way pliantly over and round obstacles toward
its freedom, is more exemplary for the mind and will than the
imperious rhetoric of the jet plane's insensibility to its surroundings. "Certainty of stone" is a phrase I have taken from another
poem in *The Shaft*, "The Gap" (*S*, 50–51). What, asks the poet, is
the meaning of your delight in noticing casually, as you are driv-
ing by, a gap in the stone wall "Where you'd expect to see / A
field gate," through which

> All you see is space—that, and the wall
>   That climbs up to the spot two ways
> To embrace absence, frame skies:
>   Why does one welcome the gateless gap?
> As an image to be filled with the meaning
>   It doesn't yet have? As a confine gone?
> A saving grace in so much certainty of stone?
>   (*S*, 51)

The answers are inherent in the questions: the wall thus lets in
the whole expanse of space, releases imagination to its task of
filling absences, opening vistas of possibility. To frame is not to
contain skies—they are uncontainable; the gap creates a view
the value of which is that, though at first meaningless to the
viewer, it gives the eye freedom. It takes you beyond certainty,
whether of stone or the oblivious certainty of a jet's flight, and
leaves you in one of two conditions: either it is the agnostic's
confession, "I do not know," or it sets you "at the edge" or on
the threshold of "a saving grace," your redemption from the
merely known. For Tomlinson, however, they are not distinct
conditions but alternative names for the invitation to the imagi-

nation potential in any encounter of the familiar with the unexpected. Living at the frontier of the known and the unknown
is its own justification: "The Gap" emphasizes not the "after-
knowledge and its map" generated by the encounter but "the
moment itself, abrupt / With the pure *surprise* of seeing" (*S*, 51,
italics mine). The sudden invasion of the mind by an awareness
of what is beyond its grasp is in itself a liberation and an enlarge-
ment. In the long view there is little significant difference between this abrupt surprise that admits a limitless world and the
"startled truth," received with "misgivings," visible in the eyes of
David's self-portrait. The agnostic is neither believer nor skeptic
but a Janus facing both ways. "I do not know" may be said with
misgiving or gratitude, but either way the saying opens a door for
an eye trained on "the further light" ("Ponte Veneziano," *SIB*, 4),
an ear attuned to distant echoes ("In Arden," *S*, 47).

The welcoming of uncertainties, ambiguities, even confusions, as potentially liberating or redemptive is the same kind of
paradox as the fortunate Fall in Christian theology. The uncertainties in Tomlinson's work mainly arise from the shifting relations of the real and the imagined; the paradoxical reality—the
fictional truth—of analogy, as opposed to the reality of fact, is
consequently a central concern of his later poetry. It is, in a
sense, the theme of "Mushrooms" (*S*, 27–28), which presents
the question of truth and illusion as a teasing conundrum. To
mistake "A stone or stain, a dandelion puff" for the mushroom
you are seeking is to be "played-with rather than deluded" by
appearances; to be "taken in" is, rather, to be "taken beyond"

> This place of chiaroscuro that seemed clear,
> For realer than a myth of clarities
> Are the meanings that you read and are not there.
>
> (*S*, 28)

Memory plays a similar role in "Dates: Penkhull New Road"
(*WI*, 7–8). Recalling the street as it had been in his youth, a
"gravely neat" memorial of mid-Victorian working-class civility,
and regretting the subsequent violation of its character ("Something had bitten a gap / Out of the stretch we lived in," *WI*, 8) in
the piety of memory, he restores the interrupted continuity and
gives it the permanence of a poem: "It took time to convince me
that I cared / For more than beauty: I write to rescue / What is no

longer there" (*WI*, 8). What is no longer there once existed and still has a mental existence; what is not there, for example, the image of a mushroom in "a stone or stain," has also, if only, a mental existence, taking you beyond mere certainties. Therefore, the poet advises,

> waste
> None of the sleights of seeing: taste the sight
> You gaze unsure of—a resemblance, too,
> Is real and all its likes and links stay true
> To the weft of seeing.
> ("Mushrooms," *S*, 27–28)

Wordplay and sound-play, which is pervasive in Tomlinson's verse, function here to confuse the distinction between analogical and linear thinking—"likes and links" appears to assimilate them—and, in the transition from "links" to "weft" (chains to threads), the distinction between thinking and seeing.

Poems now not only draw attention to the element of illusion in the truth of poetry but also express relish of the disparities between fact and appearance exploited by poems—as, for instance, between bales of hay and the "scattered megaliths" they resemble ("Hay," *F*, 14). On the skyline at nightfall they seem to be—and this is what so delights the imagination—

> A henge of hay-bales to confuse the track
> Of time, and out of which the smoking dews
> Draw odours solid as the huge deception.
> (*F*, 14)

The metaphor, "henge of hay-bales," in *confusing* (the neutral word would be "identifying") the two things, wins a victory over time: the megalithic appearance in evening light is at once as "solid" as the thing itself—"a resemblance, too, / Is real"— and a "huge deception" that is appreciatively embodied in the "lavish" sensuousness of the whole poem. Imagination, says "Hawks" (*WrW*, 25), enables us to do the impossible: namely, to share, though we cannot understand, the ecstasy of birds that "after their kind are lovers" and, in defiance of our earthbound limits, "ride where we cannot climb the steep / And altering air, breathing the sweetness / Of our own excess." The poet is doing what many poets have done with their skylarks and nightingales, eagles and windhovers, but never with quite this contented poise between doing it and knowing it can't be done. Specifically, the sense of immoderateness, of overstepping limits, in "excess" is qualified by the etymological meaning, appropriate here, of merely going beyond (compare "exceeding the place it guesses" in "Nature Poem," quoted above). Going beyond ourselves "we are kinned / By space we never thought to enter": that kinship and that entry are at once real and illusory, the claim to them is at once sober truth, carefully measured in the language, and intemperateness. The poem is both a confession and a celebration of the imagination's inordinacy.

"Face and Image," in *American Scenes*, was the first poem to say openly, "Let be / this disparateness" between, for example, the face we see and our (loving) image of it:

> mouth, eyes and forehead,
> substantial things,
> advance their frontier
> clear against all imaginings.
> (*AS*, 3)

The gap between "the buzzard's two-note cry" and our translation of its meaning, or for that matter between the interpretation of its presence implicit in the silence of the small birds and, swayed by our admiration of its beauty, the image *we* have of it, is the theme of "Translating the Birds" (*S*, 53). The difference between the two poems lies in the latter's emphasis on the fact of disparity rather than on the injunction to "let be"—widening rather than closing the gap, increasing the tension between the thing itself and poetry's humanization of it. The poem expresses ironical awareness of an opposition between the other reality of the buzzard, "Thrusting itself beyond the clasp of words," and man's desire, "eager always for the intelligible," to "instruct those throats what meanings they must tell"; the irony informs the contrast—in "Beauty does not stir them, realists to a man"—between man's aesthetic appreciation of the predator and the response of its potential victims. The poet's admiration of what the small birds "do not linger to admire," the imagination's gift to reality, is reflected in the poem's opulent language: "The flash of empery that solar fire / Lends to the predatory ease of flights" (*S*, 53). The sun, indeed, here performs the office of metaphor—

lending to the bird an imperial stature and dignity that do not belong to it—and symbolizes the power and artifice of art, which in a *flash* of eloquence bestows on the buzzard's "predatory ease of flight" its own dominion over its created world. The "empery" of art recalls "the mind's imperious geometry" writing its "signature" on the unknowable in "A Self-Portrait: David." The mistrust conveyed by "imperious" is also admitted, with a certain *sang-froid* in "Translating the Birds," when the poet predicts that men will credit "with arias, minstrelsy," the small birds "who've only sung in metaphor"; but the depreciatory realism of this phrase is modified—the *sang-froid* perfects the bland—by an equal delight in the triumphant exercise of imagination: metaphor, as man's link with the world he inhabits, is both arbitrary and indispensable; art is imperious but also imperial.

In many of the later poems skepticism and affirmation, as it were, exchange properties. The *fiction* of analogy is the subject of "Fireflies" (*F*, 39), analogy that nevertheless serves to express the poet's enchantment with the seeming world created by the pinpoints of light in the darkness: "that close world lies / Pulsing within its halo, glows or goes . . . cosmos grows out of their circlings. . . . You could suppose the whole of darkness a forming rose" (*F*, 39). The scarcely avoidable pun on "lies," so placed, points to the fiction without discrediting it. The crisscross of outer and inner rhymes—the quoted lines and phrases only give a glimpse of the full effect—add a riddling confusion to the interplay between the real and the possible; the boundaries disappear between what is there and not there ("glows or goes"), between the solidity of "rose" and the conjectural existence of "suppose." It is appropriate that "In Arden" should provide a rationale for these echoes. "The depths of Arden's springs / Convey echoic waters," voicings of an unseen Eden

> Overflowing, as it brims its surfaces
>   In runes and hidden rhymes, in chords and keys
> Where Adam, Eden, Arden run together
>   And time itself must beat to the cadence of this river.
>
> (*S*, 47)

The "hidden rhymes" are runic connections created by the wizardry of poetry: magically, "Adam, Eden, Arden run together."

The echoes increase the richness of interplay, enhance our pleasure in it at the same time as they enhance our consciousness of
the artifice. It is clear now, almost explicit, that Eden is a creation
of poetry, the concentration and aspiration of the mind; language itself is the master of time.

This perceptual, or epistemological, and linguistic agnosticism—the basic uncertainty about what can be known and what
can be said that I have been illustrating—includes a specifically
religious agnosticism, one that underlies all Tomlinson's poetry
but has only become overt in recent collections. Yet here, too,
agnosticism rings with the tones not of doubt but of affirmation.
Sacramental language has long been a feature of Tomlinson's
verse; what is new is that the Christian associations of certain
key words in his poetic vocabulary, discreetly used, are not
firmly separated from their supernatural significance. "To See
the Heron" (*S*, 30–31) catches a moment of visual perfection in
language that, as the poem proceeds, gradually increases its religious charge (the italics here and in the next quotation are
mine): "To see the heron rise," "this *raised* torch," "this leisurely
sideways / wandering *ascension*." No sooner is the heron's transfiguration into a resurrected body completed than it is immediately restored to earth. The heron untransfigured is nothing
more than a bird searching for its prey:

> *risen*
> it is darkening now
> against the sullen sky blue,
> so let it go
> unaccompanied save by the thought
> that this is autumn and the stream
> whose course its eye is travelling
> the source of fish. . . .
>
> (*S*, 30–31)

The poem's intention, however, is to be not cynical but paradoxical: the heron is both itself and a vehicle of revelation. The paradox has the same elements as that represented by the gulls in
"The Faring" (*S*, 25), which were, in the poet's recollection of an
extraordinary day, simultaneously birds in a storm "above sea-
sonable fields," "intent / On nothing more than the ploughhand's

nourishment," and seeming messengers from an "unending sea" of space, whose presence for the observing-participating poet "rhymed here with elsewhere."

Tomlinson's concern with the religious question is most noticeable—at least I have become more conscious of it—in a recent volume, *The Flood* (1981). Plainly in several poems poetry is being offered as a sufficient "recompense" for the failed promise of revealed truth. This, at least, is one way of "translating" the Wordsworthian episode recorded in "The Recompense" (*F*, 8–9, resembling similar epiphanies in *The Prelude*, both in content and in narrative technique). The poet and his companion "climbed the darkness" to view the comet predicted for that night; they "waited" but "no comet came, and no flame thawed / The freezing reaches of [their] glance." "Unwillingly" they took themselves and their disappointment back down again, but, facing in the opposite direction, found in the "climbing brightness" of the "risen moon" "recompense for a comet lost": forfeiting the hoped-for prodigy, they turned instead to the opportunity of self-transcendence offered by the mere "rarenesses" ("Images of Perfection," *S*, 20–21) of sense experience. We

> Could read ourselves into those lines
> > Pulsating on the eye and to the veins,
> Thrust and countercharge to our own racing down,
> > Lunar flights of the rooted horizon.
> > > > ("The Recompense," *F*, 9)

In his fine elegiac sequence "For Miriam" (*F*, 4–7) Tomlinson recalls how he had played the advocate for traditional Christianity against the heresies of an eccentric woman preacher, not as a believer but as a "pagan" pleading for "poetry forgone"; in the light of his own sacramental imagery, it is interesting that he should muster all his "rhetoric" to defend specifically the doctrine of the incarnation.

Religious affirmation has been, so to speak, relocated. There are poems now, however, that proclaim their paganism not by appropriating and revaluing the language and images of Christianity but by contrasting the two ways of believing. "Under the Moon's Reign," which gives its title to a group of poems in *The Way In*, is to the best of my knowledge the first poem to probe the implications of this antithesis: the contrast there is between the twilight that was "a going of the gods" and the transformation wrought by moonlight—let us call it, at the risk of banality, the moon of imagination. In the confusion of twilight we

> Were looking still for what we could not see—
> The inside of the outside, for some spirit flung
> From the burning of that Götterdämmerung. . . .
>
> (WI, 17)

But the moon's transfiguration of the landscape is effected by "no more miracle than the place / It occupied and the eye that saw it"; "Drawing all into more than daylight height" indicates, in a favorite construction (compare "more than earth" in "At Holwell Farm," "more than bread" in "A Farmer's Wife"), that the seeming miracle of its "steady lightning" is not other than just an extension of natural and human existence. If this poem faintly recalls Elizabeth Bishop's "A Miracle for Breakfast," "San Fruttuoso" (F, 34–37), in its form of offhand anecdotal narrative and its lightly sardonic wit, it distantly resembles another kind of Bishop poem. The poet takes the ferry in rough seas; divers don their suits and slip underwater: the two actions alternate in counterpoint. The poet's is a world of sun, bodies, "an ill-lit sky," and violent motion: the divers "assume / alternative bodies," pursuing purposes—"whatever it is draws them downwards"—that Tomlinson treats with an affectation of polite puzzlement and incredulity throughout. That "alternative" is a coolly disdainful substitution for "resurrected" becomes apparent in the whimsical description of the divers levitating around the sunken statue of *Cristo del mare*, "buoyed up by adoration" "like Correggio's sky- / swimming angels," performing "slow-motion pirouettes / forgetful of body, of gravity"—and we may be sure that gravity also means "proper seriousness." The poem begins with salt—"Sea salt has rusted the ironwork trellis"—and toward the end, thankfully after the uncertainties of his passage, the poet reaches the quay "with salted lips": the salt of corrosive time, then, the acrid taste of an unignorable reality, in the presence of which the charming antics of the divers seem the merest frivolity. It is in keeping that, in an implied comparison with the "baroque ecstatic devotion" of the circling divers in the postcard of *Cristo del mare*, Tomlinson should show a humorous preference for the mother who "has the placid / and faintly bovine look / of a Northern madonna." Juxtaposition of a late poem, "Thunder in Tuscany" (*F*, 40), with a comparable early poem, "Ponte Veneziano" (from which I have already quoted), may serve to isolate this shift of focus in his recent work. Both depict stone figures in postures that in the eyes of the poet express and affirm exemplary attitudes. In "Ponte Veneziano" the fixed gaze of the two figures, "Tight-socketed in space . . . / Stripping the vista to its depth," projects strength of mind and will: undistractable concentration, unrelaxing singleness and tenacity of purpose, strictness of judgment, a disciplined commitment to what is necessary, and, as "It broods on the further light," the "utmost" of what is possible. Staring into the circle formed by a bridge-vault and its reflection,

> They do not exclaim,
> But, bound to that distance,
> Transmit without gesture
> Their stillness into its ringed centre.
> (*SIB*, 4)

In contrast with the steady light and stillness of "Ponte Veneziano," the scene of "Thunder in Tuscany" is cinematically dramatic, and the figures, far from being "without gesture," are almost flamboyantly expressive: lightning illuminates a facade of "statues listening," giving fragmentary glimpses of features "Taut with the intent a body shapes through them / Standing on sheerness outlistening the storm." The "stillness" of the Venetian figures epitomizes the peculiar quality of their attention and stoicism: a sort of stoicism also characterizes the mood of "Thunder in Tuscany," but the image here projects tension and challenge. The illusion of an abyss conveyed by "sheerness"—recalling as it might the "slow abyss" eating away the fields, in "The Compact: At Volterra" (*WrW*, 13–14), and the grit of those who farm the land up to the very edge, "Refusing to give ground before they must"—perhaps will justify the suggestion that the attitude in which these statues are caught "outlistening," looking to survive, with knowledge of something beyond the storm, is an image of post-Christian daring.

The obverse of Tomlinson's affirmative agnosticism is an *ironic* sense of the disparities—between fact and appearance, thing and image, reality and imagination—that his poetry has chosen to embrace and to celebrate. An incidental implication of my comments on "Translating the Birds" was that irony and celebration ride together; I would suggest that in the poems of the seventies they are never far apart. "Translating the Birds" balances the realistic, respectful silence of the small birds in the presence of the buzzard against the loud rhetoric of the aroused imagination and sets poetry's "eagerness" to translate what it sees and hears into the language of the mind against a precise perception of the mind's limits and a readiness to applaud what is "beyond the clasp of words"; only a slight shift in perspective transmutes the double consciousness at play here into the ironic poise of the so-called "Histories" grouped together in *The Shaft*. Irony is an insurance against the hubris of imagination. In poems that reflect and reflect on Tomlinson's experience, irony plays a muted accompaniment to the mind's eagerness to possess and to transform what it contemplates. Conversely, in his treatment of others' attempts to possess their lives—his portraits, for example, of the revolutionaries Charlotte Corday and Danton and his interpretation of the painter David's self-portrait—and in his humorous exposure of contemporary anecdote's failure to give coherence and meaning to the poet Denham's life, irony dominates. Contraries in "Translating the Birds" are welded into complementarities: the simultaneous acknowledgment and defiance of limitation hints an irony but leaves no crack for it to enter by. The disparity, however, between the foreground of Corday's and Danton's partial, subjective readings of reality and the impersonal background of time's "links of consequence," of history, which is the poet's knowledge of the *whole* story, is the gap that in those poems admits irony (for example, the gap between Corday's intention, "to have brought peace" by her "faultless blow," and "the Terror still to come," the future she could not foresee). The guillotine,

> the blade
> Inherited the future now and she
> Entered a darkness where no irony
> Seeps through to move the pity of her shade.
>   ("Charlotte Corday," *S*, 4)

What she cannot feel the poem provides—irony leaves space for pity, restrained pity for the disproportion and incompleteness of her life. The combination of irony and pity in these portraits produces the equivalent of the balance of positive realism and (let us call it) positive romanticism in poems like "Translating the Birds."

The tragic irony of Danton's situation is that he has mistaken the part for the whole; he not only has exchanged his full humanity for the partial satisfactions afforded by political power but also, now that he realizes his mistake, pursues the opposite satisfaction of the senses with an equally unbalanced intensity:

> He fronts the parapet
> Drinking the present with unguarded sense:
>
> The stream comes on. Its music deafens him
> To other sounds, to past and future wrong.
> ("For Danton," *S*, 6–7)

I am reminded by the phrase "unguarded sense," implying values that can easily be misconceived, of certain emphases in Calvin Bedient's description of Tomlinson's imagination in *Eight Contemporary Poets*. It is not possible to summarize his lengthy examination of the subject, but a fair impression of the kind of balance he strikes in his assessment is conveyed by this sentence: "Though obviously far from being ample, headlong, or richly empowering, neither, on the other hand, is it faint or apologetic."[7] I disagree: I find it ample and richly empowering. One wonders, however, what conception of imagination is implied by "headlong." If one knew, it might tell us why he thinks Tomlinson's is "unobtrusive and stopped-down." I want to conclude this essay with a brief consideration of the issues raised by this description. By implication, a *guarded* sense of the present is the standard by which, in the lines quoted above, Danton's attitude is being judged. It might be assumed that a guarded sense of things is what Mr. Bedient conceivably means by a "stopped-down" imagination. It is an understandable but wrong assumption. For "guarded" in this context would mean not defensive but circumspect—that is, attentive to all circumstances that may affect decision. And should circumspection seem a modest liter-

7. Calvin Bedient, *Eight Contemporary Poets* (New York: Oxford University Press, 1974), p. 14.

ary virtue, let me remind the reader of Eliot's definition of wit in his essay on Andrew Marvell: "a constant inspection and criticism of experience. It involves, probably, a recognition, implicit in the expression of every experience, of other kinds of experience which are possible."[8] Circumspection is a part of wit. The "unguarded," *headlong*, oblivious immersion in the pleasures of the present shuts out consciousness of "past and future wrong" and hides from Danton the significance of the stream's inexorable progress ("the links of consequence / Chiming his life away"). The "unguarded" vision is one blind to the *whole* truth: conversely, a guarded vision would be one that opens the mind to *all* circumstances, to the present and its contraries. Imagination for Tomlinson is, as I have said, the faculty that brings to what the senses perceive an inner sense of what is not present— we may call them contraries or "other kinds of experience which are possible." The critical, vigilant, self-doubting—in a word, circumspect—approach to experience recommended in these lines, far from bottling up imagination (the genie in a bottle figure, I suspect, lurks somewhere in the shadows of Mr. Bedient's prose), is precisely what *empowers* and gives it *ample* range.

8. T. S. Eliot, "Andrew Marvell," in his *Selected Essays* (1932; reprint, New York: Harcourt, Brace, and World, 1964).

Three Prehistoric Masks (1973)

Part III

The Painter

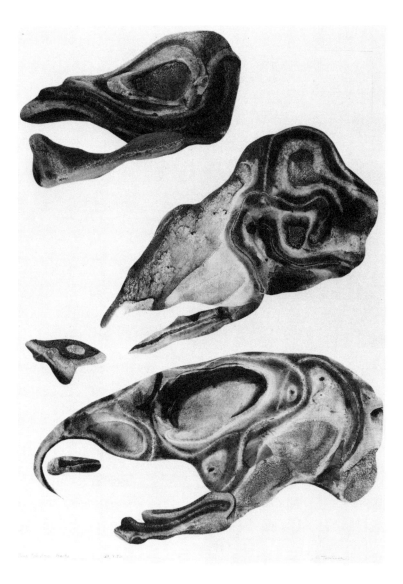

Ruth Grogan

12. Language and Graphics

As a very young man Charles Tomlinson wrote and illustrated his own Blake-Whitman prophetic books. Words were his predominant public medium from his first volume of poetry in 1951 until about 1969, but many poems on painters (Constable, Van Gogh, Cézanne) and his remark, "Visual art has stayed major whereas poetry since the 'grand old men' has dwindled: it has no equivalents for Pollock, de Kooning, or Arshile Gorky," attest to a continuous leaning toward the visual arts.[1] Reviewers have almost monotonously described his poetry as painterly, referring to his observant eye for color, tonalities of light, and fluid patterns. Recently two volumes of reproductions of Tomlinson's own graphic work have appeared—*Words and Images* (1972) and *In Black and White* (1976)—the outcome of a renewed confidence that he is fundamentally as much a painter as a poet.[2]

In Black and White is prefaced by one long essay by Octavio Paz and three short prose meditations by Tomlinson. These short essays dwell on the parallels between his poetry and painting, their joint interest in "the threshold of perception" (*BW*, 22), and the interplay in both of light and dark, lucidity and mystery. Their central preoccupation, however, is the role of chance in art, the way patterns arise fortuitously in words or paint, to be

---

Ruth Grogan is Associate Professor of English at York University, Toronto. She has written articles on Charles Tomlinson and on William Carlos Williams. "Language and Graphics" was originally published as "Charles Tomlinson: Poet and Painter" in *Critical Quarterly* 19 (1977): 71–77.

1. Hamilton, "Four Conversations," p. 83–84.
2. [Editor's note: These were Tomlinson's current collections of his graphics at the time this essay was originally published (1977). More recently, Tomlinson has published his graphics in *Eden: Graphics and Poetry* (Bristol: Redcliffe Press, Ltd., 1986).]

seized on and extended by the alert imagination of the artist. The admission of randomness into the process of making a work of art, whether verbal or visual, seems to be for Tomlinson a way of restricting the ego, bringing "otherness" to bear on the imagination, and feeling his way toward unforeseen and unpredictable meanings. Octavio Paz calls it, more sweepingly, a way of transforming fate into free choice (*BW*, 14).

But the poet and painter in Tomlinson stand in a more antithetical relation than any of these essays would suggest. If his earlier poetry aimed on the whole toward moderation, precision, lucidity, selflessness, and a balanced encounter between human and natural, and if Donald Davie's term for him—Augustan—seemed appropriate,[3] then one has to acknowledge a departure in at least one group of these paintings. The paintings I am referring to are unexpectedly chthonic and menacing, exposing as it were an oneiric underside of his imagination. My thesis will be that the process of painting seemed to release energies that in unprecedented ways trouble the poetry as well. The disturbance can be seen in some of the poems that were written at the time of his return to painting and were selected to accompany the reproductions in the composite volume *Words and Images*; it is skirted in the introductory essays of *In Black and White*, and surfaces occasionally in his more recent work.

"The Chances of Rhyme" (*WW*, 59) is the poem Tomlinson chose to discuss in his prefatory essay, "Poet as Painter" (*BW*, 16–19). In the tradition of poems about writing poetry—which must by now have reached the status of genre—this poem is a re-enactment of a confident submission to fortuitous aural and etymological sequences in language. It began, so Tomlinson recalls, in the rhyme of "chance" with "dance." Ruminating on this "nutrifying" accident, he found himself scribbling: "The chances of rhyme are like the chances of meeting—/ In the finding fortuitous, but once found, binding" (*WW*, 59). The poet is compelled by benign energies of the language itself into an Edenic realm of un-bestial beasts:

> Yes. We are led, though we seem to lead
> Through a fair forest, an Arden (a rhyme
> For Eden)—breeding ground for beasts

---

3. Davie, Introduction to *The Necklace*, p. xvi.

Not bestial, but loyal and legendary, which is more
    Than nature's are. . . .

(WW, 59)

Taking chances, as defined here, is not an act of extremity (a term of reproach in Tomlinson's moral lexicon):

    the fortuitousness
Of art [is not] something to be met with only
    At extremity's brink . . .

  · · · · · · · · · · · · · ·

    To take chances, as to make rhymes
Is human, but between chance and impenitence
    (A half-rhyme) come dance, vigilance
And circumstance (meaning all that is there
    Besides you, when you are there). And between
Rest-in-peace and precipice,
    Inertia and perversion, come the varieties
Increase, lease, re-lease (in both
    Senses); and immersion, conversion—of inert
Mass, that is, into energies to combat confusion.
    Let rhyme be my conclusion.

(WW, 59)

"Like the weaver," says Merleau-Ponty, in a passage that Tomlinson has quoted, "the writer works on the wrong side of his material. He has to do only with language, and it is thus that he suddenly finds himself surrounded by meaning."[4] Weaving the chances of rhyme into a poem is paradigmatic of how other kinds of accidents—"the chances of meeting" for example—are accommodated with time and attentiveness to the pattern of a life; Tomlinson elsewhere[5] relates this poem to one on the ripening into friendship of a chance meeting with Octavio Paz, a poem in which, as he notes, chance becomes "event," and "event" rhymes with "consent." Taking chances, accepting contingencies, can be seen as part of Tomlinson's larger morality, his "containment of self."[6]

4. Maurice Merleau-Ponty, "Indirect Language and the Voices of Silence," in his *Signs*, trans. Richard C. McCleary (Evanston: Northwestern University Press, 1964), p. 45; quoted by Tomlinson in "Not in Sequence of a Metronome . . . ," p. 53.
5. Rasula and Erwin, "Interview," p. 409.
6. Hamilton, "Four Conversations," p. 84.

In his graphic techniques Tomlinson takes chances in three ways: by the use of photo-collage, decalcomania, and black-and-white. Decalcomania is a technique invented by the surrealists in which diluted paint or ink is crushed between two surfaces and the resulting random forms are used as the suggestive basis for a new picture. Tomlinson uses glass, rough paper, sponges, and so on for his surfaces, getting granular, stippled, chiaroscuric textures on his pages reminiscent of such things as hardened lava, bundles of rod-shaped cells, lichen stains on rock, and cloud-shapes. With these textures and stains as a basis, he pushes the paint around, adjusts, extends; sometimes he uses scissors rather than brush, and by pasting on cut-out shapes, especially from black-and-white photographs, adds more sharp-edged semi-random juxtapositions and planes of reference. In his graphic, as in his poetic technique, we become aware that choice and chance, deliberation and consent are bound together, each contributing at every moment of the process, interactive, and in the final event indistinguishable.

Some of the works in *Words and Images* and *In Black and White*, listed below, can be arranged on a scale of increasing intricacy in their morphological, metamorphic, and metaphorical patterns. Spongy surfaces composed of tiny bosses and fibers, viscous swirls, caverns, and saliencies shift, dissolve, and refocus under our eyes, inviting interpretation on scales that vary from cosmic to microorganic. In these contexts color would restrict interpretation, and Tomlinson's monochromism serves as much to liberate fantasy as to express his moral and aesthetic austerity.

"Into distance" (*Images*, 31; *BW*, pl. 22) and "Land and water" (*Images*, 8; *BW*, pl. 10). In these relatively simple images the decalcomaniacal stains suggest volcanic landscape, craters, escarpments, and rocky plateaux, severe and uninhabited.

"Deep structure" (*Images*, 11; *BW*, pl. 23). This is a more chiaroscuric composition in which porous inky stains become lichen and cloudscapes as well as fissures in the earth.

"Composition 1" (*Images*, 25; *BW*, pl. 14). Here lava bubbles, fissures, and geological strata exist in the interior of cut-out amoebic or pebble shapes. Two flat-bottomed island shapes give depth to the picture plane, making the other shapes float somewhere between.

"Origins of the Milky Way" (*Images*, 5; *BW*, pl. 25), "Small galaxy" (*Images*, 29), and "Centrifugal" (*Images*, 23). These expand Tomlinson's morphology into cosmic realms.

"Landscape with bathers" (*Images*, 27; *BW*, pl. 28). The whole picture interiorized, a polymorphous reverie of lunar terrain, scabrous lichen stains, ciliated cell structures, and skyscapes, within an immense skull-shape, reminiscent perhaps, considering Tomlinson's interest in Henry Moore, of Moore's drawings of elephant skulls. In "Poet as Painter" Tomlinson remarks that in some of his paintings he has "tried to push outward from the contained forms of the skulls—my own skull, perhaps" (*BW*, 18). Cut-out egg shapes and amoeba shapes are superimposed, each with its own textured interior, and more clearly than in the earlier works two or three of these are merging into monolithic human form. Inside one of the eggs there is an incongruously tiny drawing of a coach and horses.

"Willendorf Grotto" (*Images*, 7; *BW*, pl. 29). Its upper and lower halves, roughly symmetrical and suggestive of the walls of a sea-cave reflected in water or the spread wings of some creature in flight, contain again the egg and amoeba shapes, some of them now with overt sexual implications. One bulbous, pockmarked pebble resembles the paleolithic Venus.

The composition dates of most of these paintings are given in *In Black and White*; interestingly enough, the sequence that I had devised solely with the purpose of showing increasing complexity of metaphorical reference turned out to be also the chronological sequence, with the exception of the second and third categories, which I had reversed. The conclusion is irresistible; in this sequence chance plays another role and has led the painter's eye and hand, not into the Edenic and moral world of "The Chances of Rhyme" but into realms very remote from humanity—into galactic space, bleak, furrowed Hebridean landscapes, volcanic craters, and microorganisms not observable by the naked eye. The Willendorf Venus, though recognizably human, has scarcely emerged from her stone matrix and survives from an unimaginably distant era in prehistory. This is not Augustan nature, not "humanity and landscape . . . held in imaginative rapport."[7] To confirm my point, visual landscapes might be compared with the landscape of the poem "Winter Encounters," a characteristic view of rural England in which fields, though wintry, mesh with houses and provide a mirroring environment for subdued but fulfilling human encounters. The key words here are encounter, pairings, interchange, and response. Tomlinson's poems, like his paintings, show him fascinated by grain,

7. Tomlinson, "State of Poetry," p. 50.

texture, and currents, though not exclusively: the stone of his poems, unlike that of his paintings, will often be the material of a house; a hill has someone walking over it; and the currents in a stream serve as an image of the flexible relentlessness of logic, a highly civilized human capacity. As Tomlinson says, "A lot of things I *write* about—houses, cities, walls, landscapes are . . . saturated in human presence and tradition" (my italics).[8] Even when nature in the poems is wintry, unnerving, or resistant to human presence, its "otherness" comes from outside the mind and does not well up from intolerable inner depths.

"Ariadne and the Minotaur," published in *Written on Water* in 1972 and selected to accompany a quartet of reproductions in *Words and Images* (20–21) entitled "Stone lips," is an anomaly in the context of Tomlinson's poems. Unlike "The Chances of Rhyme," this is a poem "At Extremity's Brink." The stone lips of this earth fissure lead into a subterranean labyrinth housing the Minotaur, and the poem is a lament, on Ariadne's behalf, that in assisting Theseus to kill the Minotaur she betrayed her own destiny:

> between the lips of stone
> appeared he whom she had sent
> to go where her unspeakable
> intent unspoken had been to go
> herself, and heaved unlabyrinthed at her feet
> their mutual completed crime—
> a put-by destiny, a dying
> look that sought her
> out of eyes the light extinguished,
> eyes she should have led
> herself to light: . . .
>
> (*WrW*, 21)

The tragedy lies in Ariadne's refusal to go over the brink, mate in the depths with her half-brother, himself half-beast, and eventually lead him back to light and the upper world. In "The Chances of Rhyme" (*WW*, 59) the beasts were "not bestial, but loyal and legendary"; here the beast is "bestial" indeed. Tomlinson's favorite images of stone, light, and language are taken up

---

8. Hamilton, "Four Conversations," p. 84.

again to yield a hellish rather than Edenic meaning. With just this exception of Eden, Tomlinson has normally avoided myth, on the grounds that it interferes between the observer and the observed. A tree is itself and not a dryad [9]—which accentuates one's suspicion that the contents of this poem come from outside the ordinary boundaries of his poetry and thus require the indirection and concealment of mythic formulation.

Tomlinson's brief prefaces to *In Black and White* obliquely touch on and withdraw from these issues. At one point he describes poems and paintings as a place of reconciliation, "where the civilized, discriminating faculties and the sense of the elemental, of origins, reinforce each other" (*BW*, 19). This is true certainly on the level of technique, but if the comment is transposed to the symbolic and psychological level, "reinforce" is hardly the word for the relationship between Ariadne and the Minotaur. In another of the prefaces Tomlinson quotes from Wordsworth to explain how compliance with chance events in paint and water brings an invasion of the mind by "ungovernable presences":

> . . . huge and mighty forms, that do not live
> Like living men, mov'd slowly through my mind
> By day, and were the trouble of my dreams. [10]

But rather than acknowledge or dwell on the menace in these images, Tomlinson proceeds immediately to reflect on lightness and translucency in paint. In discussing and rejecting the surrealists' use of chance, Tomlinson concludes that "visual art," and by implication poetic art, is "not an unleasher of 'the subconscious,' but a cure for blindness" (*BW*, 22); "Ariadne and the Minotaur" shows that this prose way of putting it suppresses an essential stage in the curative process. Ariadne's tragic failure is precisely a failure to descend into the depths, unleash and submit to that ungovernable presence from the subconscious, the Minotaur, before bringing it back alive to the light of day. The Minotaur's blindness—and her own, if the syntactical ambigu-

---

9. Rasula and Erwin, "Interview," p. 407.
10. William Wordsworth, *The Prelude, or Growth of a Poet's Mind* (1805 text), edited by Ernest de Selincourt, a new edition corrected by Stephen Gill (London and New York: Oxford University Press, 1970), p. 12. Tomlinson cites this passage in *BW*, 20.

ities of the poem are attended to—could have been cured only by this threefold venture of descent, submission, and deliverance.

My hypothesis is that these menacing and ungovernable presences, though in retrospect occasionally discernible in the earlier poetry, were brought more distinctly to the foreground only in the medium of paint and only when Tomlinson permitted chance to generate, if not govern, his painting. Some of the graphic works, as I arranged them, show how his remote landscapes, having been emptied of the humans who inhabit his poetic landscapes, can then metamorphose toward those disturbing sexual or chthonic images equally remote from the ordinary daylight experience and human scale of his earlier poetry. The Ariadne poem, transposing these elements into myth, expresses both a fear of meeting them and a fear of not meeting them; one might say that in effect the poem kills off the human forces lurking in the dark concavities of the paintings across the page and then weeps for their demise.

One of Tomlinson's recent critical articles, on Isaac Rosenberg's plays, seems to be working through themes related to those of "Ariadne," though on an ostensibly historical and literary topic. It is concerned with the tension in Rosenberg's plays between "primal energies and conscious purpose," "primitive vigour and . . . 'largeness' of understanding," "the fear of wasted possibilities," and "the need for tragic acceptance."[11] The article is densely, even tortuously, argued and is rather untypical of Tomlinson's critical style. It would be foolish to make predictions from such hints, except to say that we may eventually see that Tomlinson's painting was not a divagation in his development but a deeply renovative impulse.

11. Tomlinson, "Fate," p. 61, 65.

Octavio Paz

Translated by Michael Schmidt

13. The Graphics of Charles Tomlinson

When I first read one of Charles Tomlinson's poems, over ten years ago, I was struck by the powerful presence of an element that, later, I found in almost all his creative work, even in the most reflective and self-contemplating: the outer world, a presence at once constant and invisible. It is everywhere, but we do not see it. If Tomlinson is a poet for whom "the outer world exits," it must be added that it does not exist for him as an independent reality, apart from us. In his poems the distinction between subject and object is attenuated until it becomes, rather than a frontier, a zone of interpenetration, giving precedence not to the subject but rather to the object: the world is not a representation of the subject—rather, the subject is the projection of the world. In his poems, outer reality—more than merely the space in which our actions, thoughts, and emotions unfold—is a climate that involves us, an impalpable substance, at once physical and mental, that we penetrate and that penetrates us.

Octavio Paz, Mexican writer and diplomat, has been awarded the Ingersoll Prize for Creative Writing, the International Poetry Grand Prix, and a Guggenheim Foundation fellowship. A member of the American Academy of Arts & Letters, he has written numerous volumes of poetry, prose, and criticism and has edited several literary reviews. Michael Schmidt is Editorial Director at Carcanet Press, which he founded with Peter Jones. He is the founding editor of *P N Review* and has written and edited several books of British poetry. He is Special Lecturer in Poetry at the University of Manchester. "The Graphics of Charles Tomlinson" was published originally in *Poetry Nation 5* 3, 1, and more recently in *On Poets and Others* by Octavio Paz (New York: Seavers Books, 1986).

The world turns to air, temperature, sensation, thought; and we become stone, window, orange peel, turf, oil stain, helix.

Against the idea of the world-as-spectacle, Tomlinson opposes the concept—a very English one—of the world as event. His poems are neither a painting nor a description of the object or its more or less constant properties; what interests him is the process that leads it to be the object it is. He is fascinated—with his eyes open: a lucid fascination—at the universal busyness, the continuous generation and degeneration of things. His is a poetry of the minimal catastrophes and resurrections of which the great catastrophe and resurrection of the worlds is composed. Objects are unstable congregations ruled alternately by the forces of attraction and repulsion. Process and not transition: not the place of departure and the place of arrival but what we are when we depart and what we have become when we arrive. . . . The water-drops on a bench wet with rain, crowded on the edge of a slat, after an instant of ripening—analogous in the affairs of men to the moment of doubt that precedes major decisions—fall onto the concrete; "dropped seeds of now becoming then." A moral and physical evocation of the water-drops. . . .

Thanks to a double process, at once visual and intellectual, the product of many patient hours of concentrated passivity and of a moment of decision, Tomlinson can isolate the object, observe it, leap suddenly inside it, and, before it dissolves, take his snapshot. The poem is the perception of the change, a perception that includes the poet: he changes with the changes of the object and perceives himself in the perception of those changes. The leap into the object is a leap into himself. The mind is a photographic darkroom: there the images—"the gypsum's snow / the limestone stair / and bone-yard landscape grow / into the identity of flesh" ("The Cavern," *AS*, 21). It is not, of course, a pantheistic claim to be everywhere and to be everything. Tomlinson does not wish to be the heart and soul of the universe. He does not seek the "thing in itself" or the "thing in myself," but rather he seeks things in that moment of indecision when they are on the point of generation or degeneration. The moment they appear or disappear before us, before they form as objects in our minds or dissolve in our forgetfulness. . . . Tomlinson quotes a passage from Kafka that defines his own purpose admirably: "to catch a glimpse of things as they may have been before they show themselves to me" (*BW*, 20).

His procedure approaches, at one extreme, science: maximum objectivity and purification, though not suppression, of the subject. At the other extreme, nothing is further from modern scientism. This is not because of the aestheticism with which he is at times reproached, but because his poems are experiences and not experiments. Aestheticism is an affectation, contortion, preciosity, and in Tomlinson we find rigor, precision, economy, subtlety. The experiments of modern science are carried out on segments of reality, while experiences implicitly postulate that the grain of sand is a world and each fragment figures the whole; the archetype of experiments is the quantitative model of mathematics, while in experience a qualitative element appears that up to now has not been limited to measurement. A contemporary mathematician, René Thom, describes the situation with grace and exactness: "A la fin du XVIIième siècle, la controverse faisait rage entre tenants des physiques de Descartes et de Newton. Descartes, avec ses tourbillons, ses atomes crochus, etc., expliquait tout et ne calculait rien; Newton, avec la loi de gravitation en $1/r^2$, calculait tout et n'expliquait rien" (At the end of the seventeenth century, the controversy raged between the followers of Descartes' physics and those of Newton. Descartes, with his whirlwinds, his atoms, etc., explained everything and calculated nothing; Newton, with the law of gravity in $1/r^2$, calculated everything and explained nothing.") And he adds, "Le point de vue newtonien se justifie pleinement par son efficacité . . . mais les esprits soucieux de compréhension n'auront jamais, au regard des théories qualitatives et descriptives, l'attitude méprisant du scientisme quantitatif" (The Newtonian point of view justifies itself fully through its efficacy . . . but those spirits who want to understand will never have, in the qualitative and descriptive theories, the attitude of quantitative scientism). It is even less justifiable to undervalue the poets, who offer us not theories but experiences.

In many of his poems Tomlinson presents us with the changes in the particle of dust, the outlines of the stain spreading on the rag, the way the seed's flying mechanism works, the structure of the swirling air current. The experience fulfills a need of the human spirit: to imagine what we cannot see, give ideas a form the senses can respond to, *see* ideas. In this sense the poet's experiences are not less truthful than the experiments carried out in our laboratories, though their truth is on another level from scientific truth. Geometry translates the abstract relationships between bodies into forms that are visible archetypes: thus, it is the frontier between the qualitative and the quantitative. But there is another frontier, art and poetry, which translates into sensible forms, that are at the same time archetypes, the qualitative relationships between things and men. Poetry—imagination and sensibility made language—is a crystallizing agent of phenomena. Tomlinson's poems are crystals, produced by the combined action of his sensibility and his imaginative and verbal powers—crystals sometimes transparent, sometimes rainbow-colored, not all perfect, but all poems that we can look through. The act of looking becomes a destiny and a profession of faith: seeing is believing.

It is hardly surprising that a poet with these concerns should be attracted to painting. In general, the poet who turns to painting tries to express with shapes and colors those things he cannot say with words. The same is true of the painter who writes. Arp's poetry is a counterpointing of wit and fantasy set against the abstract elegance of his plastic work. In the case of Michaux, painting and drawing are essentially rhythmic incantations, signs beyond articulate language, visual magic. The expressionism of some of Tagore's ink drawings, with their violence, compensates us for the sticky sweetness of many of his melodies. To find one of Valéry's watercolors among the arguments and paradoxes of the *Cahiers* is like opening the window and finding that outside the sea, the sun, and the trees still exist. When I was considering Tomlinson, I called to mind these other artists, and I asked myself how this desire to paint came to manifest itself in a meditative temperament such as his—a poet whose main faculty of sense is his eyes, but eyes that think. Before I had a chance to ask him about this, I received, around 1970, a letter from him in which he told me he had sent me one of the *New Directions Anthologies*,[1] which included reproductions

1. [Editor's note: See *New Directions 34: An International Anthology of Prose and Poetry*, ed. James Laughlin with Peter Glassgold and Frederick R. Martin (New York: New Directions, 1977), pp. 155–63. Paz cites *Agenda* as the journal in the original essay but corrects it in the reprint of the essay in *In Black and White*.]

of some of his drawings done in 1968. Later in 1970, during my stay in England, I was able to see other drawings from that same period—all of them in black and white, except for a few in sepia; studies of cow skulls, skeletons of birds, rats, and other creatures that he and his daughters had found in the countryside and on the Cornish beaches.

In Tomlinson's poetry, the perception of movement is exquisite and precise. Whether the poem is about rocks, plants, sand, insects, leaves, birds, or human beings, the true protagonist, the hero of each poem, is change. Tomlinson hears foliage grow. Such an acute perception of variations, at times almost imperceptible, in beings and things, necessarily implies a vision of reality as a system of calls and replies. Beings and things, in changing, come in contact: change means relationship. In those Tomlinson drawings, the skulls of the birds, rats, and cows were isolated structures, placed in an abstract space, far from other objects, and even at a remove from themselves, fixed and immovable. Rather than a counterpointing of his poetic work, they seemed to me a contradiction. Missing were some of the features that attract me to his poetry: delicacy, wit, refinement of tones, energy, depth. How could he recover all these qualities without turning Tomlinson the painter into a servile disciple of Tomlinson the poet? The answer to this question is found in the work—drawings, collages, and decalcomania[2]—of recent years.

Tomlinson's painting vocation began, significantly, in a fascination with films. When he came down from Cambridge in 1948, he had not only seen "all the films" but also was writing scripts that he sent to producers and that they, invariably, returned to him. This passion died out in time but left two enduring interests: in the image in motion, and in the idea of a literary text as support for the image. Both elements reappear in the poems and the collages. When the unions closed the doors of the film industry against him, Tomlinson dedicated himself energetically to painting. His first experiments, combining *frottage*,

2. "Decalcomania without preconceived object or decalcomania of desire: by means of a thick brush, spread out black gouache, more or less diluted in places, upon a sheet of glossy white paper, and cover at once with a second sheet, upon which exert an even pressure. Lift off the second sheet without haste." Óscar Domínguez, quoted in *Surrealism* by Roger Cardinal and Robert Stuart Short.

oil and ink, date from that period. Between 1948 and 1950 he exhibited his work in London and Manchester. In 1951 he had the opportunity to live for a time in Italy. During that trip the urge to paint began to recede before the urge to write poetry. When he returned to England, he devoted himself more and more to writing, less and less to painting. In this first phase of his painting, the results were indecisive: *frottages* in the shadow of Max Ernst, studies of water and rocks more or less inspired by Cézanne, trees and foliage seen in Samuel Palmer rather than in the real world. Like other artists of his generation, he made the circuit around the various stations of modern art and paused, long enough to genuflect, before the geometric chapel of the Braques, the Légers and the Gris's. During those same years—getting on toward 1954—Tomlinson was writing the splendid *Seeing Is Believing* poems. He ceased painting.

The interruption was not long. Settled near Bristol, he returned to his brushes and crayons. The temptation to use black (why? he still asks himself) had an unfortunate effect: by exaggerating the contours, it made his compositions stiff. "I wanted to reveal the pressure of objects," he wrote to me, "but all I managed to do was thicken the outlines." In 1968 Tomlinson seriously confronted his vocation and the obstacles to it. I refer to his inner inhibitions and, most of all, to that mysterious predilection for black. As always happens, an intercessor appeared: Seghers. Tomlinson was wise to have chosen Hércules Seghers— each of us has the intercessors he deserves. It is worth noting that the work of this great artist—I am thinking of his impressive stony landscapes done in white, black, and sepia—also inspired Nicolas de Staël. Segher's lesson is not to abandon black, not to resist it, but to embrace it, walk around it as you walk around a mountain. Black was not an enemy but an accomplice. If it was not a bridge, then it was a tunnel: if he followed it to the end, it would bring him through to the other side, to the light. Tomlinson had found the key that had seemed lost. With that key he unlocked the door so long bolted against him and entered a world that, despite its initial strangeness, he soon recognized as his own. In that world black and white proved to be rich, and the limitation on the use of materials provoked the explosion of forms and fantasy.

In the earliest drawings of this period, Tomlinson began with the method that shortly afterward he was to use in his collages: he set the image in a literary context and thus built up a system of visual echoes and verbal correspondences. It was only natural that he should have selected one of Mallarmé's sonnets in which the sea snail is a spiral of resonances and reflections. The encounter with surrealism was inevitable—not to repeat the experiences of Ernst or Tanguy but to find the route back to himself. Perhaps it would be best to quote a paragraph of the letter I mentioned before: "Why couldn't I make their world my world? But in my own terms. In poetry I had always been drawn to impersonality—how could I go beyond the self in painting?" Or put another way, how to use the surrealists' psychic automatism without lapsing into subjectivism? In poetry we accept the accident and use it even in the most conscious and premeditated works. Rhyme, for example, is an accident; it appears unsummoned but, as soon as we accept it, it turns into a choice and a rule. Tomlinson asked himself: What in painting is the equivalent of rhyme in poetry? What is *given* in the visual arts? Óscar Domínguez answered that question with his decalcomania. In fact, Domínguez was a bridge to an artist closer to Tomlinson's own sensibility. In those days he was obsessed by Gaudí and by the memory of the dining room windows in Casa Batlló. He drew them many times: What would happen if we could look out from these windows onto the landscape of the moon?

Those two impulses, Domínguez's decalcomania and Gaudí's architectural arabesques, fused. Tomlinson describes the process: "Then, I conceived of the idea of cutting and contrasting sections of a sheet of decalcomania and fitting them into the irregular window-panes. . . . Scissors! Here was the instrument for choice. I found I could draw *with* scissors, reacting *with* and *against* the decalcomania. . . . Finally I took a piece of paper, cut out the shape of Gaudí's window and moved this mask across my decalcomania until I found my moonscape. . . . The 18th of June 1970 was a day of discovery for me: I made my best arabesque of a mask, fitted it round a paint blot and then extended the idea of reflection implicit in the blot with geometric lines." Tomlinson had found, with different means from those he used in his poetry but with analogous results, a visual counterpoint for his verbal world: a counterpointing and a complement.

The quotations from Tomlinson's letter reveal with involuntary but overwhelming clarity the double function of the images, be they verbal or visual. Gaudí's windows, converted by Tomlinson into masks, that is, into objects that *conceal*, serve him to *reveal*. And what does he discover through those window-masks? Not the real world: an imaginary landscape. What began on 18 June 1970 was a fantastic morphology. A morphology and not a mythology: the places and beings that Tomlinson's collages evoke for us reveal no paradise or hell. Those skies and those caverns are not inhabited by gods or devils; they are places of the mind. To be more exact, they are places, beings, and things revealed in the darkroom of the mind. They are the product of the confabulation—in the etymological sense of that word—of accident and imagination.

Has it all been the product of chance? But what is meant by that word? Chance is never produced by chance. Chance possesses a logic—is a logic. Because we have yet to discover the rules of something, we have no reason to doubt that there are rules. If we could outline a plan, however roughly, of its involved corridors of mirrors that ceaselessly knot and unknot themselves, we would know a little more of what really matters. We would know something, for instance, about the intervention of "chance" both in scientific discoveries and artistic creation and in history and our daily life. Of course, like all artists, Tomlinson knows something: we ought to accept chance as we accept the appearance of an unsummoned rhyme.

In general, we should stress the moral and philosophical aspect of the operation: in accepting chance, the artist transforms a thing of fate into a free choice. Or it can be seen from another angle: rhyme guides the text but the text produces the rhyme. A modern superstition is that of art as transgression. The opposite seems to me truer: art transforms disturbance into a new regularity. Topology can show us something: the appearance of the accident provokes, rather than the destruction of the system, a recombination of the structure that was destined to absorb it. The structure validates the disturbance, art canonizes the exception. Rhyme is not a rupture but a binding agent, a link in the chain, without which the continuity of the text would be broken. Rhymes convert the text into a succession of auditory equivalences, just as metaphors make the poem into a texture of semantic equivalences. Tomlinson's fantastic morphology is a world ruled by verbal and visual analogies.

What we call chance is nothing but the sudden revelation of relationships between things. Chance is an aspect of analogy. Its unexpected advent provokes the immediate response of analogy, which tends to integrate the exception in a system of correspondences. Thanks to chance, we discover that silence is milk, that the stone is composed of water and wind, that ink has wings and a beak. Between the grain of corn and the lion we sense no relationship at all, until we reflect that both serve the same lord: the sun. The spectrum of relationships and affinities between things is extensive, from the interpenetration of one object with another—"the sea's edge is neither sand nor water," the poem says—to the literary comparisons linked by the word "like." Contrary to surrealist practice, Tomlinson does not juxtapose contradictory realities in order to produce a mental explosion. His method is more subtle. And his intention is distinct from theirs: he does not wish to alter reality but to achieve a *modus vivendi* with it. He is not certain that the function of imagination is to transform reality; he is certain, on the other hand, that it can make it more real. Imagination imparts a little more reality to our lives.

Spurred on by fantasy and reined in by reflection, Tomlinson's work submits to the double requirements of imagination and perception: one demands freedom and the other precision. His attempt seems to propose for itself two contradictory objectives: the saving of appearances and their destruction. The purpose is not contradictory because what it is really about is the rediscovery—more precisely, the re-living—of the original act of making. The experience of art is one of the experiences of Beginning: that archetypal moment in which, combining one set of things with another to produce a new, we reproduce the very moment of the making of the worlds. Intercommunication between the letter and the image, the decalcomania and the scissors, the window and the mask, those things that are hard-looking and those that are soft-looking, the photograph and the drawing, the hand and the compass, the reality that we see with our eyes and the reality that closes our eyes so that we see it: the search for a lost identity. Or as Tomlinson puts it best: "to reconcile the I that is with the I that I am." In the nameless, impersonal I that is, are fused the I that measures and the I that dreams, the I that thinks and the I that breathes, the I that creates and the I that destroys.

Charles Tomlinson

14. Poet as Painter

"The Poet as Painter" is not an altogether adequate title for what I want to talk about this evening. Although I can read to you from my poems, I shall not be able to show you my pictures. All I can do there is to mention the appearance of a book of my graphic work, *In Black and White*, introduced by Octavio Paz and published by Carcanet Press. Perhaps some of you were even present earlier this year at my exhibition at the Cambridge Poetry Festival. What I shall be speaking of is chiefly the *materia* the poet and painter have in common. "We live in the centre of a physical poetry," says Wallace Stevens. This is surely the basic fact that would make a poet want to paint or, if he couldn't do that, to comprehend the painter's way of regarding the physical poetry they both share. It is because of this same basic fact of "[living] in the centre of a physical poetry" that Samuel Palmer's follower, Edward Calvert, could write of "a good poem whether written or painted." "To a large extent," says Stevens, "the problems of poets are the problems of painters, and poets must often turn to the literature of painting for a discussion of their own problems." One could add to this remark of Stevens that they not only turn to the literature of painting but also help create that literature. Stevens's *Opus Posthumous* has for its epigraph a passage by Graham Bell on the integrity of Cézanne, a painter Stevens has commented on memorably more than once. Besides Stevens, Rainer Maria Rilke, D. H. Lawrence, William Carlos Williams are all poets who have written penetratingly about Cézanne. All found in him a reflection of their own problems as writers as they fought preconception and subjectivity in

---

"Poet as Painter" was delivered as an address 16 October 1975 to the Royal Society of Literature and published in their collection *Essays by Divers Hands: Innovation in Contemporary Literature*, n.s. 9, edited by Vincent Cronin, FRSL (Woodbridge, Suffolk: Boydell Press, 1979).

their art. "It is the crisis in these paintings that I recognized," says Rilke, "because I had reached it in my own work." D. H. Lawrence observes, "Cézanne felt it in paint, when he felt for the apple. Suddenly he felt the tyranny of mind, the enclosed ego in its sky-blue heaven self-painted." And Williams states, "Cézanne—The only realism in art is of the imagination. It is only thus that the work escapes plagiarism after nature and becomes a creation." So Cézanne looms gigantically over literature as well as over painting, as the forerunner of a new sensibility and a new inventiveness. Indeed, Cézanne—to traverse the common ground between poet and painter in the other direction—composed many poems of his own. As a young man, he wrote:

> A tree, shaken by raging winds,
> Waves in the air, like a gigantic corpse,
> Its naked branches which the mistral sways.

As an old man, he made good this vision in an astonishing water color that acquired the title "Bare Trees in the Fury of the Wind." Whatever the final product, the point of departure was the same: "We live in the centre of a physical poetry."

To Cézanne and his meaning for poetry I shall return. But, first, let me add to the title of my lecture, a subtitle, which will permit me to explore the center of that physical poetry in which Stevens says we live. My subtitle is "The Four Elements," and the place of exploration is the Potteries where I was born. The element that touched most persistently on the imagination there of the child as growing artist was water. For that region of smoke and blackened houses, of slag-heaps, cinder paths, pitheads, steelworks, had for its arterial system a network of canals. The canals brought back the baptismal element to a landscape by day purgatorial and by night infernal. The canals were not the only bringers of water into that place whose atmosphere, according to Arnold Bennett, was as black as its mud. One must not forget the great pools that formed in the pits where marl was dug for tile-making: as the pits were gradually abandoned, nature re-invaded, greenness appeared beside the water and fish in it. Fish! It was their existence, not just in the marl pools but in the canals, that helped bring back contemplation into lives lived out in the clatter of mines and factories. The fishing club, the Sunday matches, long hours watching the rufflings and changes of water, something both sane and mysterious came from all this. Why mysterious? Because the fisherman, if he is to be more than a random dabbler, must acquire an intuitive knowledge of the ways of fish and water, and within his stillness, at the center of his capacity to wait and to contemplate, there is a sense that is ready to strike at the exact moment, that even knows, perhaps, how to lure into its own mental orbit creatures he cannot even see under that surface on which his whole attention is concentrated. Piscator is an artist, as Walton knew. His discipline, looking out from himself, but with his inner faculties deeply roused, might make a poet or a painter of him if he had the latent powers within.

So much for water. What of earth and fire in this same Midland childhood? "The district"—the Potteries, that is—says Bennett, "comprehends the mysterious habits of fire and pure, sterile earth." He means, of course, the action of fire on the potting clay. My own most remembered and most dwelt on experience of the physical poetry of fire concerns the making of steel rather than the making of pots. And it was an experience, principally, of fire by night. When the furnaces were tapped by night, or when molten metal was poured in the great open sheds of the steel works, immense dazzling shafts of fire flared outward to be reflected in the waters of the nearby canal. Thus the remembered experience was also of fire associated with water, of fire not as the opposite of water but as mingling with it, kindling reflections in that element and also in the onlooker. To see was also to see *within*.

You gained this experience by following the canal beyond the factory established by Josiah Wedgwood in the eighteenth-century, in the place named by him Etruria. You went on until the canal cut through the center of the Shelton Bar-Iron and Steel Works. And you went by night, so as not to be seen, because children were not particularly welcome there. Etruria—Etruria Vale to give it its full name—had long since lost the nymphs one might associate with the name. But the red jets and glarings from molten steel, and from the furnaces seen in the canal, confronted one with a sense of the primal and the elemental such as nymphs themselves were once thought to symbolize in relation to landscape. And, after all, a dryad would only be a veil be-

tween yourself and a tree once your eyes had been opened by
this other more intense nakedness. For, with the soot drifting
down through the darkness onto your hair, you had experienced fire as the interior of water.

Earth, like air, fared badly in the district. "Its atmosphere as
black as its mud" was Bennett's verdict. Earth, like air, took on
the tinge of blackness. Earth was close to the sterile earth not
only of pots but also of slag-heaps and cinder paths. For all that,
gardeners coaxed miracles out of the sooty allotments that
crowned the slopes where Etruria Woods had once flourished.
As for air—air was something of a joke. There were local post-
cards showing bottle-ovens and factory chimneys all smoking at
once with dark hints of houses and perhaps a drab church-
tower. These cards carried stoical titles like, "Fresh Air from the
Potteries." At school, when the potteries "stoked-up," it was
sometimes difficult to see over to the far side of the playground.
A familiar image returns from that time, of black smoke mount-
ing from a factory chimney and, caught by the wind, fraying out
across and into the air. Air was an element that yet had to be
created there. It was, in part, the search for air, as well as
for water, that drew the fishing clubs out to the surrounding
countryside, still along those canals, that seemed to lead back
to Eden.

So of the four elements it was water that held the imagination
of the child as growing artist—water fire-tinged, water promis-
ing a cleansing, an imaginative baptism, rocking, eddying, full
of metamorphoses.

I left the district in my early twenties and subsequently lived
among many landscapes both urban and rural—London, Italy,
New Mexico, the northern United States, the Cotswolds. I think
it was Liguria and Tuscany and then Gloucestershire that taught
me the way men could be at home in a landscape. And how necessary this different view of things was, in order to place those
earlier experiences of streets that threatened to enclose you, to
shut you off from a wider and more luminous world, from intui-
tions of what Ezra Pound calls "the radiant world where one
thought cuts through another with clear edge, a world of moving energies, magnetisms that take form. . . ." I wanted to recover that "radiant world" in poems, and by doing so I seemed
to have lost touch with the Midlands. But the Midlands were al-

ways present as one term in a dialectic, as a demand for completeness subconsciously impelling the forms of one's art, even demanding *two* arts where the paradisal aspect of the visual could perhaps be rescued and celebrated.

Coming back to the Potteries almost thirty years later, I saw how much the world of my poems depended on the place, despite and because of the fact that they were an attempt to find a world of clarities, a world of unhazed senses, an intuition of Edenic freshnesses and clear perception. I tried to concentrate the history of all that into a short poem called "The Marl Pits":

> It was a language of water, light and air
>   I sought—to speak myself free of a world
> Whose stoic lethargy seemed the one reply
>   To horizons and to streets that blocked them back
> In a monotone fume, a bloom of grey.
>   I found my speech. The years return me
> To tell of all that seasoned and imprisoned:
>   I breathe familiar, sedimented air
> From a landscape of disembowellings, underworlds
>   Unearthed among the clay. Digging
> The marl, they dug a second nature
>   And water, seeping up to fill their pits,
> Sheeted them to lakes that wink and shine
>   Between tips and steeples, streets and waste
> In slow reclaimings, shimmers, balancings,
>   As if kindling Eden rescinded its own loss
> And words and water came of the same source.
>
> $\qquad\qquad\qquad\qquad\qquad\qquad$ (*WI*, 10–11)

Can my "psychoanalysis of water," to appropriate a term of Gaston Bachelard, point to any single prompting insight, any happy combination of perception and intuition that unifies the attitudes of poet and painter? Pondering this question, I remembered an early poem, "Sea Change" (*N*, 7), formally quite simple in that it seeks to catch the nature of water—this time, the sea— in a series of images, "uneasy marble," "green silk," "blue mud," then is forced to concede their inadequacy: they are like

> white wine
> Floating in a saucer of ground glass

On a pedestal of cut glass:

A static instance, therefore untrue.

(N, 7)

Much later—the better part of twenty years later—in a formally much more complex poem, "Swimming Chenango Lake," I watch a swimmer watching water. Here is an extract from the opening:

Winter will bar the swimmer soon.
 He reads the water's autumnal hesitations
A wealth of ways: it is jarred,
 It is astir already despite its steadiness,
Where the first leaves at the first
 Tremor of the morning air have dropped
Anticipating him, launching their imprints
 Outwards in eccentric, overlapping circles.
There is a geometry of water, for this
 Squares off the clouds' redundances
And sets them floating in a nether atmosphere
 All angles and elongations: every tree
Appears a cypress as it stretches there
 And every bush that shows the season,
A shaft of fire. It is a geometry and not
 A fantasia of distorting forms, but each
Liquid variation answerable to the theme
 It makes away from, plays before:
It is a consistency, the grain of the pulsating flow. . . .

(WW, 3)

I pondered this passage, along with that earlier poem "Sea Change," to find out the constant that governed my attitude as poet and painter. Poems based like this—as are the many landscape poems I have written—on exposure to and observation of the fleeting moments of visual sensation; poems that endeavor to catch this fleeting freshness and unite it to a stable form where others may share in it; poems such as these look away from the merely personal. And so does painting where the presence of the external world is strongly felt, where the painter is concerned—I quote Rilke on Cézanne—with "the incarnation of the world *as a thing carrying conviction*, the portrayal of a reality become imperishable through his experiencing of the object." To make the reality of water imperishable! The painter must acquire great formal power to achieve that: he who looks into water, and into the changing world of perception that water represents, looks into the heart of time.

Cézanne himself was very conscious of this problem for the painter—how to reconcile sensation and form without bullying your picture into a willful unity, a triumph of personality at the expense of a truth to relationship: "There mustn't be a single link too loose," Joachim Gasquet reports him as saying,

> not a crevice through which may escape the emotion, the light, the truth. . . . All that we see disperses, vanishes; is it not so? Nature is always the same, but nothing remains of it, nothing of what comes to our sight. Our art ought to give the shimmer of duration with the elements, the appearance of all its changes. It ought to make us taste it eternally. . . . My canvas joins hands. . . . But if I feel the least distraction, the least weakness, above all if I interpret too much one day . . . if I intervene, why then everything is gone.

Long before I read that conversation with Gasquet, I wrote a poem called "Cézanne at Aix," a kind of manifesto poem where I wanted my poetry to take its ethic of perception from Cézanne, an ethic distrustful of the drama of personality of which romantic art had made so much, an ethic where, by trusting to sensation, we enter being, and experience its primal fullness on terms other than those we dictate:

> And the mountain: each day
> Immobile like fruit. Unlike, also
> —Because irreducible, because
> Neither a component of the delicious
> And therefore questionable,
> Nor distracted (as the sitter)
> By his own pose and, therefore,
> Doubly to be questioned: it is not
> Posed. It is. Untaught
> Unalterable, a stone bridgehead
> To that which is tangible
> Because unfelt before. There
> In its weathered weight
> Its silence silences, a presence
> Which does not present itself.

> (*SIB*, 34)

What impressed me about Cézanne, and what on my own humbler level I wanted for poetry, was the entire absence of self-regard. "Cézanne's apples," says D. H. Lawrence, "are a real attempt to let the apple exist in its own separate entity, without transfusing it with personal emotion." Cézanne must surely have felt the narrowing lure of what Lawrence calls "personal emotion" here. Cézanne *in himself* was threatened by misunderstanding, neglect, ill health and was prone to deep melancholy. Had he chosen to ignore nature or merely to dramatize that self and impose it on nature, his pictures would have wanted the liberating Mediterranean radiance that we find there. Even his self-portraits lack introspection. Rilke, once more, supplies the classic comment. He writes to his wife, "How great and incorruptible this objectivity of his gaze was, is confirmed in an almost touching manner by the circumstance that, without analyzing or in the remotest degree regarding his expression from a superior standpoint, he made a replica of himself with so much humble objectiveness, with the credulity and extrinsic interest and attention of a dog which sees itself in the mirror and thinks: there is another dog."

In speaking of Cézanne's incorruptible objectivity, it is clear that Rilke was not thinking of the purely imaginary and outmoded objectivity of nineteenth-century positivistic science—the objectivity that supposed a complete division between the observer and the observed. The objectivity with which Rilke credits Cézanne implied an outward gaze that would draw the sensuous world closer to the inner man and that would narrow the gap between abstraction and sensation, between intellect and things. As Merleau-Ponty reflects in his great essay "Eye and Mind"—an essay that begins by quoting Gasquet's book on Cézanne—"Quality, light, colour, depth which are there before us, are there only because they awaken an echo in our body and because the body welcomes them. . . . Things have an internal equivalent in me; they arouse in me a carnal formula of their presence."

So much for Merleau-Ponty. I wanted to earn the right to use the artistic ethic of Cézanne as a basis for poetry, and I believe it made possible to me a range from natural landscape to civic landscape. It seemed to me a sort of religion, a bringing of things to stand in the light of origin, a way, even, of measuring the tragic fall from plenitude in our own urban universe. But let me make a confession. As a painter, I could find no direct way of using this inheritance. I confronted the four elements, but the only way I could resolve them in paint was to will their cohesion, to intervene, to put personal pressure on my forms in the shape of an anxious black outline. Time and again, I would approach the expression of some realization, only to disfigure it with black. I could find no way of letting the given suggest to me forms that could elude the preconceptions of the too-conscious mind and the too-conscious hand, blackening nature as surely as the factory chimneys of my boyhood had blackened it. Black became an obsession. Although I continued to draw, little by little I lapsed from painting, partly under pressure from this insoluble dilemma, partly because the time that might have gone to finding an answer went into earning a living. For fifteen years, almost nothing except the poems; then, in 1970, after a renewed, intensive spell of drawing, a solution appeared almost casually.

I think, once more, of Wallace Stevens, and that entry in his *Adagia* that reads, "The aspects of earth of interest to a poet are the casual ones, as light or colour, images." By "casual," I take it that he refers to the fortuitous nature of art—the way one may find its deepest meaning on a dull street corner, in an old pair of shoes, in the chance conjunction of the totally unforeseen and the apparently unrelated. Suddenly things knit up—the canvas joins hands, in Cézanne's words. You cease to impose and you discover, to rephrase another aphorism of Stevens. And you discover apparently by chance. But what is chance? And if one accepts it, does it not cease to be chance?

The element of chance that helped resolve my problems as a painter was the surrealist device known as a decalcomania. Briefly, the recipe for this is the one drawn up by Óscar Domínguez in 1936: "By means of a thick brush, spread out black gouache more or less diluted in places, upon a sheet of glossy white paper, and cover at once with a second sheet, upon which exert an even pressure. Lift off the second sheet without haste." Well, the result of this process, as the pigment separates out into random patterns, can be a lot of wasted paper, occasionally a very beautiful entire image, sometimes interesting fragments that prompt and defy the imagination to compose them into a picture. You can alter what is given with a brush, or you can both alter and recombine your images by going to work with scissors and paste and making a collage. The weakness of this technique is that it can lead to a flaccid fantasy of imaginary animals, or of lions turning into bicycles. Its strength lies in its challenge to mental sets, in the very impersonality of the material offered you and that you must respond to. A very unCézannian undertaking, and yet what I have called the ethic of Cézanne—submission to the given, the desire to break with preconceived images of the given, the desire to seize on and stabilize momentary appearances—this ethic, once applied, can lead your decalcomania away from the arbitrariness of fantasy toward the threshold of new perceptions.

I had followed Domínguez very literally: "Spread out black gouache," he says. Max Ernst, using this technique for the basis of some of his best pictures, clearly employs several colors. Almost blindly, I reached for my old enemy, black. I continued to use it and to use that color only. The first move was to paint the black on to a wet surface and the first thing you saw was the strokes of pigment fraying out into the water just as the smoke of your childhood had frayed out into the air. There seemed an odd rhyme here between the one experience and the other. And as I covered sheet after sheet, altered, blotted, painted with brush, finger-tips, pieces of string, and then cut up and recombined, I saw black become dazzling: I saw the shimmer of water, light and air take over from the merely fortuitous: I saw that I was working now as poet *and* painter once more.

The "merely" fortuitous! *There* is a theme for them both: the fact that "chance" rhymes with "dance" is a nutrifying thought for either poet or painter. As is that other fortuity, that in the south of England, they are pronounced "darnce" and "charnce," a source of wonder to the Midlander, as no doubt *his* pronunciation is to the southerner. There seems no intrinsic reason why these two words should have much to do with each other. And there seems no intrinsic reason, either, why the strokes of a brush covered in pigment, the dabbing of a paint-covered finger, the dashes, slashes, or dots a painter makes, should have much to do with a face, a landscape, a stone, or a skull. Turner grew an immensely long eagle's talon of a thumbnail in order to scratch out lights in his watercolors. It seems fortuitous that these jabbings into the surface of watercolor paper should come to represent luminosity.

"Chance" undoubtedly rhymes with "dance," and meditation on this fact feeds the mind: chance occurrences, chance meetings invade what we do every day, and yet they are drawn into a sort of pattern, as they crisscross with our feeling of what we are, as they remind us of other happenings or strengthen our sense of future possibility. Poetry is rather like this, also. Something seemingly fortuitous sets it off—a title, say, out of the blue, asking for a poem to go with it, a title like "The Chances of Rhyme," and you find yourself writing on the back of an envelope:

> The chances of rhyme are like the chances of meeting—
> In the finding fortuitous, but once found, binding. . . .

Already, you have started to knit up those chances, with "finding" and "binding" reinforcing the pattern, and before long the chances of rhyme are becoming the continuities of thought, and you continue writing:

> To take chances, as to make rhymes
> Is human, but between chance and impenitence
> (A half-rhyme) come dance, vigilance
> And circumstance. . . .

Yes, that makes sense. It seems to be getting somewhere: a pattern in the words, a pattern in the thought, a pattern in the way the line settles mostly for four main stresses, sometimes stretches to five, mostly dances back to four. To handle measure thus seems a human thing to do: your recurrences are never so pat as to seem simply mechanical, your outgrowths never so rambling or brambled as to spread to mere vegetation. A human measure, surrounded by surprises, impenetrable and unknowable, but always reasserting itself, this could be a salutary aim—one in which rhythm and tone are both allies—faced as we always are by the temptation to exaggerate and to overvalue the claims of self:

"The Chances of Rhyme"

The chances of rhyme are like the chances of meeting—
    In the finding fortuitous, but once found, binding:
They say, they signify and they succeed, where to succeed
    Means not success, but a way forward
If unmapped, a literal, not a royal succession;
    Though royal (it may be) is the adjective or region
That we, nature's royalty, are led into.
    Yes. We are led, though we seem to lead
Through a fair forest, an Arden (a rhyme
    For Eden)—breeding ground for beasts
Not bestial, but loyal and legendary, which is more
    Than nature's are. Yet why should we speak
Of art, of life, as if the one were all form
    And the other all Sturm-und-Drang? And I think
Too, we should confine to Crewe or to Mow
    Cop, all those who confuse the fortuitousness
Of art with something to be met with only
    At extremity's brink, reducing thus
Rhyme to a kind of rope's end, a glimpsed grass
    To be snatched at as we plunge past it—
Nostalgic, after all, for a hope deferred.
    To take chances, as to make rhymes
Is human, but between chance and impenitence
    (A half-rhyme) come dance, vigilance
And circumstance (meaning all that is there
    Besides you, when you are there). And between
Rest-in-peace and precipice,
    Inertia and perversion, come the varieties
Increase, lease, re-lease (in both
    Senses); and immersion, conversion—of inert
Mass, that is, into energies to combat confusion.
    Let rhyme be my conclusion.

                           (*WW*, 59)

Painting wakes up the hand, draws in your sense of muscular
coordination, your sense of the body, if you like. Poetry also, as
it pivots on its stresses, as it rides forward over the line-endings,
or comes to rest at pauses *in* the line, poetry also brings the

whole man into play and his bodily sense of himself. But there is no near, actual equivalent in painting for tone and rhythm adjusted by line lengths and by pauses within and at the ends of lines. There is no near equivalent because the medium is so very different. You may write with a pencil, but once you come to draw with it, what a diverse end those marks serve. But the fortuitous element is still there—the element of meeting something you didn't expect, something that isn't yourself. And once you attend to it, whatever you are starts to see an interesting challenge to its own relaxed complacency. Quite by accident you find, on a beach, the skull of a sea bird, for instance. You could put it in a cabinet or forget it in a safe place, but instead you draw it. You begin to know far more about the structure of that particular skull, as eye and pencil try to keep up with each other.

There is a lot, though, you can't know about—the mysterious darkness of its interior, the intriguing and impenetrable holes and slots where something or other has now rotted away and left a clean emptiness. The cleanliness, the natural geometry of the skull suggest the idea of surrounding it in a geometry of your own—carefully ruled lines that set off the skull, that extend it, that bed it in a universe of contrasting lines of force. Just as rhyme dancing with thought led you through to a world of human values, so skull and line build up and outward into a containing universe.

Now, there is something very resistant about this skull. You feel you could etch a very tiny poem on it called, perhaps, "To Be Engraved on the Skull of a Cormorant." To do so you would have to be both tough and careful with it—

> as searching as the sea
> that picked and pared
> this head yet spared
> its frail acuity.
> (WW, 45)

And so you go on to write a whole poem:

> across the thin
> façade, the galleried-
> with-membrane head:

narrowing, to take
the eye-dividing
declivity where
the beginning beak
prepares for flight
in a still-
perfect salience:
here, your glass
needs must stay
steady and your gross
needle re-tip
itself with reticence
but be
as searching as the sea
that picked and pared
this head yet spared
its frail acuity.

(WW, 45)

And so a poem comes out of this find, as well as drawings. But that interior darkness goes on bothering you. How could I relate it, you think, to the little universe my lines netted together around it?

This particular problem was solved by forgetting about it. Or by seeming to forget and doing something else. Three years after making a drawing, "Long-beaked Skull," I did a decalcomania-collage called "The Sleep of Animals": here two skulls are filled by a dream of the landscapes the bird and animal presences have been moving through. The dream articulates the darkness. I try to suggest a whole world in each head. There is the hint that this sleep is, perhaps, death in which both the head and nature are now one.

In writing poetry, you sometimes run aground on silence, and it takes months or sometimes years to learn what it is you wish to say. In the meantime, you are half-consciously turning the problem over, while, at the same time, furthering the knowledge of your medium. Among the techniques I had worked with between "Long-beaked Skull" and "The Sleep of Animals" were those I have described—collage and decalcomania. I had suddenly seen something rather like—though not yet *much* like—

two skulls merged in the landscape of my decalcomania, my chaos of crushed pigment floating in water. Instead of continuing to paint, once the sheet had dried, I cut out the skulls with scissors, glued new shapes on to them, then fitted them into a quite rigorous design held together by ruled lines, and called it "The Sleep of Animals." I realized I had discovered a response to the dark, unenterable interior of that first bird's skull. My response seemed to have arrived instantaneously, but—again like poetry—the formal pattern had taken up chance elements, had been the result of conscious and subconscious processes and of that strange, unifying movement of recognition when, reaching for the scissors, what I'd found became what I'd chosen. "Chance" rhymed with "dance" once more.

Why, as an artist, should one return so obsessively to the shape of the skull, whether animal or human? I do not believe that one comes back to it merely as a *memento mori*—though *that* element is present too. What seems equally important is the skull seen as a piece of architecture. It resembles a house with lit façade and shadowy interior. However much it possesses of bleak finality, it always involves one in the fascination of inside and outside, that primary lure of the human mind seeking to go beyond itself, taking purchase on the welcoming or threatening surfaces of the world, and both anxious and enriched because of the sense of what lies behind or beneath those surfaces. I tried to make this knowledge present to myself in many drawings, particularly of animal skulls. I tried also to articulate this knowledge with words, in the form of poem-in-prose called "Skullshapes."

Skulls. Finalities. They emerge towards new beginnings from undergrowth. Along with stones, fossils, flint keel-scrapers and spokeshaves, along with bowls of clay pipes heel-stamped with their makers' marks, comes the rural detritus of cattle skulls brought home by children. They are moss-stained, filthy with soil. Washing them of their mottlings, the hand grows conscious of weight, weight sharp with jaggednesses. Suspend them from a nail and one feels the boneclumsiness go out of them: there is weight still in their vertical pull downwards from the nail, but there is also a hanging fragility. The two qualities fuse and the brush translates this fusion as wit, where leg-like appendages conclude the skulls' dangling mass.

Shadow explores them. It sockets the eye-holes with black. It reaches like fingers into the places one cannot see. Skulls are a keen instance of this duality of the visible: it borders what the eye cannot make out, it transcends itself with the suggestion of all that is there beside what lies within the eyes' possession: it cannot be possessed. Flooded with light, the skull is at once manifest surface and labyrinth of recesses. Shadow reaches down out of this world of helmeted cavities and declares it.

One sees. But not merely the passive mirrorings of the retinal mosaic—nor, like Ruskin's blind man struck suddenly by vision, without memory or conception. The senses, reminded by other seeings, bring to bear on the act of vision their pattern of images; they give point and place to an otherwise naked and homeless impression. It is the mind sees. But what it sees consists not solely of that by which it is confronted grasped in the light of that which it remembers. It sees possibility.

The skulls of birds, hard to the touch, are delicate to the eye. Egglike in the round of the skull itself and as if the spherical shape were the result of an act like glass-blowing, they resist the eyes' imaginings with the blade of the beak which no lyrical admiration can attenuate to frailty.

The skull of nature is recess and volume. The skull of art—of possibility—is recess, volume and also lines—lines of containment, lines of extension. In seeing, one already extends the retinal impression, searchingly and instantaneously. Brush and pen extend the search beyond the instant, touch discloses a future. Volume, knived across by the challenge of a line, the raggedness of flaking bone countered by ruled, triangular facets, a cowskull opens a visionary field, a play of universals.

(WW, 51–52)

In both graphic and poetic art, I like something lucid surrounded by something mysterious. I see poems and pictures as the place where the civilized, discriminating faculties and the sense of the elemental, of origins, reinforce each other. I go back, time and again, to the idea of a seascape

> with illegible depths
> and lucid passages,
> bestiary of stones,
> book without pages . . .
> ("On Water," *WrW*, 3)

and a poem seems to be composing itself that could well be a picture, or several pictures:

> "Furrow" is inexact:
> no ship could be

converted to a plough
travelling this vitreous ebony:

seal it in sea-caves and
you cannot still it:
image on image bends
where half-lights fill it

with illegible depths
and lucid passages,
bestiary of stones,
book without pages:

and yet it confers
as much as it denies:
we are orphaned and fathered
by such solid vacancies:
            (*WrW*, 3)

When words seem too abstract, then I find myself painting the
sea with the very thing it is composed of—water, and allowing
its thinning and separation of the pigment to reveal an image of
its own nature. I spoke earlier of bringing things to stand in the
light of origin. When you paint with water and are painting the
image of water, you return to it, as to all primal things, with a
sense of recognition—water! We came from this. "Human tears,"
says the scientist, "are a re-creation of the primordial ocean
which, in the first stages of evolution, bathed the first eyes."
Perhaps the carnal echo that the contemplation of water awakens
in us sounds over those immense distances of time. Or if that
thought is too fanciful, when from the ruck and chaos of black
paint I find myself paradoxically creating a world of water, light
and air, perhaps that same chance is somewhere present in the
deed, which led a boy by night along a dark canal in a blackened
city and showed him fire unquenchably burning within water.
    I conclude with a final poem, entitled "At Stoke":

I have lived in a single landscape. Every tone
        And turn have had for their ground
    These beginnings in grey-black: a land
        Too handled to be primary—all the same,

The first in feeling. I thought it once
    Too desolate, diminished and too tame
To be the foundation for anything. It straggles
    A haggard valley and lets through
Discouraged greennesses, lights from a pond or two.
    By ash-tips, or where the streets give out
In cindery in-betweens, the hills
    Swell up and free of it to where, behind
The whole vapoury, patched battlefield,
    The cows stand steaming in an acrid wind.
This place, the first to seize on my heart and eye,
    Has been their hornbook and their history.

(WI, 5)

Cloudheads (1970)

Part IV

Postscript

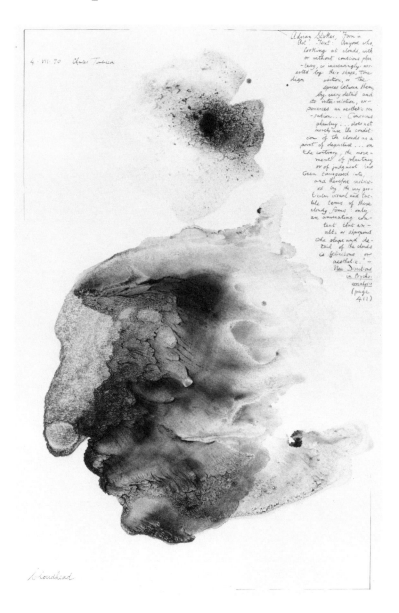

Richard Swigg and Charles Tomlinson

15. Tomlinson at Sixty

Richard Swigg and Charles Tomlinson first discussed some of the issues of this interview after a recording session at the University of Keele, where Tomlinson is currently putting all his poems on tape. Swigg, who is supervising this undertaking, then compiled a list of questions, and, back in Gloucestershire, Tomlinson wrote his answers to them.

RS Do you feel that making these recordings for Keele and so close to the place where you were born—Stoke-on-Trent—has taken you back to beginnings?

CT It has in several ways. It's made me sense the continuity with those days when I was at school here and starting dimly to apprehend, while studying French, German, and Latin in wartime, that Europe existed and that in trying to write, as I did round about sixteen, I was joining in something bigger than myself, that, as a boy from an ordinary English background, I was entering into conversation with all those mighty foreigners we'd been learning to read—Ovid, Racine, Hugo, Lamartine, Baudelaire, Heine, Rilke. I was particularly lucky in having extremely well-educated teachers of French and German. What schoolboy in Stoke in 1986 has started on Baudelaire *and* Rilke? Cecil Scrimgeour, our French master—someone very active in the WEA in these parts—and one of the finest teachers ever, also gave us marvelous classes on tragedy. I think one of the most moving experiences I had was when he was explaining Aristotle's *Poetics* to us and suddenly I found my heart was beating

Richard Swigg, Senior Lecturer in English at the University of Keele, England, is the author of *Lawrence, Hardy, and American Literature.* He has written numerous articles on Tomlinson and has supervised the recording by Tomlinson of his collected poems.

twenty to the dozen just at the thought that here I was in fifth century B.C. Athens on Thursday afternoon bandying around words like catharsis and anagnorisis. I looked out the window and there was the same old potbank smoking away down the street.

RS Did you feel your education drew you away from your home background?

CT My parents believed in education, and so what successes I had were a pleasure to them. We must have been a more sensible lot in Stoke than that lot up in Leeds, to judge from the way the poet Tony Harrison writes. We were virtually all working-class children—I hardly knew what the middle classes were till I got to Cambridge—and no teacher ever tried, as in Harrison's case, to change my accent—and this was a grammar school, mind you, nothing experimental about it. Also, you'd never have used a term like "working class" to describe yourself. You might have spoken of working people, ordinary people. Working class is one of those labels dear to the theoretical, and it covers up immense differences. I notice that Harrison's father had a telephone and used to spit in the fire. My father never rose to the first and he'd never have descended to the second. At school we didn't know what snobbery was. We knew there *were* snobs, of course, but we were sure they all lived in Newcastle-under-Lyme, not in the five towns. Certainly there was a narrowness and constriction about things, but I think it was more a growing out of certain rather stale attitudes than a self-conscious rejection of anything that one went through. It was far more organic, I mean, than most publicized accounts of the process admit. You have only to know France and Italy to realize that the English "class system" is one of the more fluid aspects of our culture.

RS Was it entirely because of the schools that poetry came into the story?

CT Largely it was. Nobody at home ever told me to go and read it. But my mother had a collected Tennyson she'd been given as a prize for home nursing (do they give nurses such prizes nowadays?), and my father had a volume of Robert W. Service and could quote the more reactionary bits of Rudyard Kipling. My grandmother—his mother—actually knew whole stretches of Scott's "Marmion," and she could recite all of Thomas Hood's "The Song of the Shirt," which she taught me as a child. She also owned a Moxon's edition of Cowper and so had by heart "John Gilpin," and it was from her I learned Cowper's phrase about "the cups / That cheer but not inebriate," so it's possible she got as far as book four of "The Task"! It's odd how these bits add up. For years I brooded on one of her phrases from "Marmion," "If I were in Lord Stanley's case. . . ." It was the word "in" that gave me much to think about. What Scott actually wrote was "place" not "case," as I discovered years later, but it was her version that mattered. And I was very struck by one of the lines from Thomas Hood, "And so with a voice of dolorous pitch"—it was the bringing together of "dolorous" and "pitch" and the rhythm of the whole line that haunted me and disturbed me. "In poverty, hunger and dirt" got me too—I felt then that "dirt" was a very daring word to use in a poem.

RS   Some of your finest poems have been concerned with rediscovery—that is, the finding of lost pathways, traditions, places, vitalities. Does the title of your new book signal a continuation of this theme in the poems?

CT   *The Return*, the title of this new book, goes back to and tries to gather up the meaning of the experience of beginning to write poems (my first real poems) in Italy in 1950–1951. This wasn't Tuscany, but Liguria, and it was close to a relatively poor village, La Serra. It was there I met a young poet, Paolo Bertolani. We were both writing our first things. He was unemployed and so was I, having rather unjustly lost the job I'd come out to take up. So when I got to England and eventually wrote "Up at La Serra" (the first of several political poems), my own fate and that of Paolo seemed closely bound up together. We then lost contact. But both of us managed to climb out of our dead end, as I realized over twenty years later when I found something by him in a magazine and at once got in touch. Like me, he was married with two girls. Unlike me, he was in the police force—and living in the same village. He's gone on to sound out the vitalities of the place in many poems and in a fine prose book. My own long poem, "The Return," celebrates our "deprived" youth, which turns out to have been full of unsuspected possibilities, and it's also an elegy for his wife, who was dying painfully and lengthily in the next room while he was at work on his last book. "The Return" tries to weigh up two poetic careers that began, as Paolo puts it, "in una Liguria minima," and that weren't going to be minimized. He dug down and in and I reached out as far afield as America and Mexico.

RS While Italy, with its land and people, has clearly had a major presence in the work from the early poems onward, what of Italian art itself, especially poetry? I am thinking here of Ungaretti's effect on you.

CT I taught myself Italian by trying to read Montale—Ungaretti came later. Montale had begun working in Liguria, too, and also out of a sense of constriction. His was a great lesson in integrity, but, like Eliot, he was the sort of poet who could hang very heavily on a younger writer. The sheer weight of his introversion and then the mysticism and worship of an absent ideal—a sort of modern re-working of *la donna* of the *dolce stil nuovo*—were utterly foreign to the habits of both myself and Paolo. Yet when I came to that part of "The Return" which characterizes Graziella, Paolo's wife, I was conscious of, as it were, glancing at Montale's own fine "Xenia" sequence, about *his* dead wife. I think it's interesting that Montale quotes there from the libretto of *Trovatore* and was a great admirer of Verdi, as I am. In Verdi there's not only the blackest pessimism but also a sort of animal resilience and a tense grace in the melodic line. Then, at the end of his life, out from under the whole heap—the heap of dead bodies, you might almost say, that, in life, had included his first wife and his children—emerges *Falstaff*, the greatest comic opera of them all.

But you asked me about Ungaretti. I read Ungaretti next, on the rocks of Liguria. And I found in his verse something that was to be brought home for me by the work of William Carlos Williams—how you can use extremely short lines, can fragment the verse line to get out of it a certain pulse and excitement in the way the whole poem runs. I even went ahead and translated a *Selected Poems* of Ungaretti—that was in the sixties—but, though I'd talked to him about it in great cordiality, he quietly sold his rights to Penguin and the next thing I knew, there was Patrick Creagh's excellent Penguin translation blocking my path. But it didn't matter. I'd learned what I needed—mostly from the early poems. There's a dreadful religiosity about some of the later things, a kind of wailing Petrarchanism, that had already tempered my enthusiasm. Though it's not there in the excellent poem about the death of his son, "You Were Shattered," ("*Tu ti spezzasti*"), which has, if you like, a sort of Verdian inconsolability and a ferocious resentment running together. At all events, most of the Ungaretti poems that really meant anything to me are available now in my Oxford University Press volume, *Translations*.

RS You spoke of how you learned to fragment the poetic line. Has your way of seeing been sharpened by your early fascination with cinema—that art of fragmenting and recombining and setting moving again?

CT I was obsessed by cinema. The kind of fluidity of movement and clarity of image I tried for cannot but have been nourished by one of the first really ambitious films I ever saw (and re-saw), Welles's *Citizen Kane*. I thought Gregg Toland's deep-focus photography there the most thrilling thing I'd ever set eyes on—to have all the levels in focus like that, right out to the small boy who is playing in the snow beyond the window while the main scene is taking place inside the room and close to the camera . . . I found it breathtaking, as I did the camera movements down staircases and across the expanses of Xanadu, Kane's house, and, later, in the seriously truncated ballroom scene of Welles's *The Magnificent Ambersons*. Even in that late, poorish film *A Touch of Evil*, Welles has a stunning opening sequence—an extended crane-shot that shows a car journey across a Mexican town—where the fluidity of the moving camera meshes with the almost balletic countermovement of pedestrians, a traffic policeman, other cars. It was Welles's fluidity combined with sharpness of focus that got me in *Kane*. I imagine even the glass paperweight in my poem on Trotsky's assassination evolved from the glass ball with the snowstorm inside it in the movie.

RS Do I take it, with your fondness for deep focus and crane-shots, your interest in film was chiefly technical?

CT Well, it *was* that, but much more than that. It was really philosophical. Let me try to explain. At the time I'm speaking of—the late forties—I thought cinema vastly more important than the novel—the novel after Joyce and Lawrence, that is (not so *outré* a point of view, actually, given one's tender age and the state of the novel in England). I looked at life much more intently via the cinema, but I went to the cinema to question as well as to admire. We had that great deluge of French films (some of them held up by the war)—Duvivier, Marcel Carné, Cocteau. But I came to feel and to resent the terrible, sapping fatalism of some of those films. They were technically well put together, and the more technically competent they became—I'm thinking of Carné's *Les Portes de la Nuit* with its shots of the Paris underground—the more grandly fatalistic they seemed to be. In the end, I came to prefer outsiders like Jean Vigo and his picture about life on the river barge, *L'Atalante*, where there's a real fight against fate, and his almost surreal film *Zéro de Conduite*, both from the mid-thirties. Indeed, I was rather taken by the surrealist cinema of the twenties and thirties, pictures like Dulac's *The Seashell and the Clergyman*, scripted by Artaud, Man Ray's *L'Étoile de la Mer*, then early Buñuel, particularly *Un Chien Andalou* and *L'Age d'Or*, and the ability of these films to move so surprisingly and rapidly from one image to the next. But finally I came to feel there was a fatalism in them, too, a mere surrender to the fortuitous and to a fluidity in which there was not enough resistance. I had to write a script of my own, along surrealist lines, to see that. This was a phantasmagoria, *The Lepidopterist*, about two children who are menaced in a garden by a mad butterfly hunter—it was somewhere between (God help us) Maeterlinck and *Dr. Caligari*, with a dash of Buñuel. Once I had it onto paper (I couldn't get anywhere near actual film-making because of the union's closed-shop policy), I saw clearly the trap of fatality—in the closing sequence a death's head moth (shades of *Chien Andalou*) gets bigger and bigger and turns into an actual skull that enlarges on the screen into massive close-up. No way to go after that but start again. So I did. I wrote another, a much longer, *Kane*-influenced script about some technocratic giant (he had a dwarf for a son, purloined from the Cocteau-Delannoy *Éternel Retour*) obsessed with harnessing the wind. He and his contraption are finally blown off a mountain by nature, who is having no more nonsense. I re-wrote the thing as a novel, *Project*

95, then decided I'd better have no more nonsense myself and started *looking* at things—smaller projects, apples, rain on the window, water, and they led back into the bigger picture—no longer a movie, but a poem! Nature—the nature of *Project 95*—was just another fatalism that was going to "solve things." One more illusion gone! To sum up my answer to your question, I admired the ability of cinema to cope with flux and movement, but I had to find my own terms whereby it wasn't all a rush into non-entity or a luxurious death-pact with fate. After all, we were at the end of a war and Europe did feel pretty smashed up and worn down even though old Adolf was off the scene.

RS From smashed up Europe, when did your thoughts actually turn to America, which is so important in your later work?

CT Not for some time. It was really accidental. The first "Americanism" was the poetic influence of Stevens, but also of Marianne Moore. Her tart tones seemed extremely tonic when Dylan of the Golden Voice was hamming away. It was the tone of American poetry that helped me beyond another luxurious romanticism—after all, I quite liked Thomas when I was up at Cambridge. And he was, of course, a genuine talent, but with bad habits of style and character. The lesson of Moore and early Stevens—mostly the more imagist poems of *Harmonium*—left me with a book on hand, *Seeing Is Believing* (1958), which I simply couldn't place in England. Just about everybody said no. Then Hugh Kenner, who had discovered and reviewed *The Necklace* (1955), with enormous generosity placed it for me with his own publisher in New York. Quite unexpectedly, I was offered a traveling fellowship on the strength of *Seeing Is Believing* and poems published in *Poetry* (Chicago), and found myself, along with Italo Calvino, Gunter Grass, Fernando Arrabal, given *carte blanche*—and money—to go wherever I wanted in the States. So that began a long and fruitful relationship with America, particularly the Southwest and ultimately Mexico. Indeed, *The Return* goes back over all that territory too. It's as if I have to keep faithfully going back and feeling out once more all the links—La Serra, Albuquerque, the desert, Chimayó, Oaxaca, so you get a bit of all of them in several of the books and perhaps even more so in *The Return*, where the American experience is still being balanced up against those youthful days in Italy.

RS We've spoken of film. But what about another art: music? In a poem of the 1950s, "Antecedents," you saw Wagner as the embodiment of one kind of romantic expression from which you diverge. Yet other kinds of music—would you agree?—seem to have been crucial to your sense of poetry.

CT That's true enough, but I feel bound to say that Wagner was crucial too. The other kinds of music—and you're probably thinking of Webern and Schoenberg—were a reaction to Wagner, but without sacrificing the astonishing orchestral range and timbres (think of Webern's *Six Pieces for Orchestra*) Wagner made possible. And where would Mahler (another unavoidable romantic) have been without the extension of tonality in *Tristan*? "He is a master of miniature," said Nietzsche of Wagner, and, I suppose, among other things, it's the miniaturism—the passages of extremely refined and delicate orchestration—that appealed to Mahler (appealed also to Debussy, even when he'd become an anti-Wagnerite). And when all is said and done, Wagner is full of extraordinary insights, wonderful forestial vistas (think what Bruckner got from those), little touches that sometimes last hardly a moment. "This monster full of detail," says Thomas Mann. It's the detail that appears . . . And yet what broadscale invention there is, too—think of the dynamic compactness of *Rheingold*, opening at the bottom of the Rhine and ending with the rainbow bridge into Valhalla, held in brilliant ironic focus by the fire god Loge's commentary—there's diagnostic art for you. It's as if in *Rheingold* Wagner just forgets about himself, loses himself in telling the story; it's as diagnostic of overweaning egotism as (say) *Kane* is—both of them, at some level, a self-diagnosis.

But, yes, you're right. I'd discovered Webern and Schoenberg just when I started fragmenting my lines, spacing them out with breath-pauses and hesitations, caught up very consciously into the fabric of the whole, like Webern's use of silences. I also enjoyed John Cage's lecture *On Nothing* (rather more than his music except for some early things for prepared piano), which is a sort of talkathon arranged around silences ("I have nothing to say / and I am saying it / and that is / poetry . . ."). He breaks up his sentences, lets in the pauses, actually makes you see that silence as well as the words is a created thing—"What we re-quire / is / silence / ; / but what silence re-quires / is / that I go on talking / . / . . ."

It's all very witty and more than witty. I suppose this kind of thing could become tediously self-conscious, as some Cage is, though he seems to be attacking the idea of self—certainly the egotistical sublime. Anyhow, I read that Cage at the right moment. Perhaps just as important as all this, but in ways I find hard to explain—something to do basically with rhythm and melodic line, I imagine—is the fact that I listen to a *lot* of music. I think I shocked Geoffrey Hill when I suggested listening to Rossini. I had in mind the marvelous Mediterranean clarity and—in the best sense—superficiality (not meddling, not moaning, forgetting the Big Questions), which is close to Anglo-Saxon common sense, after all. Interesting, isn't it, that the song Kane's mistress sings is Rossini's "*Una voce poco fa!*"

RS You've confessed to being drawn to romanticism—Wagner, Bruckner, Mahler. Is there a discrepancy here with the fact that some critics have spoken of your "Augustan" qualities as a poet, and with your involvement with Dryden and Pope?

CT You see, I don't think there is this clean break, anyway, between the Augustans and romanticism. What could be more "romantic"—surreal, if you like—than Dryden's feeling for Ovid and for metamorphosis? His greatest work—his Ovid translations—pivots on all that. I find Pope as sensuous as Keats and I find his "Eloisa to Abelard" more passionate—if that's one of the measures of romanticism—than Shelley, whose passions are too often self-induced and shrill. But Pope, unlike a lot of Shelley, can place his own sexual feelings, his tracing of art and eroticism to common sources, within a framework which isn't resonating all the time to "me, me, me!" So what critics call "Augustanism" in my case is probably the attempt to situate all I've learned from romanticism—and this means not just Wagner and Mahler, but Wordsworth, Coleridge (particularly the conversation poems), Constable, Turner—within reach of a distrust of the ego, within reach of a flexible awareness that, no, you can't have things *your* way all or even most of the time, you must respect what is other than you as you respect people in a conversation. You don't want to bawl them down and you don't want to bawl down the universe. But you do want an awareness of things that is both passionate and balanced.

RS You've been called a religious poet. Do you think this is a helpful description or possibly a misleading one?

CT The trouble is that, sooner or later, you're going to be dragged willy-nilly into somebody's fold of believers and asked to sign on the dotted line and to subscribe to however many articles it is one is supposed to believe in. I happen to think, with Santayana, that "religious doctrines would do well to withdraw their pretension to be dealing with fact." It's no longer possible to reinstate seventeenth century, basically medieval criteria of belief—criteria from times when it was virtually possible to believe *anything*. It seems to me that my poetry is religious in the sense that I am awed by things that exceed my grasp and I am awed by the mystery of a universe that refuses to be tidied away. And this brings one back to that vexed question of the poet's "self" and the role it plays in his poems. In my poems, self has to justify its existence in relation to what is other. In a rather personal book like (say) *The Flood*, it is vulnerably confronted with an actual flood that threatens to sweep it away, with death that one day will, and with the dream of a vast apocalyptic flood that is about to destroy the universe (the long shadow of Wagner again?). In that particular poem, "The Epilogue," the self is unsupported except for love which is, perhaps, a religious awareness too. In life the self is actually supported by one of our greatest inheritances, our language, but the religious have long ceased to care about language in throwing overboard the splendor of their Bible and their prayer book in exchange for a "message" mediated in the language of newspapers and magazines. I think, too, that poetry stands by a certain ungainsayableness that religion knew about before it went soft in the nineteenth century and then stayed soft. Before that, it could still find words that were a true currency for much of experience, which is what poets, after all, in their own different way still try to do, which is what I am trying to do with the fact of death and fidelity to places and people in *The Return*. As I have written there:

> Place is always an embodiment
> And incarnation without argument.

In my next book, *Annunciations*, on which I am working now, I shall go on with this attempt to redefine Christian concepts, something I've been doing quietly for a long time.

Kathleen O'Gorman

Bibliography

I. Works by Charles Tomlinson

Poetry and Graphics

Alan Brownjohn, Michael Hamburger, Charles Tomlinson. Penguin Modern Poets 14. Baltimore: Penguin Books, 1969.
America West Southwest. San Marcos, Texas: San Marcos Press, 1970.
American Scenes and Other Poems. London: Oxford University Press, 1966.
Collected Poems. Oxford and New York: Oxford University Press, 1985.
Eden: Graphics and Poetry. Bristol: Redcliffe Poetry, 1985.
The Flood. Oxford and New York: Oxford University Press, 1981.
In Black and White: The Graphics of Charles Tomlinson. Cheadle: Carcanet Press, 1976.
The Matachines. San Marcos, Texas: San Marcos Press, 1968.
The Necklace. 1955. Reprint. London: Oxford University Press, 1966.
Notes from New York and Other Poems. Oxford and New York: Oxford University Press, 1984.
A Peopled Landscape: Poems. London and New York: Oxford University Press, 1963.
Relations and Contraries. Poems in Pamphlet 9. Aldington, Kent: Hand and Flower Press, 1951.
Seeing Is Believing. 1958. Reprint. London: Oxford University Press, 1960.
Selected Poems 1951–1974. Oxford and New York: Oxford University Press, 1978.
The Shaft. Oxford and New York: Oxford University Press, 1978.
"Solo for a Glass Harmonica." *Poems in Folio 7*. San Francisco: Westerham, 1957.
To Be Engraved on the Skull of a Cormorant. London: The Unaccompanied Serpent, 1968.
The Way In and Other Poems. London: Oxford University Press, 1974.
The Way of a World. London: Oxford University Press, 1969.
With Austin Clarke and Tony Connor. *Poems*. London and New York: Oxford University Press, 1964.
With Octavio Paz. *Airborn / Hijos del Aire*. London: Anvil Press Poetry, 1981.
With Octavio Paz, Jacques Roubaud, and Edoardo Sanguineti. *Renga: A Chain of Poems*. 1970. Reprint. New York: George Braziller, Inc., 1972.

Words and Images. London: Covent Garden Press, 1972.
Written on Water. London: Oxford University Press, 1972.

Nonfiction

The Poem as Initiation. Hamilton, New York: Colgate University Press, 1967.
Poetry and Metamorphosis. Cambridge, England: Cambridge University Press, 1983.
"Some Americans: A Personal Record." *Contemporary Literature* 18 (1977): 279–304.
Some Americans: A Personal Record. Berkeley and London: University of California Press, 1981.

Editor, Translator

Editor. *Marianne Moore: A Collection of Critical Essays*. Twentieth Century Views. Englewood Cliffs and London: Prentice-Hall, 1969.
Editor. *The Oxford Book of Verse in English Translation*. Oxford and New York: Oxford University Press, 1980.
Editor. *William Carlos Williams: A Critical Anthology*. Harmondsworth: Penguin, 1972.
Editor. *William Carlos Williams: Selected Poems*. 1976. Reprint. New York: New Directions, 1985.
Translations. Oxford and New York: Oxford University Press, 1983.
Trans. *Ten Versions from Trilce*, by César Vallejo. San Marcos, Texas: San Marcos Press, 1970.
Trans. *Versions from Fyodor Tyutchev 1803–1873*. London: Oxford University Press, 1960.
Trans. with Henry Gifford. *Castilian Ilexes: Versions from Antonio Machado*. London: Oxford University Press, 1963.

Essays

"Abundance, not too much: The Poetry of Marianne Moore." *Sewanee Review* 65 (1957): 677–87.
"Aerial Perspective in the Valley of Vision." Review of *The Parting Light: Selected Writing of Samuel Palmer*, edited by Mark Abley. *P N Review* 13, 2 (1987): 52–53.
"America: Imagination and the Spirit of Place." *National Review* 11, 6 (1961): 86–87, 103.
"Black Mountain as Focus." *The Review* 10 (1964): 4–5.
"Coleridge: 'Christabel.'" In *Interpretations: Essays on Twelve English Poems*, edited by John Wain. London and Boston: Routledge and Kegan Paul, 1972.
"Dove sta memoria: in Italy." *Hudson Review* 33 (1980): 13–34.
"Dr. Williams' Practice." *Encounter* 29 (November 1967): 66–70.
"Edward Thomas." *Poetry* 95 (1959): 52–54.
"Experience into Music: The Poetry of Basil Bunting." *Agenda* 4, 5–6 (1966): 11–17.

"Fate and the Image of Music: An Examination of Rosenberg's Plays." *Poetry Nation* 3 (1974): 67–69.

"From Amateur to Impresario." *Times Literary Supplement*, 14 December 1979, 135.

Introduction to *A New Kind of Tie: Poems 1965–68*, by Simon Cutts. Seattle: Tarasque Press, 1972.

Introduction to *The Manoeuvering Sun: An Anthology of Verse by People Who Live or Work in the Bristol Area*, compiled by Alan Crang. N.p., n.d.

"Isaac Rosenberg of Bristol." *Local History Pamphlets* 53. Bristol: Bristol Branch of the Historical Association, 1982.

"Ivor Gurney's Best Poems." *Times Literary Supplement*, 3 January 1986, 12.

"Last of Lands." *New Statesman* 61 (28 April 1961): 674.

"Looking Out for Wholeness." *Times Literary Supplement*, 3 June 1983, 575.

"Marianne Moore: Her Poetry and Her Critics." *Agenda* 6, 3–4 (1968): 137–42.

"The Middlebrow Muse." *Essays in Criticism* 7 (1957): 208–17.

"Mr. Pound on Literature." Review of *Literary Essays of Ezra Pound*, edited by T. S. Eliot. *Spectator* 192 (19 February 1954): 212.

"Not in Sequence of a Metronome." *Agenda* 10, no. 4 (1972–73): 53–54.

"Of Charles Reznikoff." In *Charles Reznikoff: Man and Poet*, edited by Milton Hindus. Orono, Maine: National Poetry Foundation, 1984.

"Of Native Things." *The Listener* 81 (20 February 1969): 242.

"Out of Liguria." *London Magazine*, n.s. 23 (February 1984): 73–76.

"Overdoing the Generosity." *Times Literary Supplement*, 25 March 1983, 286.

"Owen as Correspondent." *Agenda* 6, no. 2 (1968): 66–70.

"Pages from an Italian Journal." *Poetry* 89 (1956): 183–87.

"Pictures From Brueghel." *Times Literary Supplement*, 21 May 1964, 435.

"The Poet as Painter." In *Essays by Divers Hands: Innovation in Contemporary Literature*, n.s. 9, edited by Vincent Cronin. Woodbridge, Suffolk: Boydell Press, 1979.

"The Poet as Translator." *Times Literary Supplement*, 22 April 1977, 474–75.

"The Poet as Translator." *Times Literary Supplement*, 26 September 1980, 1067–68.

"Poetry and Possibility: The Work of Robert Duncan." *Agenda* 8, 3–4 (1970): 159–70.

"The Poetry of Christina Rosetti." *Poetry* 89 (1957): 385–90.

"Poetry Today." In *The Modern Age*. Harmondsworth: Penguin, 1961.

"Poets and Mushrooms: A Retrospect of British Poetry in 1961." *Poetry* 100 (1962): 104–21.

"Pull Down Thy Vanity." *Poetry* 98 (1961): 263–66.

"A Rich Sitter: The Poetry of Lorine Niedecker." *Agenda* 7, no. 2 (1969): 65–67.

"Robert Creeley in Conversation with Charles Tomlinson." *The Review* 10 (1964): 24–35.

"Rock Bottom." *Poetry* 89 (1957): 260–64.

"Some Aspects of Poetry Since the War." In *The New Pelican Guide to English Literature: The Present* 8, edited by Boris Ford. Harmondsworth: Penguin, 1983.

"The State of Poetry—A Symposium." *The Review* 29–30 (1972): 48–51.

"Street Ballads." *Poetry* 91 (1958): 400–402.

"The Tone of Pound's Critics." *Agenda* 4, no. 2 (1965): 46–49.

"Wilfred Owen." *Poetry* 106 (1964): 41–43.

"Yeats and the Practising Poet." In *An Honoured Guest: New Essays on W. B. Yeats*, edited by Denis Donoghue and J. R. Mulryne. London: Edward Arnold, Ltd., 1965.

II. Works about Charles Tomlinson

Barker, Jonathan. "An Awareness of Delight." *Times Literary Supplement*, 17 July 1981, 816.

Beaver, Harold. "Crossing Rebel Lines." *Parnassus* 10 (Spring- Summer 1982): 117–24.

Bedient, Calvin. *Eight Contemporary Poets*. New York: Oxford University Press, 1974.

———. "On Charles Tomlinson." In *British Poetry Since 1960: A Critical Survey*, edited by Michael Schmidt and Grevel Lindop. Manchester: Carcanet Press, 1972. [First published in *Iowa Review* (Spring 1970): 83–101.]

———. "Poetry Comfortable and Uncomfortable." Review of *The Shaft*, by Charles Tomlinson. *Sewanee Review* 87 (1979): 296–304.

———. Review of *Written on Water*, by Charles Tomlinson. *New York Times Book Review*, 29 April 1973, 7.

Bergin, Thomas G. Review of *Translations*, by Charles Tomlinson. *World Literature Today* 59 (Winter 1985): 163.

Bergonzi, B. "Modern Metamorphoses: From Ovid to Ezra Pound." Review of *Poetry and Metamorphosis*, by Charles Tomlinson. *Encounter* 61 (July–August 1983): 79–81.

Bewley, Marius. "Poetry Chronicle." *Hudson Review* 17 (1966): 479–93.

Bolt, Sydney. "Not the Full Face." *Delta*, no. 40 (1967): 4–9.

Booth, Phillip. Review of *Seeing Is Believing*, by Charles Tomlinson. *Christian Science Monitor*, 26 March 1959, 11.

Brown, J. L. Review of *The Oxford Book of Verse in English Translation*, edited by Charles Tomlinson. *World Literature Today* 55 (1981): 539–40.

Brown, Merle. "Divisiveness in Recent English Poetry." *Boundary* 8 (1980): 279–95.

———. *Double Lyric: Divisiveness and Communal Creativity in Recent English Poetry*. New York: Columbia University Press, 1980.

———. "Intuition and Perception in the Poetry of Charles Tomlinson." *Journal of Aesthetics and Art Criticism* 37 (1979): 277–93.

Brownjohn, Alan. Review of *The Way of a World*, by Charles Tomlinson. *New Statesman* 78 (5 December 1969): 830.

Carbo, Nicholas Andrew. "The Poets of Renga: Octavio Paz, Jacques Roubaud, Edoardo Sanguineti, and Charles Tomlinson." Ph.D. diss., New York University, 1977.

Carey, John. Review of *American Scenes*, by Charles Tomlinson. *New Statesman* 71 (17 June 1966): 894.

Carruth, Hayden. "Abstruse Considerations." *Poetry* 106 (1964): 243–44.

Chamberlin, J. E. "Poetry Chronicle." *Hudson Review* 26 (1973): 395–96.

———. "Poetry and Confidence." Review of *The Way In*, by Charles Tomlinson. *Hudson Review* 28 (1975): 119–35.

Ciardi, John. Review of *Seeing Is Believing*, by Charles Tomlinson. *Saturday Review* 41 (27 September 1958): 32.

Clayre, Alasdair. "The Poetry of Charles Tomlinson." *London Magazine*, n.s. 3 (May 1963): 47–57.

———. Review of *The Necklace*, by Charles Tomlinson. *Encounter* 29 (November 1967): 77.

"Coming in from the Cold." Review of *The Way In*, by Charles Tomlinson. *Times Literary Supplement*, 8 November 1974, 1265.

Cookson, William. "Charles Tomlinson and Robert Creeley." Review of *American Scenes* and *The Necklace*, by Charles Tomlinson. *Agenda* 4, 5–6 (1966): 64–66.

Corn, Alfred. "Fishing by Obstinate Isles: Five Poets." Review of *Selected Poems 1951–1974*, by Charles Tomlinson. *Yale Review* 68 (1979): 400–10.

Cushman, Jerome. Review of *The Way of a World*, by Charles Tomlinson. *Library Journal* 95 (1970): 1848.

Darenberg, Karl H. "Charles Tomlinson: 'Winter Encounter.'" In *Die Moderne Englische Lyrik: Interpretationen*, edited by Horst Oppel. Berlin: E. Schmidt Verl., 1967.

Davie, Donald. Introduction to *The Necklace*, by Charles Tomlinson. 1955. Reprint. London: Oxford University Press, 1966.

———. "See and Believe." Review of *Seeing Is Believing*, by Charles Tomlinson. *Essays in Criticism* 9 (1959): 188–95.

———. *Thomas Hardy and British Poetry*. New York: Oxford University Press, 1972.

Davies, Harold L. "The Poetry and Poetics of Charles Tomlinson." Ph.D. diss., Syracuse University, 1974.

Donoghue, Denis. "In the Scene of Being." *Hudson Review* 14 (1961): 233–46.

———. "The Proper Plenitude of Fact." In *The Ordinary Universe: Soundings in Modern Literature*, by Denis Donoghue. New York: Macmillan, 1968.

Dorn, N. K. Review of *Seeing Is Believing*, by Charles Tomlinson. *San Francisco Chronicle*, 23 November 1958, 13CB.

Dunn, Douglas. "Redundant Elegance." Review of *The Way In*, by Charles Tomlinson. *Encounter* 44 (March 1975): 85–89.

Eagleton, Terry. "Structures and Connections: New Poetry." Review of *The Way In*, by Charles Tomlinson. *Stand* 16, 3 (1975): 73–78.

Edwards, Michael. "American Lessons for English Ends." *Times Literary Supplement*, 21 March 1986, 308.

———. "Charles Tomlinson: Notes on Tradition and Impersonality." *Critical Quarterly* 15 (Summer 1973): 133–44.

———. "Charles Tomlinson's Seeing and Believing." In *Poetry and Possibility*, by Michael Edwards. New York: Macmillan, 1987.

———. "The Poetry of Charles Tomlinson." *Agenda* 9, 2–3 (1971): 126–41.

———. "'Renga,' Translation and Eliot's Ghost." *P N Review* 7, 2 (1980): 24–28.

———. "Renga: ¿Un nuevo género literario?" *Plural* 23 (1973): 36–37.

———. Review of *The Way of a World*, by Charles Tomlinson. *Adam: International Review* 340–42 (1970): 52–57.

Elliot, Alistair. Review of *Poetry and Metamorphosis*, by Charles Tomlinson. *Times Literary Supplement*, 14 October 1983, 1120.

Enslin, Theodore. "A Precision in Two Languages." Review of *American Scenes*, by Charles Tomlinson. *Poetry* 109 (1966): 112–14.

Falk, Colin. "Dreams and Responsibilities." *The Review* 2 (1962): 3–18.

Fenton, James. "Poetry and Self-Regard." Review of *The Way In*, by Charles Tomlinson. *New Statesman* 88 (6 December 1974): 832–34.

"Flick of Feeling." Review of *American Scenes*, by Charles Tomlinson. *Times Literary Supplement*, 2 June 1966, 496.

Flint, F. C. Review of *A Peopled Landscape*, by Charles Tomlinson. *Virginia Quarterly Review* 39 (1963): 680.

Flint, R. W. "Hard Way to Beauty." Review of *Selected Poems 1951–1974* and *The Shaft*, by Charles Tomlinson. *New York Times Book Review*, 31 December 1978, 9.

Ford, Boris, ed. *Poetry Today. The Pelican Guide to English Literature.* Vol. 7. Harmondsworth: Penguin, 1961.

Fraser, G. S. Review of *A Peopled Landscape*, by Charles Tomlinson. *New York Review of Books*, 20 February 1964, 12.

"From Waterways to Soupy Streams." Review of *The Way In*, by Charles Tomlinson. *Times Literary Supplement*, 20 October 1972, 1249.

Galassi, Jonathan. Review of *Written on Water*, by Charles Tomlinson. *Poetry* 123 (1973): 113.

Getz, T. H. "Charles Tomlinson's Manscapes." *Modern Poetry Studies* 11 (1983): 209–18.

Gibbons, Reginald. "With So Exact a Care." Review of *The Shaft*, by Charles Tomlinson. *Agenda* 16, no. 2 (1978): 52–58.

Gibson, James, ed. *Let the Poet Choose*. London: Harrap, 1973.

Gioia, Dana. Review of *The Flood*, by Charles Tomlinson. *Hudson Review* 34 (1981–1982): 579–94.

Gitzen, Julian. "British Nature Poetry Now." *Midwest Quarterly* 15 (1974): 323–37.

———. "Charles Tomlinson and the Plenitude of Fact." *Critical Quarterly* 13 (Winter 1971): 355–62.

Grogan, Ruth. "Charles Tomlinson: Poet as Painter." *Critical Quarterly* 19 (Winter 1977): 71–77.

———. "Charles Tomlinson: The Way of His World." *Contemporary Literature* 19 (1978): 472–96.

Gould, Alan. "Control and Parsimony." *Poetry Australia* 72 (October 1979): 54–59.

Gunn, Thom. "Seeing and Thinking." Review of *Seeing Is Believing*, by Charles Tomlinson. *American Scholar* 28 (1959): 390–96.

Halfmann, Ulrich. "'Negotiations': Zur Subjekt/Objekt-Beziehung in de Lyrik Charles Tomlinsons." *Anglia* 98 (1980): 68–84.

Hall, Donald. Review of *Some Americans: A Personal Record*, by Charles Tomlinson. *New York Times Book Review*, 1 March 1981, 12.

Hamburger, Michael. *The Truth of Poetry: Tensions in Modern Poetry from Baudelaire to the 1960s*. Harmondsworth: Penguin, 1972.

Hamilton, Ian. "Four Conversations." *London Magazine*, n.s. 4 (November 1964): 64–85.

Hardie, Joseph Keith, Jr. "'Mouthers and Unmakers': Theories of Language in the Work of Flann O'Brien, Walker Percy, and Charles Tomlinson." Ph.D. diss., University of Oregon, 1983.

Harvey, Arthur. "'Naked Nature' and 'Negotiations.'" *New Poetry* 19 (April 1971): 3–8.

Hayman, Ronald. "Observation Plus." *Encounter* 35 (December 1970): 72–73.

Hennessy, Michael. "Charles Tomlinson." In *Critical Survey of Poetry*, edited by Frank N. McGill. Englewood Cliffs, N.J.: Salem Press, 1983.

———. "Discovering America." Review of *Some Americans: A Personal Record*, by Charles Tomlinson. *Contemporary Literature* 23 (1982): 254–58.

———. "Perception and Self in Charles Tomlinson's Early Poetry." *Rocky Mountain Review of Language and Literature* 36 (1982): 95–102.

———. Review of *The Flood*, by Charles Tomlinson and *Airborn / Hijos del Aire*, by Charles Tomlinson and Octavio Paz. *Library Journal* 106 (1981): 2240.

———. "Thematic Development in the Poetry of Charles Tomlinson." Ph.D. diss., Boston College, 1979.

Hirsch, Edward. "The Meditative Eye of Charles Tomlinson." *The Hollins Critic* 15, 2 (1978): 1–12.

———. "'Out There is the World': The Visual Imperative in the Poetry of George Oppen and Charles Tomlinson." In *George Oppen: Man and Poet*, edited by Burton Hatlen. Orono, Maine: National Poetry Foundation, 1981.

Homberger, Eric. *The Art of the Real: Poetry in England and America Since 1939*. London: J. M. Dent & Sons, Ltd., 1977.

———. "The Objectivists." *Akros* 17 (April 1982): 42–51.

Hughes, J. W. Review of *The Way of a World*, by Charles Tomlinson. *Saturday Review* 53 (8 August 1970): 33.

John, Brian. "The Poetry of Charles Tomlinson." *Far Point* (University of Manitoba) 3 (Fall-Winter 1969): 50–61.

Kenner, Hugh. "A Creator of Spaces." Review of *The Necklace*, by Charles Tomlinson. *Poetry* 88 (1956): 324–28.

———. "Next Year's Words." Review of *Seeing Is Believing*, by Charles Tomlinson. *Poetry* 93 (1959): 335–40.

Kinsella, Thomas. Review of *A Peopled Landscape*, by Charles Tomlinson. *New York Times Book Review*, 24 November 1963, 46.

Kirkham, Michael. "Charles Tomlinson." In *British Poetry Since 1970: A Critical Survey*, edited by Peter Jones and Michael Schmidt. New York: Persea Books, 1980.

———. "Negotiations." Review of *American Scenes*, by Charles Tomlinson. *Essays in Criticism* 17 (1967): 367–74.

———. "Philip Larkin and Charles Tomlinson: Realism and Art." In *The New Pelican Guide to English Literature: The Present* 8, edited by Boris Ford. Harmondsworth: Penguin, 1983.

Koehler, Stanley. "The Art of Poetry VI." *Paris Review* 8 (Summer-Fall 1964): 111–51.

Lasdun, James. Review of *Poetry and Metamorphosis*, by Charles Tomlinson. *New Statesman* 107 (3 February 1984): 26.

Lattimore, Richard. Review of *The Oxford Book of Verse In English Translation*, edited by Charles Tomlinson. *Hudson Review* 35 (1982): 154–58.

Law, Pam. "Notions of Excellence." *Poetry Australia* 47 (1973): 75–80.

Lee, L. L. "Charles Tomlinson as American Un-American." *Contemporary Poetry: A Journal of Criticism* 2, 2 (1977): 11–15.

Levertov, Denise. "An English Event." *Kulchur* 2, 6 (1962): 3–9.

Longley, Edna. Review of *Poetry and Metamorphosis*, by Charles Tomlinson. *Notes and Queries*, n. s. 32 (1985): 413–15.

Lucas, J. Review of *Notes From New York*, by Charles Tomlinson. *New Statesman* 107 (22 June 1984): 23–24.

MacCraig, Norman. Review of *A Peopled Landscape*, by Charles Tomlinson. *New Statesman* 66 (5 July 1963): 20.

McDonald, G. D. Review of *Seeing Is Believing*, by Charles Tomlinson. *Library Journal* 83 (1958): 2846.

Mariani, Paul. "Charles Tomlinson." In *A Usable Past: Essays on Modern and Contemporary Poetry*, by Paul Mariani. Amherst: University of Massachusetts Press, 1984.

———. "Tomlinson's Use of the Williams' Triad." *Contemporary Literature* 18 (1977): 405–15.

Marsack, Robyn. "Elegy and Celebration." *P N Review* 8, 5 (1981): 57.

Marten, Harry. "Tomlinson's American Relations." Review of *Selected Poems 1951–1974*, by Charles Tomlinson. *Prairie Schooner* 53 (1979): 280–82.

Martz, Louis L. "Recent Poetry: Roethke, Warren, and Others." *Yale Review* 56 (1967): 274–84.

Molesworth, Charles. "British Poetry: Crossing the Borders." Review of *Written on Water*, by Charles Tomlinson. *The Nation* 16 (1974): 346–48.

"The More Deceived." Review of *The Necklace*, by Charles Tomlinson. *Times Literary Supplement*, 6 October 1966, 916.

Mott, Michael. "Recent Developments in British Poetry." Review of *The Way of a World*, by Charles Tomlinson. *Poetry* 118 (1971): 102–14.

Murphy, Rosalie, ed. *Contemporary Poets of the English Language*. London and Chicago: St. James, 1970.

O'Driscoll, Dennis. Review of *The Flood*, by Charles Tomlinson. *Agenda* 19, nos. 2–3 (1981): 79–81.

O'Gorman, Kathleen. "Phenomenology of Perception in the Early Poetry of Charles Tomlinson." Ph.D. diss., University of Notre Dame, 1981.

———. "Space, Time and Ritual in Charles Tomlinson's Poetry." *Sagetrieb* 2 (Summer-Fall 1983): 85–98.

Orr, Peter. "Charles Tomlinson." In *The Poet Speaks*, by Peter Orr. New York: Barnes and Noble, 1966.

Palmer, Penelope. Review of *The Way In*, by Charles Tomlinson. *Agenda* 13, no. 2 (1975): 66–67.

Pawling, Geoffrey. "A Way Into England." *Delta* 54 (1975): 10–16.

Paz, Octavio. "En blanco y negro." In *In/Mediaciones*, by Octavio Paz. Barcelona: Editorial Seix Barral, 1979.

Pinsky, Robert. *The Situation of Poetry: Contemporary Poetry and Its Traditions*. Princeton: Princeton University Press, 1976.

"Poetry." Review of *American Scenes*, by Charles Tomlinson. *Virginia Quarterly Review* 42 (1966): cxl.

Pritchard, William H. "Aboard the Poetry Omnibus." Review of *Notes from New York*, by Charles Tomlinson. *Hudson Review* 37 (1984): 327–42.

———. "In the British Looking-Glass." Review of *The Way In*, by Charles Tomlinson. *Parnassus* 4 (Spring-Summer 1976): 225–34.

"Questionnaire on Rhythm." *Agenda* 10–11, 4 and 1 (1972): 7–58.

Rae, Simon. Review of *The Flood*, by Charles Tomlinson. *New Statesman* 102 (4 September 1981): 19.

Raine, Craig. "The Age of Austerity." Review of *Selected Poems 1951–1974* and *The Shaft*, by Charles Tomlinson. *New Statesman* 96 (4 August 1978): 154.

Rasula, Jed, and Mike Erwin. "An Interview with Charles Tomlinson." *Contemporary Literature* 16 (1975): 405–16.

Regan, Robert. Review of *American Scenes*, by Charles Tomlinson. *Library Journal* 91 (1966): 3442.

Review of *A Peopled Landscape*, by Charles Tomlinson. *Times Literary Supplement*, 9 August 1963, 610.

Review of *Seeing Is Believing*, by Charles Tomlinson. *Kirkus* 26 (1958): 329.

Review of *The Shaft*, by Charles Tomlinson. *Choice* 16 (March 1978): 82.

Review of *The Way In*, by Charles Tomlinson. *Choice* 11 (February 1975): 782.

Review of *The Way of a World*, by Charles Tomlinson. *Times Literary Supplement*, 29 January 1970, 104.

Riggan, W. "The 1984 Jurors and Their Candidates for the Neustadt

International Prize for Literature." *World Literature Today* 58 (1984): 55–56.

Robinson, P. J. E. "Responsibilities and Distances: The Moral of the Poet in the Work of Donald Davie, Roy Fisher and Charles Tomlinson." Ph.D. diss., University of Cambridge, 1982.

Rosenthal, M. L. "The American Influence on the Coots of Hampstead Heath." *Antioch Review* 22 (1962): 189–201.

———. "Contemporary British Poetry: Charles Tomlinson." In *The New Poets: American and British Poetry Since World War II*, by M. L. Rosenthal. London: Oxford University Press, 1967.

———. *The Modern Poets: A Critical Introduction*. New York: Oxford University Press, 1960.

Ross, Alan, and Charles Tomlinson. "Words and Water: The Poetry of Charles Tomlinson." *London Magazine*, n. s. 20 (January 1981): 22–39.

Ruddick, Bill. Review of *The Way In*, by Charles Tomlinson. *Critical Quarterly* 17 (Summer 1975): 181–85.

Ruthven, Greystiel. "Charles Tomlinson—An Introduction." *Gemini/Dialogue* 3 (January 1960): 30–33.

Saunders, William S. "Artifice and Ideas." *Delta* 59 (1979): 35–40.

———. "A Peopled Landscape." *Delta* 56 (1977): 10–15.

———. "Reaching Beyond Desire: Charles Tomlinson's Poetry of Otherness." Ph.D. diss., University of Iowa, 1975.

Schlessinger, Sheila. "'Hawk, Thrush and Crow': The Bird Poems of Tomlinson and Hughes." *Theoria* 59 (October 1982): 51–61.

———. "The Poetry of Charles Tomlinson." M. A. thesis, University of South Africa, 1978.

Schmidt, Michael, ed. "Charles Tomlinson at Fifty: A Celebration." *P N Review* 5, 1 (1977): 33–50.

———. "In the Eden of Civility." Review of *Selected Poems 1951–1974* and *The Shaft*, by Charles Tomlinson. *Times Literary Supplement*, 1 December 1978, 1406.

———. *An Introduction to Fifty Modern British Poets*. Pan Literature Guides. London: Pan, 1979.

———. "On Charles Tomlinson." *P N Review* 13, 2 (1986): 70–72.

———. "Stretching the Language." Review of *The Oxford Book of Verse in English Translation*, edited by Charles Tomlinson. *The Listener* 104 (1980): 732–33.

———, trans. "In Black and White: The Graphics of Charles Tomlinson." In *On Poets and Others*, by Octavio Paz. New York: Seaver Books, 1986. (First published in *Poetry Nation 5* Vol. 3, 1. Reprinted in *In Black and White: The Graphics of Charles Tomlinson*, by Charles Tomlinson. Cheadle: Carcanet Press, 1976.)

Shapiro, Harvey. Review of *Seeing Is Believing*, by Charles Tomlinson. *New York Times Book Review*, 22 June 1958, 4.

Shivpuri, Jagdish. "Charles Tomlinson: Earlier Poetry." *Siddha* (Siddharth College, India) 12 (1978): 7–22.

Sisson, C. H. Review of *The Oxford Book of Verse in English Translation*, edited by Charles Tomlinson. *Times Literary Supplement*, 3 October 1980, 1093–94.

Skelton, Robin. "Britannia's Muse Awakening." Review of *American Scenes*, by Charles Tomlinson. *Massachusetts Review* 8 (1967): 352–66.

———. "Britannia's Muse Revisited." *Massachusetts Review* 6 (1965): 829–39.

Smith, William J. Review of *American Scenes*, by Charles Tomlinson. *Harper's*, August 1966, 89–92.

Spears, Monroe K. "Shapes and Surfaces: David Jones, with a Glance at Charles Tomlinson." *Contemporary Literature* 12 (1971): 402–19.

Spector, R. D. Review of *The Necklace*, by Charles Tomlinson. *Saturday Review* 50 (11 February 1967): 39.

———. Review of *A Peopled Landscape*, by Charles Tomlinson. *Saturday Review* 47 (1 February 1964): 38.

Spiegelman, Willard. "The Rituals of Perception." Review of *Selected Poems 1951–1974* and *The Shaft*, by Charles Tomlinson. *Parnassus* 7 (Spring-Summer 1979): 151–64.

Srawley, Stephen. "A Note on Musical and Poetic Rhythm." *Agenda* 10–11, 4 and 1 (1972): 114–22.

Stanton, Richard J. "Charles Tomlinson and the Process of Defining Relationships." *North Dakota Quarterly* 45, 3 (1977): 47–60.

Steiner, George. Review of *The Oxford Book of Verse in English Translation*, edited by Charles Tomlinson. *P N Review* 7, 5 (1980): 19–20.

Stevenson, Anne. "Night-time Tongue." Review of *The Shaft*, by Charles Tomlinson. *The Listener* 100 (13 July 1978): 62–63.

Sutton, Walter. Review of *A Peopled Landscape*, by Charles Tomlinson. *The Nation* 198 (1964): 589.

Swann, Brian. "English Opposites: Charles Tomlinson and Christopher Middleton." *Modern Poetry Studies* 5 (1974): 222–36.

———. "Proteus." Review of *Poetry and Metamorphosis*, by Charles Tomlinson. *P N Review* 10, 2 (1983): 53–54.

Swigg, Richard. "Reading the World." Review of *The Flood*, by Charles Tomlinson. *P N Review* 6, 7 (1982): 63–64.

———. Review of *Translations*, by Charles Tomlinson. *Times Literary Supplement*, 27 April 1984, 452.

Szirtes, George. Review of *Airborn / Hijos del Aire*, by Charles Tomlinson and Octavio Paz. *Times Literary Supplement*, 4 September 1981, 1019.

Tartt, Alison. Review of *Some Americans: A Personal Record*, by Charles Tomlinson and *The Oxford Book of Verse in English Translation*, edited by Charles Tomlinson. *Library Journal* 105 (1980): 2574.

Thwaite, Anthony. *Poetry Today: 1960–1973*. Edinburgh: R. & R. Clark, Ltd., 1973.

Tobias, R. Review of *Poetry and Metamorphosis*, by Charles Tomlinson. *World Literature Today* 58 (Winter 1984): 111.

Vendler, Helen. "A Quarter of Poetry." Review of *The Way In*, by Charles Tomlinson. *New York Times Book Review*, 6 April 1975, 4–5, 29–38.

Watkins, Evan. "Charles Tomlinson: The Poetry of Experience." In *The Critical Art: Criticism and Community*, by Evan Watkins. New Haven: Yale University Press, 1978.

Weatherhead, Andrew Kingsley. "Charles Tomlinson." In *The British Dissonance: Essays on Ten Contemporary Poets*, by A. K. Weatherhead. Columbia: University of Missouri Press, 1983.

———. "Charles Tomlinson: With Respect to Flux." *Iowa Review* 7 (Fall 1976): 120–34.

Wesling, Donald. "The Inevitable Ear: Freedom and Necessity in Lyric Form, Wordsworth and After." *ELH* 36 (1969): 544–61.

White, R. S. Review of *Poetry and Metamorphosis*, by Charles Tomlinson. *Review of English Studies*, n.s. 36 (1985): 601–03.

Wilkinson, David. "Charles Tomlinson and the Narrative Voice." *Dutch Quarterly Review of Anglo-American Letters* 14, 2 (1984): 110–24.

Williams, William Carlos. "Seeing Is Believing." Review of *Seeing is Believing*, by Charles Tomlinson. *Spectrum* 2 (Fall 1958): 189.

Wilmer, Clive. Review of *Some Americans: A Personal Record*, by Charles Tomlinson. *Times Literary Supplement*, 5 February 1982, 141.

Wilson, Robert Jr. "Not Awfully Plain." Review of *American Scenes*, by Charles Tomlinson. *Carleton Miscellany* 8 (Winter 1967): 103–07.

Wood, Michael. "We All Hate Home: English Poetry Since World War II." *Contemporary Literature* 18 (1977): 305–18.

Woodward, Anthony. Review of *Poetry and Metamorphosis*, by Charles Tomlinson. *Unisa English Studies* (University of South Africa, Pretoria) 21, 2 (1983): 68–69.

Young, Alan. "Rooted Horizon: Charles Tomlinson and American Modernism." *Critical Quarterly* 24 (Winter 1982): 67–73.

Young, V. Review of *Selected Poems 1951–1974* and *The Shaft*, by Charles Tomlinson. *Hudson Review* 31 (1978–1979): 677–92.

Index

Permissions

"An Agnostic's Grace" by Michael Kirkham reprinted by permission of *P N Review*.

"Poet as Painter" by Charles Tomlinson reprinted by permission of Redcliffe Poetry Press.